TWAYNE'S WORLD AUTHORS SERIES

A Survey of the World's Literature

Sylvia E. Bowman, Indiana University

GENERAL EDITOR

GERMANY

Ulrich Weisstein, Indiana University

EDITOR

Gottfried August Bürger

(TWAS 270)

GOTTFRIED AUGUST BÜRGER

Gottfried August Bürger

By Wm. A. LITTLE

University of Virginia

Twayne Publishers, Inc. :: New York

ISBN 0–8057–2185–1

MANUFACTURED IN THE UNITED STATES OF AMERICA

186004

TO MY DEAR WIFE,
MARY

Preface

The present volume is intended to serve as an introduction to the life and works of Gottfried August Bürger. It is hoped that it may find an audience among those who have a knowledge of German as well as among those who do not. Bürger was a man of many sides and many talents. His accomplishments as a poet are not restricted to "Lenore," and the complexities of his personal life ranged far beyond the tangled and unhappy course of his first marriage. To the extent that this study can illuminate his career and achievements, it will have achieved its purpose. To the extent that it can generate a renewal of interest in Bürger, it will have succeeded.

One of the major problems in dealing with Bürger is that of arriving at a definitive text of his works. Another is that of finding them. The edition edited by Karl Reinhard (1796–1802) does not offer a critical text, nor can it be regarded as an "Ausgabe letzter Hand." It was "heavily" edited, and ever since the early nineteenth century scholars have regarded it with some misgiving. The excellent critical edition of Bürger's poetry prepared by Ernst Consentius (1911, 1914[2]) has been out of print and unavailable for over half a century, and the more comprehensive edition of Wolfgang Wurzbach (1902), though generally excellent, is equally unobtainable. On the other hand, there has never been a "complete" edition of Bürger's works; one editor includes some things and excludes others; one will rely on Reinhard's versions of the poems, another on the 1789 edition (which has finally come to be accepted as a sort of "Ausgabe letzter Hand"). The edition by Wurzbach comes as close to being complete as any, but even that scholar omitted numerous writings, including "Die Republik England."

The problems which obtain with the texts are also present with the correspondence. In 1974 it will have been a century since the publication of Bürger's letters by Adolf Strodtmann. In the intervening decades, a very sizable volume of correspondence, both to and from Bürger, has come to light, but it remains either unpublished or published in journals which are not generally accessible. Unfortunately, the recent reprint of Strodtmann (1874) brings us no closer to a complete edition of the correspondence.

To a large extent, all biographies of Bürger must ultimately rely on the work of Dr. Ludwig Christoph Althof (1798), the poet's long-time friend and physician. The other early biographies, such as those included in Meusel, Ersch & Gruber (see bibliography), are less reliable. In his biography of Bürger (1900) Wolfgang Wurzbach continued to depend on Dr. Althof, but he also had at his disposal the correspondence which had been published in the interval. I must acknowledge my own debt to Althof, Strodtmann and Wurzbach, although I have felt that the latter's profound sympathy for Bürger sometimes clouded his critical judgment. At the same time, Wurzbach, more than anyone else in this century, is responsible for making Bürger available to the German public. I do not know of any previous biography in English.

The translations in the present study are my own, and in preparing them I have aimed at blending accuracy and intent. Hesitant to attempt poetic renderings, I have supplied all translations in prose. Several of the ballads particularly, "Lenore," (with a translation by Sir Walter Scott) exist in English verse translations, and these can be found without difficulty if a comparison is desired. When translating for precision and accuracy, I have used normal double quotes, but when allowing myself more freedom, I have preferred single quotes.

Finally, I should acknowledge that I am indebted to many people in many ways for assisting me in this work. I should like to thank the Summer Research Committee of the University of Virginia for the support which has enabled me to finish the book at this time. I express my gratitude as well to the Library of the University of Virginia for its many excellent and helpful services. In England, where all the actual writing was done, I owe particular thanks to Professor J. P. Stern, our kind and gracious host in Cambridge. For his having arranged our visit in Cambridge and for his help in innumerable ways I am deeply grateful. I appreciate also the very generous assistance given me by the University Library of Cambridge.

Finally, I wish to thank my good wife, Mary, not only for her material help, which has been inestimable, but for all her understanding, patience, and encouragement, which has been inexhaustible.   Wm. A. L.

Contents

Chronology

1778	Assumes editorship of the *Göttinger Musen-Almanach*.
	First edition of collected poetry: *Gedichte*.
	Birth of a daughter, Marianne, March 15.
1780–	Leases a farm at Appenrode.
1784	
1782	Birth of a natural son, Emil (1782–1841) to Molly and Bürger.
1784	Retires as Magistrate at Altengleichen.
	Death of Dorette July 30.
	Joins the faculty of Göttingen University without salary, September 29.
1785	Marries Augusta Marie Wilhelmine Eva Leonhart (1758–1786) Molly, June 17.
	December 25, birth of a daughter, Auguste Anna Henriette (1785–1847).
1786	Death of Molly, January 9.
1787	Is awarded an honorary degree (Dr. philos.) by the University of Göttingen.
1789	Second edition of collected poems, *Gedichte*.
	Elise Hahn (1769–1833), the "Schwabenmädchen," first comes to his attention.
	Promoted to Professor extraordinarius, Göttingen, in October.
1790	Marries Elise Hahn, in Stuttgart in September. Returns to Göttingen.
1791	Schiller's review of Bürger's *Gedichte* appears in the *Allgemeine Literatur-Zeitung*, January.
	August 1, birth of a son, Agathon (1791–1813).
1792	Divorce from Elise (end of March).
1793	Partnership with Girtanner; publication of *Politische Annalen*.
1794	Dies in Göttingen on June 8.

CHAPTER 1

Gottfried August Bürger: Volksdichter

GOTTFRIED August Bürger occupies a place of some distinction in the history of German literature, yet the chronicle of his life reads like a catalogue of misfortunes, mistakes, frustrations, and disappointments. Confusion is also present and in fact marks the very beginning of Bürger's existence, for even the year of his birth was for generations a subject of debate: was it on December 31, 1747, or January 1, 1748, that Bürger was born in the village of Molmerswende in the precinct of Falkenstein and the bishopric of Halberstadt? Bürger and his family always celebrated his birthday on January 1, and that date also appears on Bürger's gravestone. On the other hand, according to the church register, the date recorded is December 31, 1747, a date that might be contested were it not that the hand in which the entry was recorded is that of the pastor of the church, Bürger's father. Evidently expecting no further entries for 1747, he drew a line and below it wrote 1748. When Gottfried August was born, evidently earlier than anticipated, the elder Bürger crossed out the line and the new year, and recorded his son's birth as an event still belonging to 1747. That date is now generally accepted. The issue is perhaps a minor one, but its symbolic significance has not been overlooked.

Uncertainty is compounded with confusion, and for nearly a century the name of Bürger's birthplace posed insuperable spelling problems. The tiny village of Molmerswende was an utterly obscure hamlet, and almost no one was quite sure (or concerned) about the exact spelling of the place. Dr. Althof, Bürger's first biographer, wrote "Wolmerswende," as did practically all subsequent biographers. Rese, who wrote the article on Bürger in Ersch & Gruber's Encyclopedia, put forward the suggestion that the first letter in the name of the town was an *M*, but might be pronounced as if it were *W*. Heinrich Döring, in his biography of Bürger (1826), went so far as to chide Richter who had, in fact, provided the correct spelling in his biographical dictionary of *Liederdichter*. Perhaps Hirschfeld went furthest afield by writing "Wolmirsword."[1] Even at the beginning of the twentieth century, the picture post cards depicting Bürger's birthplace still showed an orthographic ambivalence: side by side one finds "Molmerschwende" and "Molmerswende."

Gottfried August was the second child and only son of Johann Gottfried Bürger and his wife Gertrud Elisabeth (née Bauer). Both parents came from the same general geographical and social background. His father (son of Johann Heinrich, a *Frei- und Rittersasse*) was born in the nearby village of Pansfelde[2] in 1706. He had studied theology at the University of Halle and in 1741 became pastor of the church in Molmerswende, where he received an annual salary of 160 Thaler. Under normal circumstances, he might have regarded with some satisfaction his marriage to Gertrud Elisabeth Bauer in the following year. Born in 1718 in nearby Aschersleben, she was the daughter of Jakob Philipp Bauer, superintendent of the St. Elisabeth Hospital in that town and a citizen of some position and means. Whatever Johann Gottfried might have wished for or expected in his wife, it is doubtful if he fully foresaw what he received. From every report Gertrud Elisabeth was a woman of exceptional crudity, parsimony, and vindictiveness. Her malice in words and deeds was, in fact, sufficiently flamboyant to establish her as something of a local legend, and tales about her still circulated well into the nineteenth century. Thus she characterized her husband's profession in noting that "Hell is plastered with the skulls of parsons, and the one empty spot left is reserved for Johann Gottfried Bürger's head."[3] Her vindictive acts were notorious and her aim impartial. On one occasion, when it appeared that the family would soon move to Westorf, she vented her special hatred for her husband's successor by damaging all the trees on the grounds of the rectory. After an unusually stormy session with her husband she would return to her father's home in Aschersleben, but always Johann Gottfried brought her back. According to her son's testimony, she was a "woman of extraordinary talents, who, with the proper education, could have been the most famous member of her sex."[4] Unfortunately, as Gottfried August acknowledged, she could barely read or write, a fact which may, in part, account for her habit of using church records for household purposes. Given her character, it is not surprising that none of her children felt particularly close to her.

Gottfried August was one of four children. His elder sister, Henriette Philippine (1744–1807), married Friedrich Gotthelf Oesfeld in 1770 and moved to Lößnitz in the Erzgebirge, where her husband was pastor of the village church. The poet's second sister, Friederike Philippine Louise (1751–1799) was perhaps closest to him. She was a woman of considerable refinement, and in her second marriage, to Heinrich Adolf Müllner, she became the mother of the dramatist Adolf Müllner. Bürger's youngest sister, Johanna Dorothea, died at the early age of sixteen (1756–1772).

Because of the very meager income paid by his church in Molmerswende, Johann Gottfried found it necessary to look for a position in a larger parish. The opportunity for a move presented itself in 1748, and he was named pastor-elect of the church in Westorf, where he would succeed the incumbent at the time of his retirement. Since Casper Abel was already 73 years old and in delicate heath, Bürger's father had every reason to believe that his fiscal situation might soon improve, Fortune, however, graced Pastor Abel with a long life, and he lived to be 89. When in 1764 Johann Gottfried finally assumed his duties in Westorf, he was himself in frail health and died a few months later. A man of easygoing temperament, he had been a remarkable counterfoil to his volatile wife. Bürger described him as a man not easily ruffled, one who enjoyed whatever amenities he could afford, and was not unduly concerned with the upbringing and education of his children. The younger Bürger was considered particularly slow ("ein erzdummer Junge") and despite (or perhaps because of) the tumultuous episodes of home instruction, his Latin was rudimentary. Because of his slow progress he was sent to be tutored in Pansfelde with the children of his godfather, Pastor Samuel Joachim Kutzbach. Bürger's struggle with Latin continued, and, although he moved slowly, and read with great difficulty, it was here that he first came into contact with classical literature and picked his way through fragments of Virgil. Until that time, Bürger's reading had chiefly consisted of biblical extracts and the Protestant hymnal. His favorite hymns were "Ein feste Burg ist unser Gott" (which he memorized), "Du, O schönes Weltgebäude," "Es ist gewißlich an der Zeit," and "O Ewigkeit, du Donnerwort!" Even in this early period, Bürger had already begun to write poetry, although none of it has survived. As he maintained, there may have been grammatical errors, but his sense of rhythm and meter was always impeccable.

In 1759 Bürger was sent to the town school in Aschersleben, and there he lived with his maternal grandfather, Johann Philipp Bauer. The latter was a man of uneven temperament, at times stubborn and insensitive and at others generous and gracious. His role during Bürger's formative years was of major significance, and Bürger's feelings towards him were mixed. Ultimately, he remembered him with respect, gratitude, and affection.

Bürger's performance at the school in Aschersleben served to confirm his parents' and his instructors' opinion that he was both slow-witted and intractable. He spent his time playing the flute, which he had more or less taught himself, and in writing poetry. Among other things, he wrote one or two particularly acid epigrams aimed at other students. One of these was not favorably received, and Bürger's punishment came swift and was evidently harsh. His grandfather interceded and succeeded in having the rector, Georg Wilhelm Auerbach, reprimanded; but the die was cast, and Bürger left the school on August 25, 1760. Immediately, his grandfather sent him to Halle, where on September 8 he matriculated at the *Pädagogium.*

The *Pädagogium* at Halle had been established some fifty years earlier, but it had already won widespread recognition for its faculty and students. The rector of the school was Johann Anton Niemeyer (1723–1765), and although he governed his establishment with the iron hand of Protestant orthodoxy, he was both fair and just. Moreover, Niemeyer was a highly perceptive judge of people, as his notes and records reveal. For some reason, he took a particular interest in his new student, and for the first time Bürger flourished academically. "Bürger, the grandson of the elder Herr Bauer in Aschersleben, has quite uncommon talents and equally great pride." Curiously enough, Niemeyer always referred to his charge as "der kleine Bürger" ("little Bürger") and his notebook entries read, "little Bürger is sick," or "little Bürger has had 4 Thaler stolen," etc. Even three years later, when Gottfried August was sixteen years old and about to graduate, Niemeyer still called him "little Bürger." From contemporary descriptions, Bürger was rather plain-looking, wiry and quite strong, but prone to frail health.

During the course of the three years he spent at the *Pädagogium*

Bürger advanced rapidly and proved himself to be a sound, if not stunning, student. His favorite instructor was a young physicist, Christian Leiste (1738–1815), who also taught French, Latin, and Greek. Under Leiste, Bürger's command of these languages improved, and Leiste encouraged him in his poetic efforts. Indeed, it was with his poetry that Bürger distinguished himself at the *Pädagogium.* Astonishingly, in less than six months after his arrival (January 29, 1761), his proficiency in Latin had progressed to the point where he was able to write and deliver an address, "contra eos qui contumeliose maledicunt." Shortly thereafter he also composed and recited a Latin "Carmen," which had been inspired by Klopstock's *Messias,* "Non titulos sed merita esse aestimanda." Klopstock's influence on Bürger at this time was considerable, and in the following year he and another student, Schmiedeberg, prepared and presented a German poem with the Latin title, "Concilium patrum et angelorum in note Golgatha." With increasing confidence in his abilities, Bürger now stepped into the poetic limelight of the *Pädagogium,* and in his third year he commemorated the fiftieth anniversary of its founding with a German ode. In the same year (1763) he hailed the Peace of Hubertusburg in another ode, in which he praised the king for having brought about the end of the Seven Years' War. Both odes were doubtless written in the Klopstockian manner, as was also his final contribution at the *Pädagogium,* an ode, "Christus in Gethsemane," presented on September 29 and 30, 1763.

Bürger's life at the *Pädagogium* seems to have been relatively uneventful. His associations with the other students were apparently cordial, but did not yield any deep or lasting friendships. The only two students who were to emerge in Bürger's later life were his roommate, Von der Reck, who later became the Prussian *États-und Kultus-Minister,* and the poet Leopold Friedrich von Goeckingk (1748–1828), whose own talents were already beginning to be recognized. Suddenly, in the fall of 1763, both Niemeyer and Bürger received letters from the latter's grandfather notifying them that he was terminating Bürger's course of study at the *Pädagogium.* This was a severe blow to Bürger, since he had come to have great affection for the school. Niemeyer's notes shed little light on the cause for the decision, but do help to explain the situation:

Bürger, grandson of the old Superintendent Bauer, received a letter, as did I, from his grandfather, that he was to leave at Michaelmas (September 29). *He is a willful old man.* His little grandson has been in "Prima" [=eleventh grade] a full half year and is about fifteen years old. *He cried and asked me not* to reassign his place, that he intended to plead for a renewal. But the old man turned him down.[5]

Nothing could dissuade the elder Bauer from his decision, and Bürger left Halle for Aschersleben, where he spent the winter of 1763–64. He was hopelessly bored during his enforced stay there, and because Auerbach was still the rector, he could not even return to the school. The only product of his stay in Aschersleben was a fragmentary poem of seventeen eight-line stanzas, having the Baroque title, "Die Feuersbrünste am 4. Januar und 1. April des 1764. Jahres zu Aschersleben, geschildert von Gottfried August Bürger, d.f.K.u. W. B."[6] Dr. Althof had an opportunity to examine it, but like Bürger's other very early efforts, it has since disappeared. In identifying himself as the author, Bürger appropriated the slightly inaccurate title, "der freien Künste und Wissenschaften Beflissener," or roughly the equivalent of the B.A. No one seemed to mind, however, and it was under these colors that Bürger registered on May 26, 1764, as a student of theology at the University of Halle. His reasons for engaging in theological studies are obscure and are also surprising in view of his mother's opinion of clerics and his father's enduring poverty. The general belief that he was prodded into theology by his grandfather is probably correct. Shortly after Bürger's arrival at Halle, his father died, after having finally assumed his duties in Westorf. His mother and his three sisters subsequently returned to the family home in Aschersleben.

Bürger's early months at Halle were probably less than satisfying. Theology was hardly the field for someone of his temperament, and although there is reason to believe that on one or two occasions he may have delivered sermons at nearby village churches, it is hard to imagine that he would have continued very long in pursuit of a clerical career. Already his thoughts were moving in the direction of philology and the humanities. He wrote a very well received thesis, "De Lucani Pharsalia," for the great lexicographer J. G. Meusel, and increasingly devoted himself to his poetic activities.

Of major importance for Bürger's career was the arrival of Christian Adolf Klotz (1738–1771) in Halle. Klotz had come from

Göttingen and was appointed professor of philosophy and rhetoric ("Beredsamkeit") in 1765. At the time of his appointment, he was twenty-seven years old. At Halle he founded and edited the *Deutsche Bibliothek der schönen Wissenschaften* (1767). As a result of his dispute with Lessing, he had attained a substantial measure of fame (or notoriety). He had been naive enough to believe that he could match wits with Lessing; it was an illusion that cost him the scholarly respect he had formerly enjoyed. It would be incorrect to assert, however, that Klotz was intellectually incapable; he was in fact a man of considerable learning and immense energy. Unfortunately, his personal life was not beyond reproach, and he was generally eschewed by the rigidly orthodox society of Halle. Nonetheless, he took much interest in his students and encouraged their studies and literary endeavors.

Shortly after his arrival in Halle, Bürger came into contact with Klotz, and the friendship which developed had a strong impact on Bürger's future. Very soon Bürger became a frequent guest in Klotz's house and also came to share the bad reputation attached to it. Klotz recognized Bürger's talent and consistently helped and advised him. He also had hopes that Bürger would be his successor at the University. For his part, Bürger was immensely receptive, and he responded by seeking Klotz's opinion on all aspects of his work. It was at Klotz's suggestion that he first addressed himself to a translation of the Latin "Pervigilium Veneris" (1767) for which he intended also to provide a commentary. It was also under Klotz's guidance that Bürger first read Herder's *Fragmente,* and at his suggestion that he began work on his translation of Homer, which was subsequently published in the *Deutsche Bibliothek* (1771). All in all, Klotz proved to be a valuable and loyal friend, despite the adverse effect the friendship may have had on Bürger's local reputation. Even after Bürger had left Halle, he maintained a correspondence with Klotz—in, of all things, Latin. His letters reveal the extent of Bürger's respect and affection for Klotz, and Klotz fully returned Bürger's feelings. He helped Bürger in a number of ways, and the friendship lasted until Klotz's death.

In 1767 Bürger's studies at Halle ended abruptly as a result of a rather unpleasant and unfortunate—but in retrospect innocuous— incident. Like many of his contemporaries Bürger belonged to one of the associations made up of students from various parts of the country ("Landsmannschaften"). These were secret and unlawful societies. The Lower Saxony Association had been dissolved, and a movement was begun in July, 1767, to form a new Lower Saxony Association of residents from the Magdeburg and Halberstadt areas. The first meeting, which was also to be the occasion for a feast, was called for July 25. Unfortunately, the authorities were informed of these developments, and the officers of the association were apprehended. Bürger, as one of the four adjutants, was an officer of rather secondary importance. Even so, he was brought to trial and, despite his plea that the club was not a "Landsmannschaft" but simply a group of good friends, he was found guilty and sentenced to 6–8 days' incarceration. The records of the hearing and the verdict (August 8, 1767) note that Bürger was studying law ("studiert Jura"). When he formally transferred from theology to law is not known, and, although it is easy to see why he gave up theology, it is not clear why he took up law. His natural inclination for the law was minimal as his correspondence shows, although he later proved to be a capable lawyer.[7]

Evidently, Bürger's grandfather, Bauer, had heard of the incident involving the "Landsmannschaften," and he once more recalled his grandson to Aschersleben—where the young jurist did his best to appease the old gentleman. The sojourn in Aschersleben was a very unhappy one; Bürger felt isolated from the world he knew, and he was even separated from his books. Fortunately, he was successful in persuading his grandfather that he should get on with his studies, and in 1768 he left for the University of Göttingen.

Although Bürger was no longer under the immediate influence of Klotz, the latter continued to play a major role in his protegé's career. If Bürger had made a social gaff in his associations with Klotz in Halle, he made an even greater blunder in Göttingen by renting rooms in the house of Klotz's mother-in-law, the widow Sachse. The house was inhabited mainly by wealthy and wild young Russians whose interests were neither intellectual nor academic. Bürger was ludicrously out of place. He did not have the money and should not have had the time, but he tried to keep up pretenses and accrued considerable debts. Repeatedly, his grandfather came to his rescue, but he warned him that he would not do so indefinitely. Bürger's residence in the Sachse household (which was to last until the widow's death in the winter of 1770–71) had a negative and retarding effect on his professional development. His stay there was marked by a series of mésalliances and unpleasant incidents, culminating in Bürger's formal complaint against another student resident (Jakob Ludwig Ratje) with whom he had frequent and violent encounters. Of considerable significance was the fact that Bürger had no strong figure on whom to model himself and whether for better or worse, there was no one in Göttingen to take Klotz's place.

During the early part of his stay in Göttingen, Bürger neglected his studies, his talents, and himself, but gradually he was beginning to make a name for himself as a poet. His earliest printed poem was "Lais und Demosthenes," which appeared in 1768 in the *Göttingschen Gelehrten Beiträgen zum Nutzen und Vergnügen/ bestehend aus Abhandlungen von verschiedenen Materien.* The next year he completed his essay on a Homeric translation, "Etwas über eine deutsche Übersetzung des Homer," which he submitted as part of his petition for membership in the Königliche Deutsche Gesellschaft zu Göttingen (founded in 1738). Despite certain misgivings and reservations, the essay was approved and Bürger became a member of the association, since it was generally acknowledged that he possessed talent as well as flair.

The year 1770 brought a significant upward swing in Bürger's affairs. Although still a resident of the Sachse household, he began to turn his attention more and more seriously to his studies and to his writing. Academically, he developed remarkably well, and for the first time he seemed to pursue his work with some intensity. A statistical account of his borrowings from the university library during the years 1769 to 1772 is quite informative:

1769	8 works
1770	37 works
1771	47 works
1772 (Jan. & Feb.)	8 works[8]

His readings were primarily, but by no means exclusively, in law. He read history, the classics, and a variety of other subjects as well. The bulk of these works were in German or Latin, but Bürger also read French and English. During this period, he was working intermittently on his Homer translation and trying to improve his Greek. At the same time, he nearly completed his translation of "Anthia und Abrokomas," by Xenophon of Ephesus which he published in 1775. With several friends he taught himself Italian and Spanish, and as late as 1798 Boie still possessed a novella Bürger had written in Spanish. Bürger's literary production steadily increased, and in 1770 he published his "Stutzertändelei" ("The Dandy's Dalliance") in the *Hamburger Unterhaltung*.

Gradually, Bürger's circle of friends increased and his intellectual and artistic interests and horizons were no longer encompassed by Frau Sachse and her boarders. He renewed his acquaintance with Heinrich Christian Boie (1744–1806), whom he had met at Klotz's home in Halle. At the time of their first meeting, Boie had not been favorably impressed by Bürger, but in the years that followed he was to become one of his closest friends and staunchest supporters.

Another of Bürger's friends at this time was Johann Erich Biester (1749–1816), who later became the editor of the *Berliner Monatsschrift* and was an influential, if not always popular, critic of the period. In 1770, Biester and Bürger founded the Shakespeare-Klub; they were joined by Boie, the historian Matthias Christian Sprengel, and several others. The members were dedicated to reading, reciting, and discussing the works of Shakespeare in the original, and their rather convoluted rules included one that required members to speak only in Shakespearean expressions (?) at their meetings— a somewhat demanding requisite, considering the fact that they were reading and declaiming Spanish, French, and Italian authors, as well as Shakespeare, at their meetings.

Clearly, Bürger was moving more and more into the literary world, and it was at about this time, toward the end of 1770, that he came to the notice of the Halberstadt poet, Johann Wilhelm Ludwig Gleim (1719–1803), otherwise known as "Vater Gleim." Gleim distinguished himself by vigorously supporting the younger generation of poets, both morally and financially. He took a particular interest in Bürger, perhaps because they both hailed from the same area. In any case, Gleim wrote to Boie early in 1772 in order to inquire about this promising young man. Gleim was also anxious to learn about Bürger's life style, since he had heard that the latter was moving in questionable company and given to drink. Plainly put, he wanted to have a complete report, and in his answer Boie supplied Gleim—and posterity—with a fairly accurate appraisal of Bürger at this stage in his life.

Herr Bürger is now living in a blameless fashion and I promise our nation not a little from his talents. They have suffered by his former life style, but they are not destroyed. I believe his entry into refined and cultured society will now make of him a complete man and easily wear off the rough edges, which are still left over from his former way of living.[9]

Although Bürger may now have qualified for refined and cultivated society, he was still stiflingly poor and his debts increased relentlessly. Certainly the time had come for him to find gainful employment, and his friends went to great lengths to assist him. Klotz even tried to intercede for him with his grandfather, but Bauer overwhelmed him with his vehemence, and Klotz wrote Bürger, in something of a daze, that there was little prospect of aid from that quarter. Klotz also nearly succeeded in securing for Bürger the post of Legationssekretär in Warsaw, but at the last minute the prospect failed.

With Gleim's entering the picture, Bürger's prospects seem to have improved. There was some talk of a position in Magdeburg, but Bürger had to admit that he could not leave Göttingen because of his debts. A visit from Gleim followed—evidently to assess the situation—and when the older poet departed he was poorer by fifty Thaler. The loan was made as an advance, but it was still outstanding thirteen years later, when Gleim came upon the note while working on his will. With his customary good grace and generosity, Gleim wrote Bürger (July, 1784) that he need not fear its being found among his effects (i.e., that he was destroying it), but that Bürger might give the sum to the trust fund which Gleim was then setting up. Bürger should be able to do this easily with the money he would earn from his translation of Homer. After all, "Pope earned 100,000 Thaler with his translation, and Bürger's Homer is better than Pope's."[10]

Even with Gleim's loan Bürger did not go to Magdeburg, nor did Gleim's other efforts come to fruition. Bürger finally found a position with a lawyer, one Dr. Hesse. Initially, he was given to understand that Dr. Hesse was satisfied with his work, and then suddenly, in the fall of 1771, he was replaced. Wurzbach's speculation about "obscure machinations"[11] may, or may not, be true.

Bürger was thus once more unemployed, and in the fall of 1771 he moved into the home of the eminent historian August Ludwig Schlözer, a professor at the University of Göttingen. His responsibilities seem to have been minimal, but so was his income, and the necessity of finding a remunerative position was pressing. During this time, Bürger continued with his own writings, although he could scarcely anticipate making his livelihood from them. Nonetheless, he was now regularly submitting works for publication, primarily to the *Göttinger Musen-Almanach.*

Bürger's correspondence in 1771 indicates that he was engaged in a number of projects, most of which never materialized. He had plans for writing epics and dramas and was also sketching out the details for a work on the Crusades. His actual accomplishments during that year included, among other things, "Das Dörfchen," and a minor occasional poem, "An M.W." Neither was published until some time later, although in 1771 he did publish a drinking song, "Herr Bacchus."

Although Bürger seems to have had ample time to pursue his own work while he was with Schlözer, his position there was perforce a temporary one. During the winter of 1771–72, the search for a position continued but with little success. Klotz had died earlier in 1771, but Gleim, Boie, and others proved to be equally loyal friends. Ultimately, it was Boie who found the solution, although it turned out to be disastrous, even in a career peppered with calamity.

Towards the end of February or the beginning of March, 1772, Bürger heard from Boie that the position of rural magistrate (Amtmann) on the assizes of the Von Uslar family would become vacant on July 1 of that year. Boie had received this information from Hofrat Ernst Ferdinand Listn. Boie recommended Bürger strongly, and Listn indicated that he was amenable to the suggestion. Listn was then living in retirement, but was guardian for two children of the Von Uslar family. At the very outset, Boie foresaw "many difficulties," but he probably had no idea how many.

The Von Uslar territories at Altengleichen were located at Gelliehausen (about a mile from Göttingen). At that time they covered six villages, and the magisterial domain of Altengleichen was under Hannoverian (i.e. British) jurisdiction, with its seat at Hannover. The Von Uslar family, to whom the magistrate was responsible, existed in a permanent state of internecine warfare. Its two main branches waged a constant war for supremacy, and their labyrinthine intrigues, schemes, and suits required constant legal counsel. The spokesman for the senior branch of the family, the

Ludolfian, was Colonel Adam Heinrich Von Uslar, and he was pitted against one Dr. Hans Von Uslar, who represented the junior, or Melchior, branch.

Given the endless legal entanglements in which the family was involved, the post of magistrate was a lucrative one. It was also an appointed post, and over a period of years the head of the senior branch of the family, Adam Heinrich, had managed to gain control of the appointment and was thus able to exercise strong influence over local affairs.

Listn had served as magistrate for twenty-five years (1742–1747) but had now more or less retired to the role of senior adviser. As guardian of two minor brothers of the Ludolfian branch, he may have believed that his recommendation for magistrate would at least be acceptable to that branch of the family. He could not make that assumption. His proposal of Bürger's name met with a startling lack of resistance by the Melchior branch of the family, but Adam Heinrich, evidently suspecting that he had been tricked, immediately insisted upon another candidate, an Assessor Oppermann from Göttingen. The junior branch of the family now galvanized itself for Bürger, and the confrontation was set up: henceforth Adam Heinrich concentrated his influence and energy on eliminating Bürger, since he had become a symbol for the opposition. Clearly the situation was a hornet's nest, and Bürger was *persona omnibus non grata* even before he had arrived—in fact, before he was even offered the post.

The pro-Bürger faction was unusually firm in its stand, and Adam Heinrich sensed that he might not prevail. Thus, he "compromised," and it was agreed that both Bürger and Oppermann should prepare legal briefs which would then be submitted for decision to the law faculty at Göttingen. Bürger wrote three briefs, one of which is lost, and one was published by Goedeke in 1873: "Relatio ex actis inquisitionalibus wider Anna Margaretha Kerlin und Katherina Margaretha Rel(icta) *Wegner* zu Bischhausen in puncto Infanticidii."[12] The law faculty at Göttingen declared that both briefs were acceptable and remained otherwise noncommittal. Adam Heinrich finally acquiesced, but he insisted that Bürger should put up a 600-Thaler bond. Given Bürger's financial situation, he might as easily have required 6,000, but in this instance, it was so clearly a vindictive act that offers of a loan were made by a number of people. Ultimately, it was Bürger's grandfather, who, having decided that Bürger had finally settled down, supplied the required sum. Bauer himself came to Gelliehausen and not only took care of the bond money but also paid many of Bürger's other debts. Unfortunately, he could still not bring himself to trust his grandson entirely, and left the bond money with Listn. It was a good and final reconciliation between grandfather and grandson; the old man died on December 31, 1772. Bürger, who had taken up his duties on July 1 of that year, was genuinely saddened and expressed his grief in the poem "Bei dem Grabe meines guten Großvaters Jakob Philipp Bauers" ("At the grave of my good grandfather, Jakob Philipp Bauer") which he caused to be privately printed by Dieterich in a single edition of one hundred copies. Significantly, Bürger never wrote a single line upon his father's death some eight years earlier, nor would he memorialize his mother when she died three years later.

Outwardly at least, Bürger's professional career advanced appreciably in 1772. He completed his studies with some distinction, as his letters of recommendation reveal. Von Selchow wrote that Bürger had attended his lectures "with the most praiseworthy and uninterrupted energy, and otherwise led a modest and discreet existence." ("mit rühmlichstem und ununterbrochenem Fleiße besuchet, und so einen bescheidenen und sittsamen Lebenswandel geführet").[13] The other letters, from Professors Meister and Pütter, confirm Von Selchow's assertion, and there is little doubt that, with the possibility of a secure position in sight, Bürger devoted himself to his studies with unprecedented vigor.

Neither his studies nor his new position at Gelliehausen took up all his time, and Bürger was able to continue his poetic career as well. The year 1772 was one of considerable literary activity in Göttingen. Bürger's friends, Boie and Biester, were extraordinarily active, the Shakespeare-Klub flourished, and there were several newcomers on the scene, including Johann Heinrich Voß. Perceptibly, a sense of program was developing among the younger poets, and it took formal shape in 1772 with the establishment of the Göttinger Dichterbund, or as the members called it, the Göttinger Hainbund. Among the founders were Boie and Friedrich Wilhelm Gotter, and in the course of time almost all of the Göttingen poets were, in one way or another, associated with the group, though not necessarily members.

The orientation of the Hainbund was vigorously Germanic in every way. Klopstock represented the highest ideal of German poetry, and Wieland and his works (tainted, as they were, by foreign influences) were vigorously rejected. The ideals of the Hainbund were lofty, and the members regarded them with esteem and reverence. It was all very pleasant, but in the long run it left little substantive impression on the German literary scene. Bürger never actually belonged to the Hainbund, although he was regularly invited to its meetings and frequently attended. Essentially his character and temperament differed (as did his poetry) from that of the Hainbund.

Bürger simply was not a "Parnassian;" he was too much attached to the earth and to the senses. Moreover, the pervasive sentimentality of the Bund was foreign to him, and the underlying incompatibility was perhaps unconsciously acknowledged in Klopstock's question to Miller,[14] "Just tell me, is Bürger really so much one of us?" Bürger probably wasn't; he was much more the "Genie" in tune with the highly charged animacy of the "Sturm und Drang." Shakespeare was his god, not Klopstock, and while the members of the Hainbund were intoning the "antique" odes of Klopstock, Bürger was immersed in reading Shakespeare and Homer.

In other areas as well, there were differences of opinion between Bürger and the Hainbund, such as their attitude towards Wieland, whom the Bund "officially" held in utter contempt. Bürger, however, had dipped freely from Wieland's well and openly acknowledged his fondness for that poet. The attitude of the Hainbund towards Wieland is symptomatic in a larger sense of the general nature of the association. The Bund tended to adopt polarized views of literature and expressed its attitudes in hyperbolic terms of approval or disapproval. In a rather unstructured and unsophisticated fashion, their attitudes reflected a vague combination of aesthetic and historical ideas. Bürger had little time for such abstractions; he was a practical poet, struggling to shape his own craft and artistic expression.

When Bürger took the position of rural magistrate at Gelliehausen, he doubtless foresaw that it would lead to considerable difficulties with Colonel Adam Heinrich Von Uslar. It is quite unlikely, however, that he anticipated the anguish and bitterness that would so thoroughly mark his tenure during the next twelve years. The forces bent upon removing him were active from the very beginning and made themselves felt directly.

In an evidently rare moment of accord, both branches of the Von Uslar family sponsored a formal complaint addressed to the Royal Court (kgl. Hofgericht) in Hannover. They requested that Bürger be dismissed on the grounds that (1) he was not a native Hannoverian and (2) that he had had almost no experience in the practice of law. Additionally, he was charged with incompetence, neglect, and numerous other failings. Listn, acting for Bürger, filed a reply, but to no avail, and Bürger was ordered to appear before the court of inquiry on December 21, 1772. In a brief written for the occasion, Bürger replied one by one to the charges and volunteered to take his oath on each item. The court finally decided for Bürger on March 18, 1773, and simultaneously instructed the Von Uslars not to meddle further in Bürger's manner of discharging his duties. The effect of this decision was to spur the Von Uslars on to even greater and more furious attempts to rid themselves of their magistrate. On July 12, 1773, their second set of charges against Bürger were dismissed, and the latter could once more return to his duties.

In his first year in office Bürger had not received any salary, and his debts were almost overwhelming. His appeals to Listn were all cordially acknowledged in a good businesslike fashion, but they never yielded any results. Listn was a man not excessively burdened with scruples, particularly in matters involving money, and before he went bankrupt several years later, he had defrauded Bürger of some 12,000 to 15,000 Reichsthaler, as well as the six hundred Thaler given him by Bürger's grandfather. As on so many previous occasions when Bürger was in straitened circumstances, it was his grandfather who came to the rescue, and even now, after his death, he was able to help once more. Bauer's will had been probated, and Bürger received 8,000 Thaler from the estate. For the moment, at least, catastrophe was averted.

Despite the constant abrasions in his personal life, Bürger could regard 1773 as a fruitful year poetically. His ambition rose steadily, and his plans ranged over a broad variety of subjects. Several of his letters contain references to a major epic poem, "Die Offenbarungen" ("The Revelations"), which, however, never materialized. He also told Boie of his plans for a middle-class tragedy in the manner of Shakespeare.[15] The inspiration for this work had come from old ballads and folk songs, and the dramatis personae of Bürger's intended play were to be the people of the village. With little or no experience in the theater, it is astonishing how pressing Bürger's urge was to write for it. "Language will be the least important thing, action will be everything. In whole scenes, there will not be a word spoken. Genius, Genius of Shakespeare, let me soar!" The excitement soon wore off, however, and as the dramatic urge cooled, Bürger turned his attention to ballads.

The year 1773 was not simply one of plans and projects but also of accomplishments; foremost among Bürger's achievements for that, or any other year was "Lenore." Even before its publication it catapulted Bürger to a level of fame that he would never reach again and from which he would never really recover. "Lenore" stands as the pivotal point in Bürger's life, and henceforth it became "Bürger—the poet of 'Lenore'." As author of this monumental ballad Bürger gained admission to the poetic pantheon, but in doing so he unavoidably took on the responsibilities that go with such a role and, in the long run these responsibilities became his albatross. For the remainder of his life, Bürger labored with the hope that he might surpass "Lenore"; unfortunately, he never equaled it. In terms of poetic achievement, 1773 was thus a major year, as, in addition to "Lenore," Bürger finished "Des armen Suschens Traum" ("Poor Suschen's Dream"), "Minnesolde" ("Love's Wages"), and "Gegenliebe" ("Mutual Love"). Bürger had also completed a second ballad, "Der Raubgraf" ("The Robber Baron"), and begun a third, "Der wilde Jäger" ("The Wild Huntsman"). The number of poems from his pen appearing in the *Göttinger Musen-Almanach* was steadily increasing, and in 1773 the first edition of his "Nachtfeier der Venus" ("The Vigil of Venus") appeared (albeit without his knowledge or approval) in the *Teutsche Merkur.* Bürger's poetic star was rapidly rising, but his personal life and career as a magistrate were mired in a morass of hassles, financial crises, grievances, and general disarray.

During his first year in office, Bürger had stayed with Listn and his wife. In the following year (1773) Listn went to Hannover on business and left Bürger alone with his wife for almost the entire year. The Frau Hofrätin was, by all accounts, a lady of exceptional grace and sensitivity. She was also something of a pietist and mystic, and believed that she was communicating with the world of spirits.

Bürger developed a great fondness for her and had high regard for her opinion. Unfortunately, the lady was in a delicate state emotionally, and in the course of the year her health seriously deteriorated. Listn found it necessary to return to Gelliehausen, and Bürger was again embroiled in turmoil: "the insane wife, the tormented, desperate husband, and me between the two."[16] The only thing to do was to leave, and early in 1774 Bürger moved to the nearby village of Niedeck.

In Niedeck he came into close and frequent contact with the family of the local magistrate, Johann Karl Leonhart, the same man before whom Bürger had sworn his oath of office two years earlier. Leonhart was gregarious, generous to the point of extravagance, and not disdainful of worldly pleasures. His enjoyment of life was restricted, however, by the need to feed and care for his (second) wife and eight children. There was never much money or food in the Leonhart household, but what it lacked materially was more than made up for by the sheer exuberance one found there. A more welcome antidote for Bürger's recent (domestic) troubles could not be imagined, and Bürger responded to this wholesome domestic scene with undisguised pleasure.

Among Leonhart's children by his first marriage were two daughters, Dorothea Marianne (Dorette) and Auguste Wilhelmine Eva (Molly), who were eighteen and sixteen years old respectively when Bürger arrived in Niedeck. Wurzbach describes their personalities as being almost diametrically opposed: "If Dorette was quiet, patient, modest, very pious, content with, and grateful for little, Molly had something lively, sensual, and unusually attractive in her manner. Molly was a thoroughly feminine and delicate nature, and at the same time incomparably more talented and brighter than her sister." Bürger was attracted to both sisters and found himself torn between them. Unfortunately, Molly had not yet reached the age of consent.

It is not always easy to understand the motivating factors in Bürger's life and it can be at times unnerving to try to ascertain why he did this or that in a given situation. His formal engagement to Dorette Leonhart in mid-February, 1774, was one of those occasions. Certainly he moved with extraordinary haste, but by nature he was always inclined to plunge rather than ponder. Perhaps the opportunity came at just the right moment in his life: he had just extricated himself from the unsavory situation at the Listns and had moved into a thoroughly attractive one with the Leonharts. It is not unthinkable that Bürger moved aggressively to assure himself a place in this wholesome and vital family at the earliest possible opportunity. In retrospect, Bürger recognized the terrible folly of his decision, but it was, unfortunately, the wisdom of hindsight.

Very shortly after his engagement to Dorette, Bürger realized the depth of his attachment to Molly, but, curiously, he did nothing to break off his engagement or even retard matters. Quite the contrary, Bürger committed himself definitively, and the wedding took place on November 22, 1774. The couple settled into the Leonhart household, where they lived until moving to Wöllmershausen during the following summer.

Both before and after the wedding and for the next ten years Bürger lived in a constant state of internal turmoil, which at times grew so intense that it threatened to topple his reason. At the same time, in his defense, it must be acknowledged that, successful or not, he made a continuing and conscious effort to honor his commitment to Dorette. As the poet recalls in his "Beichte" ("Confession") of 1790:

> I have had *two sisters* for wives. In an extraordinary way, too complicated to narrate here, I happened to marry the one *without loving her*. Indeed, even as I approached the altar with her, I bore in my heart coals of the most glowing passion for the other one, who, at that time, was still a child and hardly fourteen or fifteen years old. I was quite aware of it; but more or less out of unfamiliarity with myself, I took it (though I could not actually deny it to myself) to be at most a mild infatuation ["kleinen Fieberanfall"] which would soon go away of its own. If I could only have had but half a glance into the cruel future, it would have been my duty, even at the altar, to retreat from the marriage vows. My "infatuation" did not go away, but rather in the course of ten years grew more and more inextinguishable, and in proportion as I loved, my love was requited by my most beloved.[17]

The events of 1774, for whatever reasons Bürger may have attributed to them, had a strongly negative effect on his poetic productivity. His engagement to Dorette seemed to silence rather than inspire him, and in the course of the whole year he could only claim to have written something less than a dozen poems. One of his letters at this time (to Boie) is particularly revealing: 'If it continues like this, I shall be dead to the muses of friendship and the whole world, simply in order to pursue love ("Minne"). I can do nothing at the moment but love ("lieben"); love on going to sleep, love on awakening, love in dreaming. Right now I cannot write ("Verse machen"), nor do I have any desire to. All ideas vanish in smoke, and I am so incapable of finding a rhyme that it seems to me as if there were not two words in the whole language that rhymed.'[18]

During the early months of Bürger's marriage, before the full outburst of his passion for Molly, he seemed to have settled down. His reputation as a poet was established; he was in touch with and sought after by the larger outside world; his duties were, for once, relatively unencumbered, and, at least for the moment, his complaints about impending financial catastrophe had lost some of their shrillness. Aware, perhaps, of the need for keeping away from Molly, but for perfectly good reasons otherwise, Bürger and Dorette proceeded with their plans to move out of the Leonhart household and establish their own home. Thus in the summer of 1775 they moved into a newly built farmhouse in nearby Wöllmershausen. By that time Bürger had become a father. On May 24, 1775, Dorette gave birth to their first child, Antoinette Caecilia Elisabeth, and Bürger's delight was immense. His love for his daughter became a focal point of unparalleled joy in his existence, and at least for a short time he could shower all his love and affection on her.

Bürger's moment of respite from routine calamity was dishearteningly brief, and his letters soon took on again the tone of frustrated and impotent rage at his work and his impecunious condition. "Annoyance after annoyance! Chicanery after chicanery! Bungling after bungling! And for the last two years no salary! And just recently cheated out of 700 Thaler, etc., etc."[19] Unquestionably, Bürger had much cause for complaint, and he was justly outraged at having been so defrauded. Unfortunately, the figure of 700 Thaler represented an overly conservative estimate; when the full account of Listn's embezzlement was published (he filed claims for bankruptcy in 1775), Bürger had lost between 12,000 and 15,000 Thaler. Given his other worries, apart from the Listn affair, it is not surprising that he began to express concern with his gall bladder.

The move to Wöllmershausen did little to subdue Bürger's feelings for Molly, and in the summer of 1775 he wrote the first of the *Molly Lieder* ("Songs to Molly"). In addition, he finished two more ballads, "Der Ritter und sein Liebchen" ("The Knight and His Sweetheart") and "Die Weiber von Weinsberg" ("The Women of Weinsberg"), of which the latter was to add considerably to his reputation. As usual, he was also full of plans: there were plans for a translation of Shakespeare's Timon monologue as well as an ambitious plan to publish a collection of German folk songs, neither of which materialized. On September 25 he completed the introduction to his translation of Xenophon of Ephesus's *Anthia and Abrocomas,* a Greek romance he had been working at, off and on, since 1770, and which he published in 1775.

Shortly before Christmas, 1775, Bürger's mother died, but there is no indication that he was unduly saddened. Inevitably there was an argument over the inheritance, this time with his elder sister, Henriette Oesfeld, but in the end Bürger received 500 Thaler and his share (one third of $74\frac{1}{2}$ acres) of farm land in Aschersleben, worth more than 4,000 Thaler. In order to receive his inheritance Bürger had to present himself in person, but as might be expected, he had to borrow four or five Louis d'or to cover the expenses of the trip.

For Bürger disaster was a way of life, and 1776 simply tended to confirm his sense of despair. In January he wrote to Goethe, "My vital juices have all dried up except my bile ("Galle") which is now the only and autonomous mistress of my whole machine."[20] The desire for escape appears repeatedly in his correspondence during these years, and it is not difficult to sympathize with it. His dual role as *pater familias* and *amicus extra curriculum* was not an easy one to accommodate to, and Bürger's attempts to do so were baleful failures. His passion for Molly was nearly beyond control, and it was impossible to suppress, much less hide. Even so, Bürger was not unaware of his duties, responsibilities, and commitments to Dorette, and he struggled to resist the temptations which faced him. He was determined to do his duty, but given Bürger's volatile and sensual nature, there was little hope of his succeeding. Matters apparently came to a head (at least between Bürger and Molly) sometime in August, and Molly tried to tear herself away. By then, however, it was too late; their lives were inextricably woven together, and though they continued to resist and swore continence, it was a hollow oath. Dorette's attitudes have never been fully revealed; certainly she was long-suffering, patient, and understanding.

The anguish of being confronted with insoluble problems in

Bürger's personal life was exacerbated by a new storm in his professional life which erupted in June. In its convolutions, the affair with Pastor Zuch is reminiscent of the Von Uslar case some years earlier. Were it not for its historical authenticity, it would beggar belief; and, indeed, it has distinctly comic overtones, although these were unfortunately muffled by the oppressive seriousness with which everyone viewed the matter. In simplest outline, it seems that Bürger, as part of his duties, had the responsibility of settling insurance claims for the area, and since the rectory at Gelliehausen had recently been damaged by fire a claim was filed by the pastor, Johann Christian Zuch. As repairs were in progress, Pastor Zuch's wife was struck on the head by a piece of fallen timber from the ruins of the building, and the next day Zuch arrived in Bürger's office in a rage. As luck would have it, one of the Von Uslars was in the office at the time, and Zuch evidently regarded this as an ideal opportunity to impress Von Uslar by vilifying Bürger. The accounts intimate that Zuch had been prodded into action by his wife, but once under sail Zuch followed the wind and flew at Bürger with breathless vigor and remarkable inventiveness, including charges that Bürger had defrauded his magisterial district. Bürger's initial reaction was to bring charges against Zuch, but on second thought he decided to let the matter drop. Zuch, however, had been exhilarated by the experience, and seeing it as potentially profitable, he now demanded that a completely new rectory be built for him; and for good measure he lodged a complaint against Bürger with the consistory. Moreover, he conspired with the now bankrupt and infamous Hofrat Listn in fabricating awesome tales about Bürger's alleged crimes. Bürger, they proclaimed, had been placed under arrest in Hannover because of embezzlement of deposited funds. In the face of such slander, Bürger was finally moved to litigate against Zuch, and although he eventually won the case, it proved one more drain on his already exhausted nervous system.

Given the variety and number of difficulties simultaneously facing Bürger, it is astonishing that he could still find time and energy to devote to his writing. For all the tribulations of the late 70s, they represent Bürger's most productive period. The year 1776 saw the completion of numerous poems, including "Abendphantasie eines Liebenden" ("Evening Phantasy of One in Love"), "Das Mädel, das ich meine" ("The Lass I Woo"), "Schön

Suschen" ("Lovely Suschen"), and several ballads, including "Lenardo und Blandine," which Bürger regarded with particular favor. In addition, Bürger resumed his work on the translation of the *Iliad*. Encouragement for the project had come from many sides; Goethe had publicly applauded it and, together with other members of the Weimar court, offered Bürger a total of 65 Louis d'or to free him, in some measure, from his financial worries and allow him the time to finish the translation.

Bürger accepted the gift and, for the time being, proceeded with the translation. Other forces, however, diverted his attention, and new and exciting plans distracted him. Work on the *Iliad* slowed, and the project was finally shelved as Bürger addressed himself to different problems. In the course of 1776, Bürger fairly burst with plans. His letters reveal that he was working on a drama of freedom, with material taken from Plutarch, a prose novella, an essay on peasant character, an essay, "Kritische Bedenken" ("Critical Misgivings"); and "Das Eselsopfer" (The Donkey Sacrifice) which was to have been a kind of *Dunciad*. Like so many of Bürger's other plans, none of these materialized.

One work which did come into being in 1776 was a pair of essays published under the title, "Aus Daniel Wunderlichs Buch" ("From Daniel Wunderlich's Book"). In these two essays, Bürger sought to articulate his own position vis-à-vis poetics and his own role as poet. Heart over mind, viscera over cerebrum, this, in rather oversimplified terms, was Bürger's view of poetics and the role of the poet. It was not a particularly sophisticated platform, nor was Bürger's program for carrying it out. It was hardly surprising, therefore, that Bürger's "Daniel Wunderlich" raised a number of eyebrows and was not greeted by universal acclaim. The following year Friedrich Nicolai published a rather tepid and academic satire, "Eyn feyner kleyner ALMANACH Vol Schönerr echterr ljblicherr Volcksljder, lustiger Reyen vnndt kleglicherr Mordgeschichte, gesungen von Gabriel Wunderlich weyl. Bencklsengerrn zu Dessaw, . . . "

Whether for his poetry or for his esthetic theories, people were listening to Bürger, and each year his audience and reputation increased. He was on first-name basis (familiar form) with Goethe, sought after as a contributor to various almanachs, and in correspondence with some of the leading literary figures of the day. Thus his lot as a poet gave him at least some cause for satisfaction, and

1777 seemed, initially, to promise continued success. Early in the year he visited Boie in Hannover and soon thereafter he met the poet, satirist, and philosopher, Georg Christoph Lichtenberg, with whom he developed a close and lasting friendship. At the end of April, 1777 the elder Leonhart died and left Bürger as guardian of his eldest son, Carl. The poet took his responsibilities with the Leonhart family very seriously; there were young children who had to be cared for, and Bürger was determined to fulfill his duties to them. Of course, a bond was required, but the size of the bond, 1,000 Thaler, was far beyond anything Bürger could procure. His search for assistance occupied the remainder of the year, and it was not until shortly before the deadline for filing in February, 1778, that he finally won the support of Kammerrat Carl August Hardenberg-Reventlow himself.

The assumption of his role as executor, and the duties it entailed, added one more burden to Bürger's life. Nonetheless, at about this time he decided to publish a separate edition of his poems. It was a long cherished dream of Bürger's, and for several years he had hoped it might eventually materialize. Thus on August 1, encouraged by Boie, Voß, and others, Bürger announced the edition and began the search for subscribers. He wrote to everyone he knew, and his friends alerted their acquaintances. The results were unexpected and staggering, for in the first six months Bürger accumulated about 1,200 subscribers, and before the book went to press the number had grown to some 2,000. Included were numerous royal personages including the Queen herself and Prince Ernst. Among the literary figures were, of course, all of Bürger's friends, plus "Frau Räthin Goethe zu Frankfurt a.M." (Goethe's mother), "Herr Lessing, Hofrath und Bibliothekar in Wolfenbüttel," et. al. It was, unquestionably, a very distinguished list, and Bürger could hardly believe his good fortune. The contract was signed with Dieterich, who later became one of Bürger's closest and most loyal friends. Bürger was able to persuade Daniel Chodowiecki, one of the most famous and sought-after engravers of the day, to furnish the illustrations. Immediately, the poet set to work. He gathered poems written earlier but never published, as well as some poems which had appeared elsewhere. He also wrote new ones, revised, filed, edited, and worked with unprecedented energy and intensity.

Unfortunately, Bürger could not entirely put aside his official duties, and these became an almost insupportable burden. He saw himself as a Prometheus chained forever to Altengleichen, with vultures gnawing daily at his entrails. He loathed it, he detested it, he hated it, and his frustration erupted volcanically at the thought that he could not escape. "My God, it's enough to perforate your soul," "it's almost as if I had been eating it with a spoon."[21] He felt himself beleagured and hounded, but worst of all trapped; and, of course, he was fundamentally right. He knew he could not earn his living with his writings; and he had a wife and daughter, to whom he felt an inviolable sense of duty.

While Bürger was moved by a sense of duty toward his wife, he was borne by a boundless love for his little daughter, and when she died, unexpectedly in December, 1777, his grief was fathomless. Apparently in the blossom of health, she had suddenly contracted a fever, withered and died within a fortnight. "I would have given anything to save this, my only joy, but all remedies were in vain." Bürger felt that nothing could equal the blow, and his letters dating from this time are testaments of sorrow.

There was no remedy for his grief, except perhaps time and work, and Bürger immersed himself in his writing and in his efforts to extricate himself from the constraints of Altengleichen. He had applied for the post at Niedeck which had been made vacant by the death of his father-in-law, but early in 1778 the decision was made to give it to someone else. Niedeck was also under Hannoverian jurisdiction, and the powers in Hannover had already had considerable experience with Bürger's work, his distaste for his position, his lack of initiative, and his endless delays and postponements. Bürger was furious, but one suspects that he was not utterly surprised by the decision.

Other prospects for change were beginning to emerge as various friends tried to help. Early in 1778 plans were made to establish a resident theater in Hannover, and Bürger was second in line as choice for director. It is hard to imagine why he should have been considered for the post; his experience with the theater was less than minimal. For one reason or another, the plan fell through, and Bürger was spared having to face that prospect. Another possibility, and quite an attractive one, was evidently eliminated by Bürger himself. He had been approached for the post of Hofrat at a small court on the Rhine. The salary was 1,000 Thaler, and his duties would have left him ample time for his writing, but Bürger somehow quashed the prospect with "a few incidental questions." The year ended as it had begun, with Bürger still rural magistrate at Altengleichen. His situation was not entirely unchanged, however, for he could look back on 1778 as a year of considerable accomplishment.

Major events had occurred in 1778, the most important, of course, being the publication of the first edition of his poems. The poet's feverish work of editing and revising proved not to have been in vain, for the critical reaction was highly favorable. Unquestionably, Bürger could regard the venture as a success, even if it did not accomplish everything he had hoped it would. The second major occurrence of the year 1778 was Bürger's assumption of the editorship of the *Göttinger Musen-Almanach*. The *Almanach* had seen three editors in almost as many years; first Boie, then Voß, then Bürger's immediate predecessor, Goeckingk, who had edited it from 1776 to 1778. Bürger remained its editor for the rest of his life, until 1794. It was an appointment of some importance, and although it required prodigious amounts of time and effort, the position yielded an annual income of 500 Thaler, and that meant a good deal to Bürger. Moreover, it was a position of influence and gave him a relatively free hand to do with the journal as he wished. As it turned out, Bürger took his editorship seriously and raised the standards and quality of the journal appreciably during his tenure.

Much of the material submitted to the editor required extensive reworking if it could be salvaged at all, and Bürger found himself not only editing the *Almanach* but rewriting other people's poetry, which was both a thankless and fruitless task, since the end product was a hybrid, neither Bürger's nor the original author's product. It is difficult to understand—given the immense drains on Bürger's time—why or how he could have involved himself with such busy-work. Beyond question, he was a man of colossal energy, but for the *Musen-Almanach* for 1779 alone he reworked thirty-three poems by a variety of minor poets. Quite clearly his commitments either exceeded his capabilities or were assumed in order to escape previous ones. The record seems to indicate the latter. Over and over, Bürger initiated projects with titanic energy and enthusiasm, but quickly lost interest as other ideas replaced them on his list of priorities.

In 1778, when Bürger became editor of the *Musen-Almanach,* he had a number of other projects underway which had been either temporarily or permanently set aside. The Homer translation represented perhaps the most flagrant case of neglect. Goethe had collected another 51 Louis d'or to encourage him to complete the work, and Bürger had graciously accepted the money. He had not, however, produced another line, a fact that Goethe never forgot. Other projects, too, had been begun and dropped, including Bürger's proposed translation of both *Macbeth* and *Ossian.* A sample of *Ossian* was to appear the following year, but it too would remain a torso. Bürger had begun his adaptation of *Macbeth* in 1777 but did not complete it until 1782.

Bürger's peripatetic manner may also be seen in his handling of his magisterial duties. He admitted that he shuffled papers like cards in order to give the impression that he was doing something, although, in effect, he accomplished nothing. The strain of applying himself, year in and out, to his detested duties began to have visibly negative effects on Bürger's health, and he complained that he could not sit, sleep, or write, and generally felt wretched. In the summer of 1778 he traveled to Hofgeismar in an effort to recover his health, but evidently with little success. In March Dorette had given birth to a girl, Marianne Friederike Henriette, but Bürger's grief at the recent loss of Antoinette, and his overwhelming discouragement did not allow him to take any particular delight in his new daughter. Marianne, who never really won her father's unqualified affection, survived into her 85th year and died unmarried in 1862. Very little is known about her. After her father's death she lived with his sister and her husband, Pastor Oesfeld.

Bürger's health and outlook never improved when he considered the state of his finances. By the end of January, 1779, the 800 Thaler he had received from Dieterich from the sale of his *Gedichte* had been devoured and there was little prospect of more to come. His annual salary could never begin to cover his living costs, even though he could now at least look forward to the additional income from the *Musen-Almanach.* In addition to his financial problems, Bürger faced an increasingly difficult domestic situation. His passion for Molly raged almost unchecked, and by the summer of 1779 it had

developed to such a point that even Dorette, who exercised un-
believable patience and forebearing, must have urged some measure
of discretion. Presumably in order to preserve a semblance of calm,
Molly went to live with her sister and her husband (Elderhorst)
in Bissendorf, where she spent the summer and stayed through
the following winter. The separation caused Bürger (and evidently
Molly as well) immense anguish, though he made a valiant effort
to hide it. Inevitably there was a marked effect on his writing, and
it fell off badly in 1779. His main occupation of the year seems to
have been with his translation of *Ossian* and with editing the *Musen-
Almanach*.

Ossian and the *Musen-Almanach* were cold comfort without
Molly, and Bürger found himself unable any longer to tolerate the
overwhelming sense of emptiness and futility which defined the
boundaries of his existence. For years he had talked and written
about the possibility of escape, of a flight to America, to the South
Seas, anywhere, to liberate himself from the pressures of his life and
domestic situation. Robinson Crusoe became his dream figure, and
Tahiti the island of refuge. In real life, however, Bürger was never
cut out to be a Robinson, and certainly he could not afford the passage to Tahiti. On the other hand, with great determination he succeeded in making at least a temporary break with his intolerable
situation at the office, and early in 1780 he leased the Appenrode
farm from General Adam Heinrich von Uslar. With Dorette, Marianne, their horse (an expensive animal that Bürger could ill afford),
and their dog, Bettelmann, he moved to the country, intent upon
becoming a farmer, living on the land and close to nature. He managed to arrange it so that his duties were handled by a substitute;
and what could not be taken care of by the latter, Bürger settled
by mail. Although the arrangement pleased him, it was not viewed
with particular favor by his superiors in Hannover.

In his determination to devote himself to farming, Bürger resolved
to give up everything connected with his former life, including his
writing, and in the weeks after his arrival at Appenrode the few
letters he wrote reveal an effervescent enthusiasm and abandon. He
was up early, riding, enjoying the scenery: "I am wallowing in my
garden like a mole."[22]

Although it is likely Bürger could tell a molehill from a mountain,
it soon became abundantly clear that he had not the foggiest,

most rudimentary knowledge of farming. To be sure, his health improved, but nothing else connected with the venture showed the slightest signs of prospering. Quite the contrary, Bürger very soon recognized the enormity of his move. As early as June, 1780, he stood face to face with financial disaster, and he wrote a desperate letter to Dieterich for help. Even with Dieterich's aid, however, the situation could not be salvaged, although it is difficult to agree entirely with Wurzbach, who says that "it was the cause of his complete financial ruin."[23] Despite the continuing losses incurred by his venture, Bürger was under lease at Appenrode and had to stay there. Moreover, when the lease ran out two years later, he was able to renew it at favorable terms, and so the family remained there until 1784.

After the initial flame of agricultural enthusiasm had died down Bürger returned to his efforts to secure a position which would allow him to resign from his Altengleichen position. There was some hope in October, 1780, that he might succeed Boie in his post as Stabssekretär (Staff Secretary) in Hannover, but the matter came to nothing. Bürger's management, mismanagement, or neglect of his current position was fairly common knowledge, and that knowledge did not constitute a particularly favorable recommendation. Each year Bürger renewed his efforts to obtain a better position, but he was to remain another three years in his detested post.

Creatively, Bürger had entered a rather long period of relative inactivity in 1780. The *Musen-Almanach* took much of his time, but beyond this he neglected his writing. At the start of his new life in Appenrode, he had stated his intention to put aside poetry, but even after his initial fever had subsided, the muse was quiescent in him. Homer, *Macbeth,* and *Ossian* all remained fragmentary or were simply *"in cursu,"* and all the former plans were apparently forgotten or shelved.

Bürger continued his search for a new position, but invariably the possibilities crumbled to dust in his hands. One such instance occurred in May, 1781, when Duke Karl August came to Göttingen on an incognito visit from Weimar. The duke arranged a special visit with Bürger and spent several—apparently pleasant—hours with him. At the conclusion of his visit, Karl August asked Bürger to accompany him as far as Heiligenstadt, and Bürger regarded this request as potentially significant. Possibly the duke might wish to invite him to accept some post or other in Weimar? Such a possibility was unlikely; the duke and other members of the court in Weimar, including Goethe, had supported the Homer translation with more than words, and they were still waiting for some sign of progress.

Bürger's letter of appeal to Goethe, written about the same time, produced no more positive results. Goethe replied cordially, but in a businesslike fashion, asking Bürger specifically what kind of a position he had in mind. Bürger's reply was a model of indiscretion. In its detail, tone, and candor, it was distressingly intemperate. The poet's wrath and frustration were understandable, but as so often happened, his venting them either did him considerable harm or prevented his improving his lot. At crucial moments, such as this, Bürger showed a sad inability to "read" people. Goethe's reaction may be deduced from the fact that he did not reply until February, 1782, in a very circumspect and distant manner, and offered Bürger little more than good advice.

Bürger's need for good advice—at least in his personal life—was probably never greater than in the concluding months of 1781. His passion for Molly was entirely out of hand, and the poet found himself morassed in his struggle to find a modus vivendi between Dorette and Molly. In every way the situation had become intolerable, and there is little doubt that knowledge of the affair was relatively public. A final impasse had been reached. With an alarming lack of concern for social approbation, Bürger, Dorette, and Molly determined upon a course of action which was, in fact, no action at all, but simply a mutual (and explicit?) agreement to acknowledge and accept the status quo. Bürger could thus continue to deport himself before the world as Dorette's husband and, in private, enjoy the pleasures of his mistress. It is hardly necessary to comment on the morality of the arrangement, but Dorette's role in this *ménage-à-trois* was hardly an enviable one. Bürger, however, adjusted rapidly in his newly defined situation. Wurzbach's assertion, that "the compromise was the best solution that could be devised, and all participants were content with it," bespeaks, quite clearly, a prejudiced point of view.[24] However satisfactory or unsatisfactory the "compromise" in the Bürger household, it seemed to work, and, in fact, lasted until Dorette's death. With amazing grace she tolerated an intolerable situation, and Bürger, by many kindresses, showed that he was not oblivious to the difficulty of her position.

In May, 1782, Molly visited Bürger's sister in Langendorf, and there on June 19 gave birth to a son, Emil (1782–1841). When Molly returned to Bürger and Dorette, the baby remained with his aunt. Molly returned and spent the following winter with her son in Friederike's home, and Emil continued to live there until 1792, when Bürger brought him to Göttingen. No scandal attached to Emil's birth, and it was due to Friederike's discreet handling of the situation that no one was aware of what had happened.

The series of personal and domestic convulsions seemed endless, and Bürger was swept breathlessly from one crisis to the next. The immediate one facing him in the summer of 1782 concerned the Leonhart estate, for which he was responsible and which had been a source of irritation, off and on, since 1777. Originally, he had been co-guardian with Carl Leonhart, of the minor children of his father-in-law; but Carl had died in 1781 leaving Bürger solely responsible, although, by that time, the only remaining minor among the Leonhart heirs was Georg. As time went on, the matter became increasingly complex and Bürger found himself entangled in a web of litigations. At one point, he was alleged to have embezzled some 10,000 Thaler, and at another he was threatened with personal arrest for an overdue report. The whole affair proved to be a continuing drain on his mental and financial resources, neither of which was ever ample. Ultimately, Bürger was "relieved" of this millstone, but not without showing ill effects. His resiliency had diminished significantly over the past few years, and his physical complaints became increasingly frequent and distressingly real. He found it necessary to give up riding altogether and even sold his horse. Moreover, he was so distracted generally that he could not concentrate, either on his work or on his writing. Goeckingk suggested, as he had before, the need for a change, for travel, but to no avail; the poet simply did not have the funds.

Bürger was coming to be obsessed by a determination to escape from his official position, and in 1782 he turned directly to Frederick the Great, with a letter imploring him to grant a position within his realm that would allow him to move there. The King's reply, through Chancellor Von Carmer, was quite favorable, although Von Carmer's efforts on Bürger's behalf proved quite as fruitless as all the others. The Minister of Education, Von Zedlitz, responded to Von Carmer's letter of inquiry with devastating disdain: "Although the present Electoral-Hannoverian Magistrate Bürger has proven an uncommon acquaintance with the ancients by the portions of Homer that he has translated and published from time to time, and has even achieved recognition and fame as a poet, he is, nevertheless, as is the case with the present-day wits who fancy themselves geniuses, unsuitable as an educator and teacher of youth. Moreover, there is really no paucity of people versed in the ancient languages, and I am particularly careful to eliminate any opportunity for youth to acquire an early inclination for poetry, as it undermines all mental faculties and suffocates the proper attitudes necessary for worthwhile activities. Thus I cannot, in good conscience, utilize Bürger in my department, much as I cherish him, etc., etc."[25] While Von Carmer was discreet enough not to forward Zedlitz's reply, the whole incident constituted one more fiasco in a long series of disappointments. Even so, external forces, which would ultimately pry Bürger loose from his official post, were already at work.

Hofrat Listn, now bankrupt, but still engaged in devious schemes of intrigue, proposed to the elder General Adam Heinrich Von Uslar that the moment was opportune to try again to remove Bürger from his position. It is possible that Listn envisaged his own return from retirement. In any case, the complaint was submitted by Von Uslar in August, 1783, and the machinery was finally set in gear which would permit Bürger to move. The charges were mostly warmed over from the earlier complaints, but Bürger was required to reply to them in writing.

In a moment of rare insight, Bürger availed himself of the opportunity to step down from his post, and did so in the most dignified manner. In his reply, he took note of every charge and refuted it. He now sensed the climate in a way that he had not done in his correspondence with Goethe, for the tone of his rebuttal is calm, and the style lucid, objective, and void of hyperbole.[26]

Bürger also stated that, regardless of the outcome of the inquiry or trial, he intended to resign from his position. In the end, he was almost totally cleared of the charges, and on December 31 he finally submitted his letter of resignation with full honor, to take effect the following "Johannis." Bürger was at last freed, and he shuddered as he looked back on "twelve years as a galley slave." He was not unaware of the "assistance" afforded him by Listn in relinquishing his post and expressed himself succinctly in the epigram, "Auf einen Erzkujon" ("To an Arch-villain"). Bürger was not one to hold a grudge, not even against an arch-villain, and when Listn approached him the following year (1785) with an appeal to forget and forgive—and to send him money—the poet set about taking up a collection to which he himself contributed.

Despite a certain lack of prudence, it must be admitted, Bürger showed considerable courage as he took leave of his post, since, at the time, he had no new position he could assume. Understandably, he sensed the urgency of the situation and again enlisted the aid of all his friends in his search for a job. His sights were now set on an academic post, as they had been for some time. Goethe had suggested as much, and Bürger had applied for such a position to Frederick the Great. Now Bürger resolutely turned all his energies in this direction, and at long last his efforts succeeded.

Through the good offices of Christian Gottlob Heyne, professor at Göttingen, and by the influence of the dean, Professor Kästner, to whom Bürger was recommended by Heyne, the decision was made to allow him to teach at the university in 1784–1785, but privately for fees, and not on salary. Heyne had suggested that Bürger seek a post on the law faculty, but Bürger had persisted in his desire to teach German history, German literature and language, and, if necessary, German civil law. "In short, I aspire to be simply a German Professor, which is to learn and to teach everything that must be interesting to learn for every German on account of his birth and his fatherland."[27]

Bürger welcomed the opportunity to teach, but his financial situation was not improved thereby. Without a salary, he was dependent on fees and on what he could make by giving private tutoring. Consequently, the security he had sought was still out of reach. Initially, he had hoped to leave Dorette in Gelliehausen (where the family had moved after leaving Appenrode), and he planned to rent quarters from Dieterich in Göttingen. It soon became clear, however, that this plan could not be carried out. Dorette gave birth to another daughter on April 29, 1784, and was unable to recover. Her health deteriorated rapidly—consumption ran in the Leonhart family— and on July 30 she died. She was in her twenty-eighth year. The baby, Auguste Wilhelmine, survived her mother by less than two weeks. Bürger was able to send Marianne Friederike (then six years old) to live with his sister and her family, the Elderhorsts, in Bissendorf, and after auctioning off most of his household belongings, he moved into Dieterich's house in Göttingen.

On September 29, 1784, Bürger assumed his new duties at the university. His mood at the time was hardly exuberant, but his financial situation was beginning to improve. After the end of the spring term, 1785, he went to visit the Elderhorsts, where Molly and Marianne Friederike were also living. On June 27, 1785, he was finally wedded to Auguste Marie Wilhelmine Eva Leonhart. Bürger had waited nearly a year after Dorette's death, but he had already waited an eternity. He could hardly believe his good fortune, and when the couple returned to Göttingen, the prospects for the future seemed bright, indeed. The fall semester was a success. Molly proved to be an excellent housekeeper, and they were able to put aside some money. On Christmas Day, 1785, Molly presented her husband with a baby daughter, Auguste Anna Henriette Ernestine. Suddenly, however, Molly became ill, developed a raging fever and died on January 9, 1786. Bürger's grief was inexpressible. It was an anguish, a sorrow from which he felt he could never recover. Marianne was boarded with the widow of Professor Erxleben in Göttingen, and her new sister was sent to Bissendorf, while Bürger desperately tried to put together the crumbled pieces of his existence.

At a time when Bürger was barely able to concern himself with them, his finances and his professional circumstances began to show signs of prospering. He was offered a professorship at the University of Pressburg in Hungary, and the prospect of an academic post in England also opened up. The thought of leaving his children and his homeland, however, made him decline the offer, and he decided to remain in Göttingen, where he hoped he might soon be promoted to professorial rank.

Bürger occupied a curious niche at the University of Göttingen, and his advancement was slow in coming. With several very distinguished exceptions, including Lichtenberg, Kästner, and Heyne, the faculty tended to hold him in some disdain, since he had no academic credentials and was a poet rather than a scholar. In addition, Bürger had gradually withdrawn from an active social life, lived quietly by himself and saw but few friends—particularly after Molly's death. In time he came to be regarded as something of an eccentric, and when A. W. Schlegel came to Göttingen he was warned to shun Bürger's company.

The disparaging attitude of the faculty toward Bürger made itself most directly felt by their reluctance to promote him. A number of younger men were called to Göttingen and promoted over his head, and Bürger, ever keenly sensitive to a slight, regarded the situation with growing annoyance, frustration, and pessimism.

It was not until September, 1787, that the title 'Doctor' was conferred upon him (in recognition of two poems, "Gesang am heiligen Vorabend" and an "Ode" written for the fiftieth anniversary of the university), and even then it was a Pyrrhic victory, since no promotion was connected with it. Bürger had another two years to wait (until October, 1789) before being promoted to Professor Extraordinarius, and even then the promotion was made with the explicit condition that he should not receive or expect to receive a salary. Again, it was little more than a title, but it persuaded Bürger to remain at the university. Four years later (March 6, 1793) Bürger submitted a very deferential request that he be put on salary, but he did not live to see it granted.

The reports concerning Bürger's effectiveness as a teacher vary greatly. For a long time after his death, the opinion was held that "the crowds of students passed him by without a thought."[28] The source of this attitude probably goes back to C. L. Woltmann, who was one of Bürger's early biographers and a former student at Göttingen. Woltmann had heard Bürger after Schiller's review had appeared in 1791, at a point when Bürger was deeply depressed, and at a time when his domestic situation had reached its nadir. If one relies, however, on the opinion of another contemporary, C. G. Lenz, the impression is quite different. Lenz was startlingly enthusiastic, "His lecture is good beyond expectation, clear, intelligible and pleasant."[29]

Over the years Bürger lectured on a variety of subjects, although his favorite field was German stylistics. In 1787–1788 he fell completely under the spell of Kant and prepared "Some Highlights of Kantian Philosophy" (publ. in 1803). "I thank God for this man as for a Savior," he wrote while he was working on his lectures. His enthusiasm was evidently contagious, for he was able to draw some seventy students to his lectures.

In the same year, Bürger distributed the announcement (which he had had published by Dieterich) for his course in stylistics: "On the Instruction of German Language and Style at Universities." Bürger was distressed that the student population at Göttingen was so peripherally oriented to the humanities, and he was determined to try to do something about it with his lectures on style and rhetoric. Thus the announcement published by Dieterich.

The piece has two major flaws. In the first place, it is long and repetitive. What Bürger wanted to say could have been said much more succinctly with equal effect. In fact, the very length of the essay contradicts one of the basic points Bürger was trying to make, i.e., come to the point, say what you have to say and stop.

The other unfortunate element was that Bürger chose legal prose style as his chief target—a choice which hardly brought him closer to the hearts of some of his most powerful colleagues in the legal faculty. He found it difficult to disguise his contempt for them and spoke disparagingly of their pronouncements from distinguished chairs ("von vornehmen Kathedern herab"). It was a classic example of Bürger's self-destructive drive.

In the months that followed Molly's death, little direction was left in Bürger's life, but the concentration of all his energies on his work gradually had its effect. Not that his health improved particularly—it never did—but very slowly he began, once again, to seek out company. His visits to Bissendorf cheered him, and he followed his youngest daughter's development with special pleasure. His elder daughter, Marianne, also gave him cause for pride, and he felt now that she had much promise. Bürger had by no means recovered by 1787, but he was again taking an active interest in the world around him. His efforts to remove himself from Göttingen in that year lacked the intensity of the Altengleichen struggles, even though they, too, came to nothing. Stolberg went to considerable trouble on his behalf, and Goeckingk, too, tried to secure Bürger a better position, but in both cases the results were negative, and Bürger remained in Göttingen.

As Bürger gradually moved back into the world of society, his interests were not in male company alone, and between 1786 and 1790 several women came to occupy a place in his life. As early as 1786 Bürger wrote to Friederike Mackenthun, "What love my poor heart is still capable of, the greatest part belongs to you above all feminine creatures I know."[30] The sentiment and expression were gracious but implied little. Among the other women who entered his life at this time, there was one, however, with whom Bürger entertained something more than a cordial social relationship. Sophia Margaretha Dorothea Forkel was the wife of the music historian Johann Nicolaus Forkel. She was a woman of modest attainment in everything but reputation, and it was, of course, Bürger's misfortune to establish a romantic liaison with such a woman. Very soon the affair was common knowledge throughout Göttingen, and though Bürger subsequently realized his error, the incident seriously damaged his reputation.

Bürger's letters written in the late 1780s contain frequent complaints about his loneliness, but they also reveal a significant improvement in his mood and outlook. He was not only involved with his courses and lectures, but he had resumed his writing. (It should be remembered that Bürger had never given up the editorship of the *Musen-Almanach,* nor had he ever entirely ceased to write. The years between 1780 and 1785 represented, on the other hand, the low point of his productivity, and from 1786 until his death in 1794 the list of completed works increased somewhat.) In 1786 Bürger finished a dozen poems for the *Musen-Almanach* in addition to writing some minor occasional poetry. In the same year he also completed his translation-adaptation-enlargement of the *Tales of Baron von Münchhausen.*

For some years Bürger had intended to publish a second edition of his poems, and as early as 1783 he had announced it as being in preparation. The success of the first edition gave him reason to be optimistic, but other matters interfered, and it was not until 1788 that he again gave it his serious attention. The subscription to the first edition had run to about 2,000, but for the second edition only 439 subscribers could be found. Nonetheless, the work went ahead, and the second edition in two volumes appeared in 1789. Bürger added many new poems to those he had included in the first edition or had subsequently published in the *Musen-Almanach.* In many cases he had also reworked older poems, and these revisions appeared here for the first time.

The critical reception was quite mixed, although A. W. Schlegel published a very strong and favorable comment on "Das hohe Lied von der Einzigen." Schlegel was a student at Göttingen at the time, and Bürger had already published some of Schlegel's poetry in the

Musen-Almanach (from 1787 onwards). (Bürger and Schlegel had become quite close during the winter of 1788–1789, at a time when Bürger had almost entirely withdrawn from society.) Bürger had very high regard for the younger poet's abilities and included one of Schlegel's sonnets in the preface to the 1789 edition.

In the spring of 1789, after the edition had finally appeared, Bürger decided to go on holiday from Göttingen. His health had shown signs of improvement, as had his mood. He went first to Jena and then to Weimar. He had sent a copy of the new edition of his poems to Goethe, together with a cordial letter, but he deliberated some time before deciding to pay the great man a personal visit. In the end Bürger decided to go, though his last correspondence with Goethe should have alerted him that Goethe was not overly well-disposed toward him. The earlier "Du" and "Ihr" had changed to "Sie," and Goethe's whole tone had become perceptibly cooler. Nonetheless, Bürger went to see the elder poet. He arrived on an afternoon when Goethe was with the composer Reichardt, and he asked that Goethe be informed of his arrival. Bürger was delighted that he had chosen a moment when Goethe was not officially occupied, as well as at the prospect of a pleasant informal chat with the two men or possibly later with Goethe alone. The servant returned and showed Bürger to an empty sitting room, where he was asked to wait. After some time, Goethe appeared alone, bowed in response to Bürger's greeting and motioned the latter to be seated. Goethe began the conversation by asking Bürger how many students were registered at the University of Göttingen and Bürger found himself totally thrown out of gear. The interview was clearly ill advised, and Bürger took the earliest occasion to terminate it. As he took his leave, Goethe bowed cordially, but remained standing in the middle of the room. Bürger was beside himself, and on the way home he composed the following epigram to Goethe:

> *Mich drängt' es in ein Haus zu gehn,*
> *Drin wohnt' ein Künstler und Minister.*
> *Den edlen Künstler wollt' ich sehn*
> *Und nicht das Alltagsstück Minister.*
> *Doch steif und kalt blieb der Minister*
> *Vor meinem trauten Künstler stehn,*
> *Und vor dem hölzernen Minister*
> *Kriegt' ich den Künstler nicht zu sehn.*
> *Hol' ihn der Kuckuk und sein Küster!*

/I was moved to enter a house,/Wherein dwelt an artist and Councillor.
/I wished to see the noble artist/ And not the work-a-day Councillor.
/But formal and cold the Councillor stood/ In front of my beloved artist
/And in front of the wooden Councillor/ I never got to see the artist.
/May the deuce and his deacon carry him off!/)

The memory of 116 Louis d'or and an unfulfilled promise lingered
long in Goethe's memory, as it did elsewhere in Weimar. Wieland
had also contributed to the Homer project, and when Bürger subsequently asked him to review the second edition of his poems, he
found it necessary to decline. Whether the two incidents were
related is a matter of speculation. Goethe later wrote a rather formal
note to Bürger expressing his disappointment that his visit had been
so brief, but by that time even Bürger realized that his relationship
with Goethe had ended.

Where one relationship ended badly in 1789, another, which
would end calamitously, was begun auspiciously. By circuitous
means Bürger received, in the fall of 1789, a very flattering poem,
which had been written and published anonymously by a young
lady in Stuttgart. Bürger was enchanted more by the sentiment than
by the poetic skill, but made determined inquiry as to the identity
of the poetess. At the same time he combed the list of Stuttgart
subscribers for the 1789 edition of his poems, and by putting this
and that together he discovered that his admirer was, in fact one
Elise Marie Christiane Elizabeth Hahn (born 1769). Bürger
responded with a poem, even before he knew her identity. Quite
soon, however, he was informed that she was attractive, intelligent,
and lively. By February, 1790, he had her portrait, and although
she was not blond like Molly and not quite what he had expected,
he felt that he could love her. It was impossible, however, to proceed
further until Elise should know something more about the poet, and
so Bürger forwarded to her his "Beichte" ("Confession"), a lengthy
and, generally, forthright autobiographical narrative-apologia.
Bürger made no secret of his sensual nature; he acknowledged
Emil as his son by Molly, as well as describing the entire Molly-
Dorette situation. If, after Elise had read his "Confession" and
still believed that it might be possible for her to be his wife, Bürger
proposed to come quietly to Stuttgart to meet her and determine if
they would be physically compatible, for sensuality also played
its role.

Elise was warned from all sides against inviting Bürger to come to Stuttgart, and it was graphically pointed out to her that at the age of twenty she would be taking on a husband twenty-two years her senior and become the stepmother to three children, the eldest of whom was only nine years her junior. Elise accepted the advice and wrote Bürger in a gracious and generous manner informing him that she could not consider marriage with him. Unfortunately, Bürger did not receive the letter; he had already left for Stuttgart. Even when the couple met, it was not overwhelming love at first sight. Nevertheless, they decided to become formally engaged. Bürger should have known better; all his relatives and all his friends warned him against taking this step, and Elise's mother had warned them both. Nothing, however, could dissuade Bürger, and he pressed his suit with determination. The marriage took place at Michaelmas, 1790, and Bürger returned to Göttingen with Elise. The marriage flourished for perhaps two weeks and then careened towards disaster. Elise was not cut out to sit at home quietly during the day while her husband was at the university. Nor was she content to spend a quiet evening at home with him. Picnics and parties became the order of the days and nights, and they spiraled in expense and notoriety. Elise insisted on being surrounded by men and was able to arrange it so that her more intimate admirers should come during the day when Bürger was away. By the winter of 1790–1791 Bürger's household and his wife's affairs were the scandal of Göttingen, and by Easter, 1791, caricatures of Bürger as cuckold were openly circulated in the town. The stories were embellished, and incidents were invented, but little embellishment or invention was necessary. The number of men who could claim the pleasure of Elise's intimacy steadily increased and included at least one baron, one count, one physician, and one student of philosophy. Bürger was not entirely oblivious to what was going on in his home, and the scenes with Elise grew in intensity. When Elise gave birth to a son in August, 1791—given the exotic name, Agathon—Bürger felt that she would surely now settle down and fulfill her maternal and conjugal duties. Bürger could not have been more mistaken; Elise virtually abandoned her son, and the child never fully recovered physically or emotionally from this early experience. Though they continued to live in the same house, Bürger took to writing letters to Elise, and on her birthday (November 17) he reminded her of her duties and responsibilities. He reprimanded her for her neglect and for her extravagances, but his complaints were in vain. She replied in a letter to him on November 30, claiming that his charges against her were without cause. By that time Elise's maid, Elisabeth, whom she had brought with her from Stuttgart, had left their employ, but Bürger sought her out and learned from her that she had acted as a messenger from Elise to her lovers. On December 10 Bürger faced Elise with this information, and a most unpleasant scene ensued, at the conclusion of which Bürger ordered Elise to swear a solemn oath of chastity and fidelity, and for her personal conduct in general. It was a hollow effort; Elise would have sworn that she was Joan of Arc and never given it a second thought. The following two months were probably the stormiest in Bürger's life, and matters went from bad to worse. The situation finally came to a head on February 3, when Bürger returned home unexpectedly and witnessed his wife's infidelity with his own eyes (through a hole he had bored in the door to Elise's bedroom). A volcanic scene followed and Bürger required Elise to sign a statement of confession before two witnesses, which she did. He submitted this document to the university administration, since it exercised jurisdiction over its faculty. On February 6 Elise left Göttingen, and on March 31, 1792, Bürger's divorce was final.

The year 1791 had been disastrous in more than one respect. In January a review which appeared in the *Allgemeine Literatur-Zeitung* effectively silenced Bürger as a creative poet. Published anonymously, it was ostensibly a review of the recent edition of *Gedichte,* but it ranged far beyond the scope of a routine review and called into question not only Bürger's poetry but even his right to call himself a poet. The author of the review was Friedrich Schiller, with whom Bürger had thought he was on good terms, and although the reviewer maintained his anonymity, it was not long before Bürger learned his identity.

Schiller began his review with a general statement on the decline of lyric poetry in the current philosophizing age. He then set forth what he believed poetry should do and its awesome responsibility as he saw it, i.e., that it should assimilate all the manners, the character, the entire wisdom of its time and, having refined it in its mirror, it should create, out of the century itself, a model for the century. Such a task surely called for mature and cultured hands. Enthusiasm alone was not enough, for the poet must seek to elevate with his

art. Schiller maintained that the true *Volksdichter* could no longer
exist, and that Bürger's claim to that title was unwarranted. It was
not enough to be popular; that was simply an added burden. The
true *Volksdichter* must select his material with the utmost care and
treat it with the utmost simplicity. Schiller examined Bürger's poetry
and found it wanting: "initiated into the mysteries of the beautiful,
the noble and the true, it should draw the *Volk* up to it, but Bürger
descends to the level of the *Volk,* where he mingles, rather than
edifies and elevates with his art." Bürger was inconsistent with his
title, for surely, Schiller said, the readers of the "Nachtfeier der
Venus" and of "Frau Schnips" were not one and the same. Schiller
lamented the inconsistency in taste and language that he encountered
within single poems; indeed, he had to confess that he could hardly
name a single poem of Bürger's which was completely free of these
impurities.

Schiller was so disturbed by these poems that he felt compelled
to state 'that the spirit presented in these poems is no mature spirit,
no perfected *(vollendeter)* spirit, that the products lack the final touch
(letzte Hand) because it is lacking in the spirit itself.' Schiller quoted,
curiously without comment, some fifty lines of the "Elegie, als Molly
sich losreißen wollte" as an example. He states that one of the first
demands on a poet is idealization *(Idealisierung)* and refinement
(Veredlung), and that this quality *(Idealisierkunst)* is lacking in
Bürger, whose muse seems generally to have too sensual a character: 'love for him is seldom anything more than sensual pleasure
or a treat for the eyes, beauty often only youth and health, and happiness only the life of pleasure. We are inclined to call the pictures
that he paints for us more a motley jumble of images, a compilation
of brush strokes, a kind of mosaic rather than ideals.'

Schiller insists that the poet must have distance; in the midst of
pain he cannot write of pain, because it is too immediate. Schiller
complains that the bitterness and pain in Bürger's poetry are actual
expressions of these emotions, and not the poetic image of them re-
created after the fact. Bürger, he maintains, is too intimate a participant; he is inextricably involved personally. Finally, Schiller repri-
mands Bürger for his constant self-praise.

At the conclusion of the review Schiller praises Bürger for his
achievements with the ballad, and he calls Bürger's sonnets "models
of their kind." Schiller urges Bürger to try to refine his work and
write with those aims in mind that he has outlined for him.

Schiller's review is brutally harsh, and needlessly so, but it is not done in the "malicious tone" Wurzbach ascribes to it.[31] Schiller explicitly points out that the extraordinary breadth and detail of his criticism should be clear proof in itself of the high esteem he has for Bürger. One does not spend that much time on a minor or insignificant poet. The fundamental problem with the essay, however, is that Schiller wanted Bürger to be something he was not, and he was judging him by criteria which were inapplicable.

Bürger tried to keep a good face on the affair and shortly afterwards asked Schütz to give Schiller his regards ('if he were the author') and tell him that he was not angry, but in "high and merry spirits."[32] In fact, Bürger was devastated. It was not enough that his marriage was disintegrating before his very eyes, but now his art, which was, ultimately, his whole purpose in life, was brought into question. Understandably, but unfortunately, he replied at once, rushing into print in the *Intelligenz-Blatt* of the *Allgemeine Literatur Zeitung* (April 6, 1791) with a reply which was quite unworthy of him. Almost at once he regretted having done so, but Schiller's response was swift and sharp. Bürger had answered none of his points, he said; he had tried to be clever rather than reasonable. Schiller said that he had taken great pains with his essay-review and had expected, in response, something more than the voice of "authority by exclamations, hairsplitting, deliberate misconstruction *(vorsätzliche Mißdeutung),* pathetic apostrophes, and burlesque tirades."[33] Bürger had called for the author to identify himself, but Schiller did not lift his "visor of anonymity."

In the privacy of his study, Bürger wrote a brief fragmentary comment, "Über mich und meine Werke. Materialien zu einem künftigen Gebäude" ("About me and my works. Materials for a future Study"), which was not published until after his death. It is a remarkable piece of calm reflection, in which he writes of his immediate public reply, "It seems to me as though I did not behave well."[34] Bürger argues that he has been misjudged by Schiller (whom he refers to by name), but acknowledges that "I am dealing with some one stronger than myself," and that he, Bürger, was not really interested in a victory over his opponent. Bürger's public response came chiefly in the form of epigrams in the *Musen-Almanach* (1793). Other than the epigrams, Bürger composed the poem, "Der Vogel Urselbst" ("The Beyourself Bird"). Schiller, who was the chief target of the piece, was impervious.

While it is not true that Bürger's death was brought on by Schiller's review, it is perhaps an understatement to say that Bürger's situation "at this time was not, in a material sense, the best."[35] It is fair to say, however, that Schiller snuffed out all but completely the creative gift in Bürger. His subsequent work consisted of very brief pieces, most of them inconsequential, numerous epigrams, and translations and adaptations. There are some fine passages in "Die Königin von Golkonde" ("The Queen of Golconda"), and a few in "Heloise an Abelard," but the translations, such as *Benjamin Franklins Jugendjahre* (*Benjamin Franklin's Youth*) and the historical work (which was probably a translation), "Die Republik England" ("The Republic of England"), were done for pecuniary reasons, and Bürger even withheld his name from the latter.

In 1791 A. W. Schlegel left Göttingen, and his contacts with Bürger became less frequent and less personal. Several years later, after Bürger had died, Schlegel reviewed his thoughts about his former mentor and published his "Bürger 1800." Kadner suggests that Schlegel was prompted to do so by three factors: (1) Schlegel rejected Schiller's use of speculative criticism and set his own historically oriented criticism in its place. (2) He felt it his duty to his mentor and teacher to afford him some kind of honorary defense, and (3) in 1800 Schlegel became the literary and personal antagonist of Schiller.[36] For whatever reason it was written, Schlegel's memorial to Bürger, is, if anything, less cordial and less sympathetic than Schiller's essay of 1791.

The years between 1791 and 1794 are marked by a sharp decline in almost every aspect of Bürger's existence. Financially he was forced to take on tasks, such as translations, that otherwise he would never have undertaken. He felt that his creative vein was exhausted and spent immense time and effort in revising his older poems (in order to bring them into line with what Schiller had said they should be). The poet of "Lenore" was accommodating himself to Schiller's criticism, and he felt the need to justify his every change. Little if anything new appeared in these years; and instead of producing new works Bürger set his hopes on a final *Luxus* Edition, for which he began to solicit subscriptions. The response was minimal, and Bürger never lived to see the edition published. Karl Reinhard began publishing it in 1796, two years after the poet's death.

Bürger's friends continued their efforts on his behalf, but all attempts failed. The poet's correspondence with Boie had ceased about 1791, and although he continued his correspondence with Goeckingk, he withdrew more and more into himself. His physician, Dr. Ludwig Christoph Althof, and the aging Dieterich remained his closest friends, although numerous friends and admirers continued to visit him. In 1793 his health began to fail rapidly, and he needed more and more urgently the services of Dr. Althof and other physicians. Doctors' bills grew beyond what he could possibly afford to pay, and he was finally forced to give his oil portrait of Molly as payment in kind to one of his physicians (Dr. Wrisberg). In despair (January 18, 1794) he ordered the sale of the lands he had inherited from his mother. By the time the property was sold, it was too late.

Consumption was a familiar foe to Bürger, and now he himself was rapidly succumbing to it. He could no longer speak above a whisper, and in the spring of 1794 it was apparent that he would not survive the summer. Had it not been for friends like Dieterich and Althof, Bürger might well have died of hunger, for he had no income or resources whatever. The phrase, "he is starving," which occurs more than once in Caroline Böhmer's letters, was not rhetorical. His friends continued to support him to the end, but consumption could not be turned back. On the evening of June 8, 1794, he could no longer even whisper to make himself understood. Dr. Althof suggested that he try writing what he wished to say, but his eyes also failed him, and as he tried to whisper "yes" to a question put to him by his physician he breathed his final breath. Bürger was 46 years old.

CHAPTER 2

Lyric Poetry

ONE of the first things Schiller remarks upon in his critique of Bürger's poetry is the decline of the lyric in their "philosophierendes Zeitalter" ("philosophizing age"), and his complaint is not without grounds or justification. With the exception of Goethe, the eighteenth century could hardly boast of having produced a host of great lyric poets. From the middle of the century, despite the growing inclination towards realism, poetry remained essentially imitative, whether of Anacreon, Horace, or Klopstock. Moreover, it remained the province of the educated (or upper) classes. Attempts to free the lyric from these restraints came from several quarters, but never with greater vigor than from Herder. Johann Gottfried Herder (1741–1803) exercised an almost unparalleled influence on German literature in the latter part of the eighteenth century, and his importance for the development of the German lyric is profound. Herder called for an end to the prolonged French and Greco-Roman hegemony. It was time, he urged, to be done with Anacreontic tapestries, to emancipate poetry from aristocratic exclusiveness and to make it accessible to ordinary people. He urged the poet to turn his glance back to that primeval and naive culture where poetry could be understood and appreciated by all. According to Herder, the poet should be direct and immediate in his presentation, and his setting should be the real and everyday world in which he lived.

Among those who responded enthusiastically to Herder's manifestoes was Bürger, since it was his natural inclination to be the kind of poet Herder urged. To be sure, Bürger's early models were Klopstock and Anacreon, and much of his early poetry clearly reflected their influence. Indeed, Rektor Niemeyer criticized the now lost "Christus in Gethsemane" because it was "zu klopstockisierend." Bürger produced several other Klopstockian imitations, but they have also been lost. It is impossible, therefore, to estimate what sort of pieces they were, but Bürger must have realized early on that he did not possess the requisite seraphic temperament.

Bürger's earliest surviving poems follow Anacreon's lead and date from his years at Halle when he was eighteen to twenty years old. They invoke familiar and not-so-familiar ancient gods: Aphrodite, Bacchus, Amor, Cytherea, Aurora, and Apollo, make frequent appearances, as do the idealized Adelines, Gabrieles, and Agathes. Although Bürger never entirely managed to shake off the Anacreontic accoutrements, they became vestigial mannerisms in his mature poetry. In many cases, the early poems are based on specific models or inspired by incidents or characters from larger works; i.e., "Lais und Demosthenes" from Book I, Chapter 8 of Aulus Gellius's *Noctes Atticae;* "An die Leier" from Pausanias, Book II; "An Amalchen" from Catullus; etc.[1] The habit of depending on external impetus continued throughout Bürger's life, and the creative process was often set in motion by something he had seen, heard, or read.

In the early 1770s, Bürger's attachment to the Anacreontic manner receded as he came under the influence of Herder and, consequently, of English literature. Moreover, Bürger was rapidly developing his own style, and although he continued to base much of his work on extant models, the stamp of his personality became increasingly apparent. Whether in adapting or in creating, Bürger insisted that originality was of primary concern: "Lieber ein unerträgliches Original als ein glücklicher Nachahmer."[2]

Originality as a concept covers numerous elements which characterize Bürger's poetry. One of the most important of these was the poet's pervasive subjectivity. Having broken away from the artificial values and responses of Rococo conventions, Bürger became one of the first among his generation of poets to introduce his own personality into his poetry, and in fact, to allow it to saturate his work. At times, to a distressing degree, Bürger permitted his own feelings, desires, affections, and annoyances to voice themselves, unrefined, in his art. This characteristic was one of the specific faults Schiller noted in Bürger's poetry, but the era of Romanticism was at hand, and the intrusion of the poet into his writings was not to be repressed.

The immediacy of Bürger's personality in his lyrics reflects his acute sensitivity to the world about him.[3] He was particularly susceptible to sensual stimuli and never sought to hide or deny this aspect of his character. In the most fundamental way, Bürger was the completely sensual man, and this facet of his character plays a significant role in his poetry; not only in the "Molly Songs," but from his earliest extant poetic pieces. "Die Sinnlichkeit hat ihre Rechte" ("Sensuality has its rights"), [4] he wrote in his "Confession" to Elise. Bürger portrayed the world not only as he felt it, but as he viewed and heard it. His intent was to reproduce, both visually and aurally, those things which affect the senses and enable the reader to conjure up the scene and the sound for himself. Ultimately, of course, Bürger sought, through a combination of all these elements, to achieve a fresh kind of realism, the kind that Goethe had created in his early drama and particularly in "Götz." The "Sturm und Drang" had found its essential expression in the drama, not the lyric, but it is clear that Bürger, especially in his ballads, aligned himself more with the "Stürmer und Dränger" than with the much less volatile poets of the Hainbund.

The realism Bürger sought to instill in his verse would make his lyrics, so the poet felt, understandable and attractive to the average man, and this was the audience for which Bürger consciously wrote. All his pronouncements about the need for poetry to be "popular," and his assertions that "popularity constituted the seal of perfection," make it clear that he wanted to be, and indeed felt himself to be, a *Volksdichter.*

It was a fuzzy, romantic vision, but Bürger saw it in realistic terms. In his letter to Daniel Chodowiecki, who had been engaged to prepare the cuts for the 1778 edition of the *Gedichte,* Bürger requested that the frontispiece portray "a simple but fashionably dressed singer or musician, who is performing on a harp or some other popular instrument before an attentive audience composed of all classes."[5] It was a great disappointment to the poet that Chodowiecki's engraving portrayed an elderly man in long robes with a full wig performing on a large harp. Bürger complained that friends and strangers began to address him as 'Vater Bürger,' a title he abhorred. Whether or not he deserved the title *Volksdichter* is a question that has been much debated. Schiller was the first to reject Bürger's claim, basing his argument on the fact that the role of *Volksdichter* was incommensurate with modern times. "Our world is no longer the Homeric one, where all parts of society were roughly on the same level as regards sensitivity and thought, and could, therefore, easily recognize themselves in the same descriptions and feelings, . . . whereas today there is a great hiatus between the select of a nation and the masses, which among other things constitutes a massive cultural difference."[6] Schiller maintained that in modern times the abyss separating the elite of a nation from the general populace was so vast that it would take a *Volksdichter* of Olympian gift to bring the two together. Whether or not he succeeded, Bürger always set himself that goal.

The great majority of Bürger's poems were first published in the *Göttinger Musen-Almanach*, and most of them were subsequently republished in either the first or the second edition of his collected poems. The idea of publishing a collected edition always appealed to Bürger, and he began to consider such a project as early as 1775—at a time when his complete poetic oeuvre only comprised some sixty poems. In 1777, however, his finished poems were much more numerous, and he formally proceeded on August 1 of that year to announce the proposed edition. Bürger promised that in scope it would "cover the alphabet in octavo." He also intended to compose a great many new poems for the edition, and by Easter, 1778, he lacked only five or six sheets. He had worked at great speed to finish on time, but lack of time as well as paper prevented his achieving entirely the goal he had set himself.

The Introduction to the first edition of the *Gedichte* was to have contained his poetic articles of faith, but had to be compressed into a relatively brief statement. It emerged as a collection of rather loosely connected ideas, suggesting that the poet had completed it under pressure. Bürger reacted with annoyance when under pressure, and in the Introduction his exasperation is aimed at his critics. He is determined to stay their barbs by an attitude of disarming honesty and almost casually feigned indifference. He acknowledges that some of the poems are good, some weak, that some will survive, while others will be forgotten; it is all the same to him. The Introduction also contains one of Bürger's earliest comments on his image of himself as *Volksdichter,* the *idée fixe* of his life.

In the light of his later "Rechenschaft über die Veränderungen in der Nachtfeier der Venus," it is significant to note that Bürger expresses contempt for poets who accommodate themselves to their critics. He will not be found among them, since he knows what he is about. What he has written he will let stand. To put together a prolix apologia would give offense to a person of sound mind.

In line with his manner of straightforward honesty (and with an eye on his critics) Bürger announces his intention to allay any suggestion that he has adapted or borrowed without giving credit, and he provides the sources for those poems which were not original with him. Apparently for private reasons he chose not to indicate the sources for most of the ballads, and he concluded his remarks with the statement: "Thus and no more is my entire confession."[7] Not quite the whole truth.

The *Gedichte* edition of 1778 contained a total of 66 poems, including the original Latin of the "Zechlied." Bürger maintained a rough chronological order, but he was not entirely consistent, despite his assertion to Boie. In order to distribute the plates with some evenness throughout the book, it was necessary to rearrange several poems slightly. Only sixteen of the sixty-five original pieces were published for the first time in this edition; the others had appeared before, mostly in the *Musen-Almanach*. Bürger completed four new ballads for the volume, and included seven of the *Molly Lieder,* although he refrained from naming her in any of them.

The response to the 1778 edition was eminently gratifying. Wieland hailed its contents as "true folk-poetry" ("wahre Volkspoesie"),[8] and felt the poems were not only polished and beautiful, but filled with "Saft und Kraft, Leib und Geist, Bild und Sache" ('sap and force, body and spirit, image and substance')[9]. Other critics supported Wieland's opinion, and as early as 1783 Bürger was working up plans for a new edition. For many reasons, including a depressingly small number of subscribers, it did not materialize until 1789. By that time, Bürger could have afforded to be much more selective in what he published, but he had lost a good deal of his earlier vitality, and as he wrote to Boie, "You would not believe how indifferent I feel towards most of my poems, with the exception of perhaps a dozen."[10] It was pressing, however, to fill up the volume, and in the same letter to Boie he confided that he would have cut "mercilessly, if it hadn't been a matter of bulk." As it developed, the 1789 edition appeared in two volumes and included, in addition to eight of Chodowiecki's plates taken from the first edition, a new frontispiece and two further plates by J. H. Meil. Of the sixty-six poems contained in the first edition Bürger reprinted all but the original Latin of the "Zechlied," and a rather vacuous "Fragment" he had hastily composed for the earlier edition. With the poems taken from the first edition Bürger made extensive but generally minor revisions, most of them concerned with nuance rather than with substance. Another change in the second edition was the elimination of all dates, although the chronology remained roughly the same. This change was necessitated by Bürger's division of the book into three parts: lyric, epic-lyric, and miscellaneous poems.

The edition of 1789 is, to all intents and purposes, the "Ausgabe letzter Hand." Even so, Bürger had hardly seen the volume through the press, when he began to plan for yet another. In September, 1789, he announced a grand, luxury edition of his poems and called for subscribers. He envisaged it as the great final edition, 'with such a selection, polish, and purity of texts . . . that no dissatisfaction could be had from it.'[11] Bürger intended to make radical revisions and eliminate numerous poems which had survived both prior editions. "Prinzessin Europa," "Frau Schnips," "Die Menagerie der Götter," "Fortunens Pranger" ("The Pillory of Fortune"), "An ein Maienlüftchen" ("To a May Breeze"), "Stutzertändelei" ("The Dandy's Dalliance"), "An Themiren," and others were to be omitted. In effect, Bürger intended to put a more dignified face to the world by eliminating these pieces, as generally he sought to revise "upwards." By early spring, 1790, no more than 130 subscribers had been found, and Bürger soon lost confidence in his project. Ultimately between 1796 and 1802 Karl Reinhard brought it out as he believed Bürger would have wanted it. Before his death, Bürger had finished several revisions in anticipation of the edition, and these revisions, as well as his omissions, were taken into account. Although Reinhard's edition was continually reprinted until the turn of our century, the 1789 edition seems at last to have prevailed as a basis for the editions which have appeared since 1900.

The first section of the 1789 edition contains the bulk of Bürger's lyric poetry. Occupying the same honored place it had held in the 1778 edition, the "Nachtfeier der Venus" stands at the very beginning. It was a poem to which Bürger returned again and again, always revising and reshaping. Moreover, it was one of his earlist lyrics, dating back to his student days at Halle (ca. 1767). It had been inspired by Klotz's remark in the *Hallische Neue Gelehrten-Zeitung* that it would be desirable if someone with Gleim's incomparable talent, or perhaps even Gleim himself, might be persuaded to undertake a translation of the Latin "Pervigilium Veneris."[12] Originally, Bürger set out to do an unrhymed translation and furnish it with a commentary but, at the suggestion of Boie, he changed his mind and decided to reproduce the poem in verse. The second version (the first one to have survived) found its way into Ramler's hands, who took his turn at filing and revising. The version published by Ramler in the *Teutsche Merkur* (1773) was not exactly what Bürger had had in mind, but he let it stand a while before revising it further. The versions subsequently published in the *Gedichte* (1778) and in the second edition (1789) show further revision, but no real substantive change. For Bürger the task became (one supposes, unconsciously) something of an intellectual exercise. He did, after all, hope that it would become a "model" German poem which future generations of poets would study and imitate. Indeed, he envisaged it as the poetic equal to the Polycletian canon for sculpture.[13]

The Latin poem itself has little substance and has been poorly transmitted to posterity. There is no certainty, in fact, that the order of lines in the extant poem is that of the original. It was written to celebrate a popular festival, a *trinoctium* dedicated to Venus Genetrix. Its tone and manner are jubilant, as the poet rejoices at the arrival of spring: 'The spring is come: tomorrow Venus (Genetrix) holds court; tomorrow is the wedding day of the rosebuds she has fostered; the Nymphs and Cupid, dangerous though unarmed, will be there; Diana must let the woods rest from the chase, for three nights long will the dancing last. Tomorrow is the day when Heaven wedded Earth, when Venus sprang from the sea, Venus who sways heaven, earth and sea, who gave Lavinia to Aeneas, Ilia to Mars. See, kine and flocks prepare, and the nightingale sings of love.'[14]

The original poem consisted of ninety-two (or perhaps ninety-three) lines of trochaic tetrameter, with a refrain at the beginning and end, and seven other times at irregular intervals. Bürger, in his adaptation, more than doubled the length of the original, and the refrain now occurs sixteen times. Moreover, the poet divided the poem into three sections ("Vorgesang," "Weihgesang," and "Lobgesang"), whereas there are no divisions in the original. This arbitrary tripartite structure does not perceptibly improve the poem. In style and tone Bürger's adaptation fits in well with the Anacreontic era in which it was begun. The vocabulary and the dramatis personae would also have been familiar to Bürger's audience.

In his "Rechenschaft über die Veränderungen in der Nacht-feier der Venus" ("Justification for the Changes in the 'Nachtfeier der Venus'"), a fragmentary essay first published by Reinhard (1797), Bürger set himself the virtually impossible task of justifying on rational, intellectual, academic, aesthetic, and poetic grounds each single change he had made in his revision of the poem. The final revision being prepared was to have appeared in the projected collector's edition. It was written two years after Schiller's review and demonstrates the latter's shattering effect on Bürger's confidence in himself and his work. It is indicative of Bürger's state of mind that he sought to reply to his critics by anticipation.

The "Rechenschaft" is a long essay, running to some one hundred pages in print. Like the poem itself, it is tripartite in structure. In the opening section, Bürger declares his intent to proceed objectively and demonstrate in what ways and to what degree the "Nacht-feier" should be regarded as an exemplary poem. He will only concern himself with form, since form, not subject matter *(Stoff)*, must operate within the matrix of language, and is therefore finite in its potential. The second section is devoted to a detailed discussion of the refrain: "cras amet qui nunquam amavit, quique amavit cras amet." It examines in detail the problems Bürger encountered in reproducing the Latin refrain in German. It cost him, he maintains, more effort that the rest of the poem put together, and he regarded it as a matter of vital importance to cast the original into German as faithfully as possible in thought and form, and simultaneously to avoid the pat phrases which were such a standard part of speech that they had lost all flavor. Moreover, he was determined to retain the antithetical element and achieve a symmetry corresponding to that of the original. Fairly soon it becomes clear that the problem meant far more to the poet than simply an academic puzzle. In his attempts to find a solution, Bürger is drawn into a spiraling maelstrom of linguistic possibilities: 'I still did not believe I had arrived at the boundaries of possibility. Consequently, I went off again on the hunt and finally put together such a collection of variants that I am ashamed to say how many. For in every idle moment, on every stroll, this unholy refrain taunted me.'[15] The refrain became an obsession which allowed of no ultimate solution. Pathetically, at the end of his discussion he submits thirty possible solutions and suggests, as he had earlier about another aspect of the refrain, that 'the purists can now take their choice.'[16]

The third section of the essay examines the other changes made in the final revision, but has no special appeal. Bürger's original intent to remain aloof and objective has been forgotten, as he explains that this or that 'displeased me' ("mißfiel mir") or, justifies modifying the word "schauet" because it 'seemed to me, I don't quite know why myself, to have something bland and inappropriate ("etwas Mattes und Ungehöriges") about it.'[17] Aside from such explanations, the concluding section offers little beyond some rather interesting but not highly original comments on metrics.[18]

Fortunately, Bürger did not experience the same kind of anguish with all his lyrics. Many of them, in fact, could stand as they had issued from the poet's pen. Bürger's early lyric, particularly, reveals an almost effortless manner. While much of it is fairly routine Anacreontic, some succeed in rising above the standard convention.

"An ein Mailüftchen" ("To a Little May Breeze," 1769) is short but effective. The poet calls on the breeze to leave the flower bed and go to the elder hedge, where Lina is waiting. 'I haven't yet had a single kiss, but surely she will not deny thee, gentle breeze. Take three kisses, let one be for me.' "Adeline" (1770) is in somewhat the same mood: when the poet sees Adeline in a formal situation he loses his confidence, but in everyday life he has it aplenty. "Amors Pfeil" ("Love's Arrow," 1772) is one of the shortest of the collection and consists of but a single thought, tersely expressed in the manner of an epigram:

> *Amors Pfeil hat Widerspitzen.*
> *Wen er traf, der laß' ihn sitzen,*
> *Und erduld' ein wenig Schmerz!*
> *Wer geprüften Rat verachtet,*
> *Und ihn auszureißen trachtet,*
> *Der zerfleischet ganz sein Herz.*

(/Love's arrow has barbs;/Whom it strikes, let it sit there,/And suffer a bit of pain./Whoever scorns the advice from one who knows,/And attempts to pull it out,/Will quite tear up his heart./)

In 1771 Bürger was attracted to the medieval German lyric of Minne (love), and in the following year he fashioned several quite graceful and delicate poems in imitation of that mode. The most successful of these quasi *Minnelieder* is the "Winterlied," in which the poet observes the world in its cold and inanimate state—the trees stand barren of leaves, and the plants and flowers lie buried beneath ice and snow. The poet is not daunted by the frost and winter, however, and he assures his audience that he will sing them no dirge, since his beloved fills him with all the joy of spring:

> *O Mai, was frag' ich viel nach dir?*
> *Der Frühling lebt und webt in ihr.*

(/O May, why do I inquire much about thee?/ Spring lives and has its being in her./)

This was probably the first of Bürger's poems to come to Goethe's attention, although the review of it in the *Frankfurter Gelehrten Anzeigen*—long thought to have been by Goethe—was actually written by Johann Heinrich Merck. Merck praised the poem and suggested that if Bürger could recapture more of those moments, he would become one of the strongest forces in putting down the 'empfindsame Dichterlinge mit ihren goldpapiernen Amors und Grazien" ('sentimental poetasters with their gold-foil Amors and Graces').[19]

Two poems of a quasi-religious nature may be noted which date from the period 1772–1773: "An Agathe" and "Danklied" ("Song of Thanksgiving"). These were written during Bürger's stay in the Listn household, while he was in close association with Listn's pietistically inclined wife. "An Agathe" (Frau Hofrat Listn) has the subtitle, 'After a conversation about her earthly sufferings and prospects for eternity.' It is not, on the whole, a very successful poem. The poet attempts to reassure the lady of the tranquility she will find in heaven. The tears she sheds here are gathered in God's hand to water the fields above; and her sighs will be the gentle breezes which will waft the palm leaves, etc. Bürger was determined to be earnest and pious, but he had little gift for this kind of poetry. The "Danklied", on the other hand, is considerably more successful. Grisebach calls it 'a rather exuberant variation on the hymn "How Great is the Goodness of the Almighty ("Wie groß ist des Allmächtigen Güte").'[20] Although Bürger's poem was taken over into some hymnals,[21] it must have been considerably revised, since the religious expressions occur in only three, or possibly four, stanzas. Otherwise, the poet is concerned with his love, Mira. The poem moves along vigorously and rapidly, and Bürger praises God for the many gifts he has bestowed on him (and, particularly, for Mira). 'It is not so important to count the number of stars in the heavens or the grains of sand on the beach. God has given him his imagination ("Phantasei"), by which he can create or destroy worlds; he can descend to hell or rise to heaven.' The poet can rejoice in the flowers of spring and in the song of the, alas, inevitable nightingale (Bürger was never quite able to resist the bird, and here, as usual, she is "Philomele"). The style of the poem is jubilant brisk, straightforward, and marked by an abundance of vivid images. For the first time, Bürger seems genuinely comfortable in dealing with anything other than Anacreontic imagery. Fire imagery (of which Bürger was very fond) appears for the first time, and although it is hardly striking, it indicates the poet's greatly increased confidence in his medium: "Dir dankt es feurig mein Gesang:/Wie meine Liebe flammt mein Dank."/"Für mich der Traube Feuergeist." ("My song thanks thee ardently!/My thanks flames like my Love,"/"For me the Fire spirit of the grape.") Done in a slightly different mood, "Herr Bacchus" (1770) is a particularly successful drinking song, in which Bürger makes the irreverent suggestions that Bacchus should supplant Apollo, and that the grape is preferable to the laurel:

> Dann wollen wir auf den Parnaß,
> Vor allen andern Dingen,
> Das grosse Heidelberger Faß
> Voll Nierensteiner bringen.

(/Then let us bring to Mount Parnassus/ Above all other things/ The great Heidelberg Vat/ Full of Nierstein wine.)

Unfortunately, the delightful salute, "Hoch, dreimal höher als Apoll,/Soll Vater Bacchus leben," did not appear in the 1789 edition.

Another drinking song, written somewhat later, is the equally lilting "Zechlied" ("Revelers' Song," 1777). In his Introduction to the 1778 edition of the *Gedichte,* Bürger acknowledged that he had based his poem on a Latin song, the "Cantilena Potatoria" by the twelfth-century English cleric-poet Walter Mapes (ca. 1140–ca. 1209), and he published the Latin original opposite his adaptation. Bürger was mistaken, however, in ascribing the poem to Walter Mapes; it was actually a version of the "Confessio" by an anonymous medieval German poet, the so-called "Archpoet." In his German version Bürger successfully retains the vigorous, sometimes coarse spirit and tone of the original. Wine is hailed as the essence of life, and it endows the poet (or drinker) with wholly unsuspected strengths and talents. At the same time, the poet continually reminds his audience of the transitoriness of life, and the theme of *memento mori* moves like an ostinato throughout the poem.

The "Spinnlied" is a highly stylized piece in the folk-song manner. Repetition and onomatopoeia abound: "Hurre, hurre, hurre!/ Schnurre, Rädchen, Schnurre!" is the refrain which occurs at the beginning of each stanza. The girl sitting at the wheel sings to it, asking it to cooperate with her in making a fine and splendid dress for the church fair, "That I may be inwardly and outwardly bright and pure,/Industrious, pious, and properly demure," and thereby attract a suitor. The song is short, to the point, couched in the simplest language, fashioned in a steady uncomplicated meter, and moves briskly; but it is no folk song. Bürger, the poet, is everywhere in evidence, from the contrived refrain to the mannered verbal juxtapositions. Equally distressing is the underlying moral sentiment, which is gratuitous in a song like this one. Much more successful as a song, though not as a folk song, is the simple "Lied," written in 1788. The Anacreontic flavor lingers on, without being overpowering. Quite the contrary, it affords a measure of elegance and buoyancy, and with the final twist at the end the effect is quite satisfying. Consisting of three four-line strophes, it expresses the poet's secret desire for a refreshing kiss from the lass with the face of spring ("Du mit dem Frühlingsangesichte"). He suggests that if she will not be gracious and give him one, he will take it for himself.

> *Und sollte dich der Raub verdrießen,*
> *So geb' ich gern den Augenblick,*
> *Die Schuld des Frevels abzubüßen,*
> *Ihn hundertfältig dir zurück.*

(/And should the theft vex you,/ Then in that very moment,/ In order to atone the crime,/I'll gladly return it to you a hundred fold.)

Bürger's native good humor was an immense asset in his youth and certainly contributed to his early success. Frequently, as in the "Spinnlied," however, the humorous poems contain a serious kernel. In "Lust am Liebchen" ("Pleasure in One's Sweetheart") the poet describes the bliss of the man who was a sweetheart. Bürger recites the joys of such a man and notes that that man lives like no prince on earth, nor does he care whether the world goes around, stands still, or turns upside down:

> Der Geist mußdenken. Ohne Denken gleicht
> Der Mensch dem Öchs- und Eselein im Stalle.
> Sein Herz muß lieben. Ohne Liebe schleicht
> Sein Leben matt und lahm, nach Adams Falle.

(/Grief, care, and the blues are lost on him:/He feels quite free and happy,/ And crows contented in his God:/*In dulci jubilo.*/)

To be sure, hyperbole plays its role in this poem, and Eva, who is a relatively routine figure, inevitably appears, but the point, that love is a moral virtue, is nonetheless effectively made.

In another poem, "Das vergnügte Leben" ("The Cheerful Life"), written in 1773, Bürger expresses the same thought, but states it in sober tones:

> Der Geist muß denken. Ohne Denken gleicht
> Der Mensch dem Öchs- und Eselein im Stalle.
> Sein Herz muß lieben. Ohne Liebe schleicht
> Sein Leben matt und lahm, nach Adams Falle.

(/The spirit must think. Without thought/Man is like the ox or ass in the stable./His heart must love. Without love/His life slinks faint and lame, [as] after Adam's fall./)

Unfortunately, Bürger concludes the poem with the pat reference to Amalia:

> Seit mir die Lieb' Amalien gegeben,
> Besitz' ich alles, was ich eben sang.

(/Since Love has given me Amalia/I possess everything I have just sung./)

Bürger's lively imagination was an indispensable adjunct to his wit, especially in his inventive use of language. The poet took a perennial delight in meter and rhyme, and his native facility with the latter produced some unusual and clever results. "Stutzertändelei" is a relatively unimpressive poem (Bürger regarded it as unworthy and intended to omit it from the great luxury edition), but it affords a glimpse of Bürger at play with rhyme:

> *Auch sollen dich belohnen*
> *Bonbon und Marzipan,*
> *Vortreffliche Makronen,*
> *Und was dir lüsten kann.*

(/We also shall reward you/ With candy and marzipan/ Excellent macaroons/ And what can please you./)

Other examples of Bürger's bizarre and witty rhymes occur both in "Das Lob Helenens": "Leier" with "Tokaier" (Lyre and Tokay); and "Herr Bacchus": "Parnaß" with "Kantorbaß." This kind of sport finds its high point (or nadir?) in "Prinzessin Europa" (1770) where Bürger allowed himself the broadest liberties "Er starb—*post Christum natum*—/Ich weiß nicht mehr das *Datum*," "Schon trommelt's zur Parade!/ Wo bleibt die Schokolade?" "Zu sehen das Spektakel/In diesem Tabernakel." Bürger was particularly fond of bilingual rhyme:

> *Mein Stier nahm frisch und froh*
> *Dies Tempo wahr, und spielte,*
> *Als sie nicht sah und fühlte,*
> *Ein neues* Qui pro quo.
> *Denn er verstand den* Jocus
> *Mit* fiat Hocus pocus.

(/My bull, brisk and happy/ Observed this tempo and played/ As if he neither saw nor felt her/A new *qui pro quo*/For he understood the *jocus*/ With *fiat Hocus pocus.*)

Bürger was not always so good-humored, and the lyric section of the *Gedichte* shows him in a variety of moods. In one instance, at least, he showed himself in quite a black humour. "Der Bauer an

seinen durchlauchtigen Tyrann" is a piece of social protest expressed with exceptional strength and candor:

THE PEASANT
TO HIS ILLUSTRIOUS TYRANT

Who art thou, Prince, that without hesitation
Your coach wheel runs over me,
Your steed tramples me down?

Who art thou, Prince, that in my flesh
Your friend, your hunting dog, unpunished
Sinks its claws and teeth?

Who are you, that through standing corn and forest
The 'Hurrah' of your hunt drives me,
Breathless, like wild game?

The corn, such as your hunt treads down,
What steed and dog and you devour,
That bread, thou Prince, is mine.

Thou, Prince, hast not, with harrow or plow,
Hast not sweat through the harvest day.
Mine, mine the industry and bread!

What! You would claim authority from God?
God distributes blessings; you rob!
You're not from God, Tyrant!

Bürger's anger is seldom so strong or so apparent as here, although there are other poems of protest (particularly during the
time of the French Revolution, in which Bürger took an active
interest). For the most part, however, the *lyrische Gedichte* are of
a much less volatile nature.

Scattered throughout the rather heterogeneous collection of
lyrics, there are a number of poems which, together, comprise the
so-called *Molly-Lieder.* They total about thirty in number and were
composed between early 1774 (about the time of Bürger's arrival
in Niedeck) and 1789.[22] In a variety of forms and styles they
chronicle Bürger's passion for Molly and may be divided (somewhat arbitrarily for the sake of discussion) into three main groups:

the early songs (1774–1776), which are characterized by anxiety and longing; the poems written between 1778 and 1784, during which time Bürger and Molly were united; and the poems of 1788–1789, in which Bürger memorialized Molly—a set of eleven sonnets, plus "Das hohe Lied von der Einzigen" and "Das Blümchen Wunderhold."

There is general agreement that the earliest of the Molly poems is "Ständchen" ("Serenade"), written probably in the summer of 1775. It is a night song, in which the poet grieves that he is not with his beloved. The first three lines establish the sing-song, quasi-lullaby effect, "Trallirum larum höre mich!/Trallirum larum leier!/ (Trallirum larum hear me,/ Trallirum larum softly,/ Trallirum larum that's what I am,/I, Sweet Darling, thy faithful one./)

This is the hour when everyone sleeps but the poet, the clock, and the weathervane. The husband sleeps with his wife, the birds sleep with their mates; and when, he asks, will it be my turn to have my beloved, complete with the blessing of the priest's hand? Having no idea when this will happen, he admonishes himself to patience. The final stanza comes almost as a benediction and is in keeping with the earlier desire that the union he longs for shall be blessed by God and by the priest. As in the rest of the poem, the rhythm and movement are gentle and quiet, and the refrain-like strumming recurs:

> *Nun lirum larum gute Nacht!*
> *Gott mag dein Herz bewahren!*
> *Was Gott bewahrt, ist wohl bewacht.*
> *Daß wir kein Leid erfahren.*
> *Ade! schleuß wieder zu den Schein*
> *In deinen zwei Guckäugelein.*

(/Now lirum larum and good night./ May God watch o'er your heart./ What God o'ersees, is well o'erseen/That we experience no harm./Ade, now close again the luster/In your two little peeking eyes./)

The "Abendphantasie eines Liebenden" is also a nocturnal poem and reiterates Bürger's longing for Molly. Whereas in "Ständchen" the poet himself moves through the darkened streets on his way to the girl, in the "Abendphantasie" he sends his thoughts to hover over her and observe her in her sleep. It is his lot that he may only look at her but not possess her, and he exclaims, "Und ewig, ach! vielleicht verbeut!" ("And forever, oh! perhaps forbidden!"). As he listens to her sleeping, and in his mind's eye watches her, he commands his thoughts to return before he becomes intoxicated. Bürger's fondness for fire imagery (as noted earlier in "Danklied") recurs here vividly in the final lines, where he exclaims:

> Du loderst auf in Durstesflammen!—
> Ha! wirf ins Meer der Wonne dich!
> Schlagt, Wellen, Über mir zusammen!
> Ich brenne! brenne! Kühlet mich!

(/You blaze up in flames of thirst!/Ha! cast yourself into the sea of bliss!/ Waves, close over me!/I burn! burn! cool me!/)

Seven exclamation marks in four lines give some indication of the intensity of Bürger's feelings. It is unfortunately not an entirely successful poem, not because of the flames of passion in his mind, but because the number of images tend to clutter rather than make for a cohesive whole. There are too many unrelated thoughts and disparate images in too brief a span.

In "Seufzer eines Ungeliebten" ("Sighs of One Who Is not Loved") Bürger continues the thought and tone he had established in the "Abendphantasie." In the "Seufzer" he now addresses Nature directly, as "my mother," and asks why, since she has apportioned love to all creatures, why he alone has been forgotten ("Warum ich bin allein vergessen?"). The real problem, however, is not that he has been forgotten, but as it emerges in the final couplet, "Denn ach! mir mangelt Gegenliebe,/Die Eine nur gewähren kann," ("For oh! I miss requited love,/Which only One can give./") The sentiment is a curious one, given the passion which bound Bürger and Molly.

The song "Trautel," (1775–76) is not markedly better than the preceding poem. Nonetheless, the movement is brisk, and the argument clever, if not wholly convincing. The poet's beloved keeps him bound quite closely to her; he may not go out of doors without her, nor eat dinner without her, even though he never glances at another woman. 'We were born for each other, must have each other, without each other we would be lost.' Despite the sprightly tempo, the image of the poet being led about on a leash by his beloved ("Sie gängelt mich an ihrer Hand") is not overly felicitous. Wurzbach, however, sees in the poem an expression of the "fervent love which binds him [Bürger] to Molly."[23]

In "Schwanenlied" ("Swan Song") (alternate title "Der Liebeskranke") ("The Lovesick Man") and "Die Umarmung" ("The Embrace") Bürger carries the thought of the preceding poems to its natural or logical conclusion: without love, there will be death. In the "Schwanenlied," he expresses his longing for death and release, with the hope that he may dissolve and pass away on his beloved's breast, while savoring a final, lingering kiss. ("Zerschmelzen und vergehen,/Vergehn an deiner Brust!/Aus deinem süßen Munde/Laß saugen süssen Tod!") A rather tasteless image, but no more so than kindred ones in "Die Umarmung." The latter poem is a similar indulgence with similar results. One of the poems to which Bürger returned again and again was "Das Mädel, das ich meine" ("The lass I Love"). Written in August, 1776, it was very warmly received, and two years later, at Lichtenberg's suggestion, Bürger wrote a parody of it, "Die Hexe, die ich meine" ("The Witch I Woo").[24] In his review, Schiller had set a "?" over "Mädel," and when Bürger revised the poem for the *Musen-Almanach* (1792), he made far-reaching changes and changed the title to "Die Holde, die ich meine." ("meine" has here the meaning of "minnen," to love.) His final revision attempted to ennoble the poem and its sentiments, but the earlier version, which Wurzbach called "the best known of all the *Molly Lieder*," is a good deal more immediate, forceful, and characteristic.[25] It is fundamentally a paean to Molly's beauty, both to her physical features and her internal loveliness. Each stanza examines a specific feature and is cast in the form of question and answer:

> *Wer hat das Rot auf Weiß gemalt,*
> *Das von des Mädels Wange strahlt?*
> *Der liebe Gott! der hat's getan,*
> *Der Pfirsichblüte malen kann;*
> *Der hat das Rot auf Weiß gemalt,*
> *Das von des Mädels Wange strahlt.*

(/Who has painted the red on white,/Which radiates from the lass's cheek?/ The good Lord, he has done it,/He who can paint the peach blossom;/He has painted the red on white/Which beams from the lass's cheek./)

The aspect of form is much more apparent in this poem than in many of the other Molly poems, and each of the eleven stanzas follows precisely this closed form, though varying slightly the words and phrases. The first stanza is an exclamation rather than a question, and it poses the general question about the miracle of her beauty, to which the following eight stanzas are a reply. The movement proceeds from her eye, to her cheeks, to her mouth, her locks, her voice, her breast, her body, and her soul (stanzas 2 through 9, respectively). The tenth stanza praises God who has created such beauty, and the final stanza contains the poet's admission that if she never turns her smile on him, it were better if he had never been born. All the images are seen in relation to natural phenomena, and the comparisons are to flowers, fruits, birds, etc.

Structurally, the poem is exceptionally tight in its totality and in the individual stanza. The first and last stanza form the frame of reference for the entire piece, and each stanza constitutes an independent structural unit within that frame. The poem is not simply a string of unrelated stanzas each of which proclaims, *ad seriatim,* various aspects of Molly's beauty; the internal movement is deliberate and conscious as it moves from the eye (which is the 'mirror of the soul') past the physical features to her spiritual qualities. The movement is from the external to the internal, and in each stanza the poet steps back slightly from his object, and, like a photographer, he takes in a larger and larger view until the beauty of her entire form ("Wuchs") is visible, at which point he comes, full circle, to a consideration of her soul.

In this poem Bürger seems chiefly to have been concerned with establishing a closely-knit form and with maintaining an absolutely consistent rhythm. In eleven stanzas of masculine iambic tetrameter, he maintained an almost oppressive regularity. The poem appears to have been conceived in the manner of a folk song, for its language and syntax are both simple and clear. All of Molly's features are defined through images, but unfortunately, many of these similes and metaphors lack life and color, and the overall effect is that Bürger informs his audience of Molly's features rather than paints them.

The idealized vision of Molly seen in "Das Mädel, das ich meine" represents but one side of the poet's feelings. Far more real was the consuming passion which grew in intensity until it threatened to destroy Bürger's fragile marriage. This was the state of affairs in 1776, when Molly made a desperate attempt to break away. Bürger's response was the "Elegie, als Molly sich losreißen wollte" ("Elegy, when Molly wanted to break away"). Written in the heat of the moment, the "Elegie" lacks any single thread of thought running through it, but rather vividly portrays the poet's overwrought emotions. In so far as it is emotive rather than substantive, there is no immediately perceptible logical sequence in the poem. It suggests in its movement a stream of consciousness, as one idea leads to the next without any preconceived pattern. Not until close to the end does Bürger pursue a single train of thought for more than one or two stanzas.

The first five stanzas of the poem announce the forthcoming struggle, and Bürger addresses himself directly to Molly (stanza one) and to God (stanza two). The conflict takes its shape in a number of antithetical terms: stanzas 1–12: God, Molly (Angel)—Idol (Bürger), hell, pain; stanzas 12–15: then and now, longing and absence—joy and presence; stanzas 23 ff: survival—downfall. Throughout, the struggle centers about the poet's inner or "better self" and his rebellious ("hochempörtes") and unconquerable heart. Stanzas five through eleven describe Molly, but not in realistic terms. She is portrayed as an angel ('if the earth has angels'), and Bürger sees her as the 'queen of queens of all grace.' The poet despairs of describing her in words. Her loveliness is ineffable and could only be told with the tongues of angels and in heavenly melodies. The following stanzas detail his relationship to her and the effect she has had on him. In stanzas sixteen through eighteen, he regrets his birth; his situation is hopeless, since no Christian altar in the world can sanction their love. The following stanzas reveal the full extent of Bürger's distraught state. In highly agitated terms the poet agonizes in a despair for which there seems to be no remedy. Finally, in stanzas thirty-one through thirty-five, Bürger offers a compromise. Like the captain of a ship, he finds himself sailing toward an island where he may not land, for the queen of the island is Molly. He will honor the proscription, but he pleads that he may be allowed to continue to sail around the island, not only to protect it from robbers' hands, but also in order that he may continually gaze on its queen.

The tone of the poem is elegiac, but in execution and expression it is volcanic, as the poet struggles to articulate his immeasurable grief. Lacking any single thematic thread which would give it continuity, it is pulled together by means of rhetorical devices: metaphor, hyperbole, and antithesis pervade the poem, but do not seem a successful substitute for substance.

One of Schiller's chief criticisms of Bürger was his lack of distance, and perhaps nowhere is this problem more apparent than in the "Elegie."[26] Bürger is creating from within the actuality of the experience, and the result is a massive personal catharsis. Unfortunately, the reader has difficulty in sharing that catharsis, because Bürger fails ultimately to project his torment; it remains his own private agony, and the reader discovers—with some embarrassment—that he is witnessing, but not participating in, an immensely personal event. It remains only to note that the effect of the poem is further weakened by its length. The fierce intensity attempted by Bürger could not be sustained throughout thirty-five stanzas without a more explicit sense of direction.

A span of about one and a half years separates the composition of "Liebeszauber" from the "Elegie," but in tone and mood the two poems are light-years apart. "Liebeszauber" ("The Magic of Love") is one of Bürger's most successful poems, and he seldom achieved, as he did here, a similar level of spontaneity and buoyancy. In "Liebeszauber," Bürger focuses upon Molly's beauty in realistic terms, and instead of describing an idealized vision, he creates the vital being directly. The girl is extremely pretty; she has a roguish eye and a roguish mouth ("Schelmenauge und Schelmenmund"), although she is perhaps not the most beautiful girl in the world—"the empress of beauties." That makes little difference to Bürger, as he confesses, continuing his feudalistic analogy:

> *Dennoch hegst du Kaiserrecht*
> *Über deinen treuen Knecht:*
> *Kaiserrecht in seinem Herzen,*
> *Bald zu Wonne, bald zu Schmerzen.*
> *Tod und Leben. Kaiserrecht.*
> *Nimmt von dir der treue Knecht!*

(/Nonetheless you retain imperial rights/Over your faithful subject/Imperial power in his heart/Now for bliss, and now for pain./Death and life, Imperial power,/The faithful servant takes from you./)

> *Schelmenauge, Schelmenmund,*
> *Sieh mich an und tu mir's kund:*
> *He, warum bist du die Meine?*
> *Du allein und anders keine?*
> *Sieh mich an und tu mir's kund.*
> *Schelmenauge, Schelmenmund!*

(/Roguish eye and roguish mouth,/Look at me and tell me/Why are you mine?/You alone and no one else?/Look at me and tell me/Roguish eye and roguish mouth./)

Searching here and there, the poet finds no answer and must conclude that the girl has magic powers ("Zaubermädel"), and he asks in the final line, "Sprich, wo ist dein Zauberstab?" ("Tell me, where is your magic wand?").

In a letter to Boie, written in February, 1778,[27] Bürger wrote that the poem had come to him "in continenti" and that he had written it down with a single stroke. In the same letter, he admitted that it was "not one of my worst." Indeed, in the critical notes to the poem, written much later, Bürger confessed that "it is one of my truest ('wahrsten') and best songs; in the most lively tone. In no other [poem] does such expressive power ('Darstellungskraft') obtain."[28] Even a casual reading of the poem confirms Bürger's opinion. The tone of the piece is set in the very first line with the direct address to the girl, "Ma'msell, look me in the face." In effect, of course, Bürger is also saying, "give me your ear; pay attention," and the mood of the poem is established at once. The language, the style, the syntax are true-to-life and easily accessible, and there is a welcome lack of Anacreontic apparatus. The brisk tempo of the trochaic tetrameter, with its couplets of alternating masculine-feminine rhyme, emphasizes the rapid internal movement of the text.

In "Mollys Wert" ("Molly's Worth"), written some five months later (July, 1778), the melancholy tone has regained its preeminence, and the poem is suffused with the sense of hopeless longing which characterizes so many of the earlier Molly songs. The underlying thought is expressed in terms of the unreal world: "O, if I could buy Molly,/For gold and precious jewels,/And if I had such," etc., or "If I were the Regent/Of all Europe/And could buy Molly." If all these things were possible, the poet would choose to have

Molly and turn his back on riches and power, to live with her in a "garden cottage." As a mere poet, however, lacking both wealth and power, he considers what he could offer and declares he would give a year of his life for every day she might be his.

"An die Menschengesichte" ("In People's Eyes") may be regarded as a sequence to "Mollys Wert" and actually follows it in the 1789 edition. The melancholic mood is retained, and the first stanza also seems to continue the theme of poverty: "And yet, sadly, I spin neither silk nor gold,/I spin only sorrow of heart for myself." Very soon it becomes clear, however, that the poet is no longer speaking for himself, as he had in the previous poem, but is addressing the public on behalf of both Molly and himself. It is not an "Ich," but a "Wir" poem. The thought is that if society can do nothing to assist the lovers in their plight, "Then leave us alone and bother us no more,/Just leave us alone." The poet strikes a note that he will subsequently return to in "Naturrecht," namely, that it would be contrary to nature to try to halt or prevent their love:

> Die Sonne, sie leuchtet; sie schattet, die Nacht;
> Hinab will der Bach, nicht hinan;
> Der Sommerwind trocknet; der Regen macht naß;
> Das Feuer verbrennet—Wie hindert ihr das?
> O laßt es gewähren, wie's kann!

(/The sun shines; the night gives shade,/The brook flows down stream, not up,/The summer wind dries, the rain drenches/Fire consumes; how can you prevent that?/O leave it alone, to do as it should./)

There is a perceptible change of tone in this poem from the previous one; frustration and annoyance are added to sadness and result in a restrained tone of defiance. The meter differs as well, and here Bürger's rare use of the amphibrach produces a drive and tempo not found elsewhere among the Molly songs.

The poem "Untreue über Alles" ("Infidelity above All," late summer, 1779) is included in the second section of the 1789 edition ("Epic-Lyric"), but as one of the Molly songs it deserves comment at this point. It is a framework poem, in which Bürger recalls his having been out in the fields alone with Molly, where they were aware only of nature and themselves. Having set the scene, the poet allows himself and Molly to speak in dialogue. Being more than a dialogue, however, the poem seeks to establish the extent to which fidelity plays a role in Molly's (and Bürger's) thinking. Initially, he wishes to know if it is simply sensuality that binds her to him. The questions and conditions become increasingly pointed, as Bürger invents unreal and unnatural situations to test her: What if the most beautiful fairy captured me and refused to grant me my freedom until I had made love to her? Molly supplies real answers to unreal questions: 'never come back unless you have been faithful to me.' As Bürger warms to his task, he lets his imagination roam and asks Molly to consider the possibility of his being turned into the "ugliest dwarf" or of her losing her beauty, or her being turned into a snake (!) if he were to refuse to accommodate the fairy. To this last proposition Bürger makes the bizarre offer to carry her (Molly-turned-snake) about with him under his shirt, so that she might still hear the heart that beat for her. The threat of death finds Molly as steadfast as ever, and she assures Bürger that she would come, herself, to take him to heaven. Bürger closes the poem by returning to the framework setting of the field. Essentially, the poem is an exercise in contrivance and is of interest chiefly as it reveals Bürger's thoughts of how he feels Molly should behave.

The poem "Himmel und Erde" (Heaven and Earth") was begun in 1773, and Bürger included its first stanza in a letter to Boie (May 6, 1773). Grisebach, in his essay on Bürger,[29] regarded it as the first of the *Molly Lieder,* though in the Introduction to his edition of Bürger's works (1872) he acknowledged that the last stanza might have been added later,[30] which, in fact, it was. Bürger put the poem aside for nearly a decade and did not finish it until very early in 1782. It is only four stanzas long, but within that short space Bürger conveys a mood of oppressive gloom. The contrast is between heaven with its fullness of blessings and the misery of reality on earth. Bürger complains that neither physician nor priest can cure him; he is sick both in body and in spirit. Long ago his joys have fled from him, and his hopes are dim, but even so, he would gladly continue his pilgrimage on earth, or even carry the burden of the world, if Molly were his. In this poem there obtains, as in no other poem since "Liebeszauber," a genuine and perceptible sentiment. The strength of "Himmel und Erde" lies in its extraordinary simplicity. The poet makes his statement with almost no

adornment and conveys in sober and solemn terms his overwhelming sense of sorrow.

"Mollys Abschied" ("Molly's Farewell") was written in May,
1782, at the time of Molly's departure for Langendorf, where she
was to bear her and Bürger's child. The poem proceeds with an impec-
cably steady and dignified movement, and the meter (trochaic
tetrameter) underscores the solemnity of the poem. Bürger speaks
here through Molly, for this is her farewell to him:

> *Lebe wohl, du Mann der Lust und Schmerzen!*
> *Mann der Liebe, meines Lebens Stab!*
> *Gott mit dir, Geliebter! Tief zu Herzen*
> *Halle dir mein Segensruf hinab!*

(/Farewell, thou man of pleasure and of pain/Man of love, staff of my
life,/God be with you, my Beloved, Deep in your heart/Let my words of
benediction resound./)

As Molly departs, she notes what Bürger might retain: a lock of
her hair, the vision of her face, or a wreath of forget-me-nots. All
these are but parts, however, of the whole, as Molly reminds him in
the final stanza:

> *Mann der Liebe! Mann der Lust und Schmerzen!*
> *Du, für den ich alles tat und litt,*
> *Nimm von allem! Nimm von meinem Herzen—*
> *Doch—du nimmst ja selbst das Ganze mit!*

(/Man of Love! Man of pleasure and of pain!/You, for whom I've done
and suffered all,/Take of everything! Take of my heart—/Yet you take,
the whole with you./)

In "Untreue über Alles" the poet had emerged only by inference,
whereas in "Mollys Abschied" he offers a full and enlightening
image of himself. He clearly recognized that he was a man of strong
emotions, and he was not hesitant to acknowledge his desires
("Lust") and drives ("Triebe"): "This scarf, which, yielding often
to your drive,/Revealed the sanctuary of my breast."

The poem is an eminently sober and serious affair, and the
elevated language accurately reflects its mood. At the same time,

a strangely ecclesiastical atmosphere prevails. The meter suggests a procession; the phrases have a biblical ring ("Mann der Liebe! Mann der Lust und Schmerzen"—"Man of Sorrows and acquainted with Grief"), and even such references as "Des Busens Heiligtum" and the "Segensruf" have religious overtones.

Structurally, "Mollys Abschied" presents the by-now familiar form for which Bürger showed such a strong and frequent preference. The opening and closing stanzas are either identical or very similar, and the body of the poem catalogues the material or thought contained in the opening stanza. By adhering to this pattern the poet could be certain of achieving a closed and rounded form.

"An Adoniden" (or as revised, "An Molly"), written in August, 1782, but revised for the 1789 edition, is one of the least successful of the Molly songs. It is a talisman poem, in which Bürger invokes an unreal conditional and speculative world to describe his love: "Were Homer to come back to life/And felt this urge and drive/ He would ascribe it to the sash ("Gürtel")/That Venus wore over her breast." The poem is brief and relatively unpretentious, but the experience is contrived and the emotions second-hand.

"Volkers Schwanenlied" ("Volker's Swan Song"), probably written in 1784, suffers from essentially the same problems as "An Adoniden." It is an imitation of the Old French "Lay de Mort," and when first published in the *Musen-Almanach* Bürger printed the original after his version. The original version has Tristan addressing Iseult; in the adaptation Bürger replaces her with Molly. Bürger's identifying himself with Volker (the great fiddler of the *Nibelungenlied*) was not a hollow reference; he did, in fact, regard himself as standing in the tradition of Volker, and in his correspondence frequently referred to himself by that name. The poet conjures up the feeling he would have if he were approaching death. It occurs to him that his situation parallels Volker's, and he proposes that his epitaph should be the couplet, "No man ever loved and suffered like Volker;/The hopeless man died therefrom." Molly, the "sweet murderess of life," is accorded her customary crowns, but the poet Fritz Stolberg, for whom Bürger has 'always had great affection,' is to inherit the poet's lyre. The whole situation is so unreal and the manner so contrived, that it is difficult to repress a suspicion that Bürger intended the poem as a caricature or travesty.[31] The situation in this poem is as unreal as the emotions it portrays. The image of Molly is twice removed—in both time and space—and Bürger's attempt to superimpose Molly and himself onto a foreign, indeed alien, model served to intensify rather than diminish the awarness of a surrogate experience. (It might be noted that Klopstock had a predilection for this kind of visionary post-mortem situation in a number of his odes.)

At long last, when all obstacles were removed and Bürger and Molly could stand together before the world as they had in private, the motivation for these passionate expressions of longing and melancholy disappeared. Molly's early death and his grief at her loss stunned Bürger into silence, and it was nearly three years before he could bring himself to commemorate her in his poetry. Once again Molly became the source of his inspiration, but now the future had become the past, and from his memories Bürger created her memorial.

The 1789 edition of the *Gedichte* contains one dozen sonnets, eleven of them devoted to the memory of Molly (the twelfth honors A. W. Schlegel). The aesthetic value of these poems is much disputed, although initially it was none other than Schiller, who, in his review, called them "models of their kind."[32] A. W. Schlegel was far less generous in his remarks in "Bürger 1800," but Schlegel regarded the sonnet as his own preserve and was not likely to hail the accomplishment of others in that area. Wurzbach agrees with Voß that the sonnet was, for Bürger, 'simply a comfortable form in which to include all kinds of poetic material of minor significance, and that fifteen years earlier Bürger would hardly have acknowledged these pieces as poetic.'[33] Whether so harsh a criticism is justified is a moot point, but there can be little disagreement that the Bürger of the sonnets is no longer the *Volksdichter* who saw the seal of perfection in popularity. Bürger's turning to formalism and to more concise and restrictive forms, such as the epigram and the sonnet, is characteristic of his later years, when the major force of his titanic energies had been exhausted.

Although it is likely that several of the sonnets may have been sketched at an earlier date, they were, for the most part, composed and put into final shape in the winter of 1788–1789, immediately prior to publication in the new edition. Petrach was Bürger's formal, and, to a certain extent, thematic model.

The tone of the sonnets is set in the introductory piece, "Die

Eine," which laments that for the poet there has never been but one beloved. Fickleness taunts him, 'why so committed to but one? . . . The world is large, and in the great world/Many girls and women still blossom beautifully and sweet." "Oh too true," admits Bürger (with a line reminiscent of Walther von der Vogelweide, "Vom Rhein/an bis zum Belt"), "but what good does it do me that Molly is the only one who pleases me?"

The elegiac mood established in "Die Eine" is continued in "Überall Molly und Liebe" ("Everywhere Molly and Love"). In changing the meter, however, from iambic to trochaic pentameter, Bürger has given the poem a more deliberate, measured movement. As with so many of the earlier Molly poems, the setting is nocturnal, and here the poet seeks out the solitude of the forest, "Night of firs and oaks," in order to escape the din of the world. In the forest, he hopes to find peace and relief from his longing. There is no quarter to which he can retreat, however, where Love will not pursue and find him, and where he will not be reminded of Molly. Barth feels that Bürger in this poem has fallen back to a coarse realistic or naturalistic style with such expressions as "to slink away from the din of the world."[34] Given the context of the poem, however, these do not seem to be unduly abrasive phrases.

In "Täuschung" ("Delusion"), the poet seeks still to wean his heart from the memory of Molly, and he searches among all the living beauties for one who might take her place. Finally, in a state of exhaustion, he creates, out of his phantasy, an image full of loveliness, and at last his heart believes itself healed—but only for the moment; for on closer view, his lingering gaze reveals to him that the vision he has conjured up is really Molly. The poem thus ends as it had begun, with the poet still under the spell of the real Molly, and the illusory world in which he had sought relief shatters, leaving him once more in the real world of grief. The two worlds of reality and phantasy find themselves constantly opposed in the sonnets, as Bürger wrestles with the one in the terms of the other. Invariably he posits the subjunctive wish, 'O, if only,' against the palpable, undeniable, inescapable indicative, and the very title of this sonnet, "Täuschung" suggests the conflicting experience— memory vs. phantasy.

"Für Sie, mein Eins und Alles" ("For Her, My One and All") retains the mood set in the previous sonnets, but holds out even

less hope. Fortune has not bestowed noble rank on him; in fact,
'Everything, as though in league against him, hurls back unheard
his every wish.' His only honor and possession in life is his poetic
laurel sprig, and even this he would gladly give up if Molly could
be his. The tone of the lament hovers between melancholy and
bitterness—that Dame Fortune has really given him nothing and
moreover, prevents his union with Molly. The poem is reminiscent
of the earlier "Mollys Wert," with the thought that money and
power might be a means of winning fair heart. A comparison of
the final lines of the two poems shows a significant similarity in
thought:

> MOLLYS WERT
>
> *Thus, gladly I would give, I swear,*
> *For every day a year,*
> *If she were mine*
> *My very own entirely.*

> FÜR SIE
>
> *Yet even this one thing, that I know,*
> *I would with pleasure give away as offering*
> *If, O Molly, possession of you were the prize.*

Here Bürger does not see Molly with the eyes of memory, but as
a reality he cannot possess. The sense of the present found in "Für
Sie, mein Eins und Alles" recurs in the sonnet "Die Unvergleich-
liche" ("The Incomparable One"). The poet begins by asking,
'what ideal of angelic phantasy could have hovered before Nature
as a model when she clothed that one spirit sent to earth from the
third heaven?' In this one case Nature has created the perfect
union of Spirit in Form and Form in Spirit. Though Molly is not
named in the sonnet, her immediate presence emerges at the conclusion. As in the previous poem, she is still very real and immanent
in the poet's mind, 'He never knew the pleasure and pain of Love,/
Who never learned how sweet her breath fans./How wonderfully
sweet her lips speak and smile.'

The ostinato of sorrow is lightened somewhat in the sonnet "Der
versetzte Himmel" ("Transposed Heaven"), where in a slightly
lighter but still quiet tone, Bürger declares his love for Molly.
For the first time the poet addresses his reader directly, as he reminds him of the directions his glance must take in order to see

heaven or hell. 'Above are the heavens, to which you cast upward your gaze, like one praying to God, and if you look down you perceive with terror and trembling the province of Satan.' That, Bürger expresses with a smile, is what most people think and say, 'but when Molly looks up at me, and I look down at her, there is all my heavenly bliss.' Unobtrusively, Bürger has constructed the octave on a series of contrasting images: the light and joy of heaven vs. the dead of night and horror; light and darkness; heaven and hell; above and below; joy and anguish; etc. In the sestet, the poet announces that what most people believe does not hold true for him, but that his truth lies in the inversion of these polarities.

In "Naturrecht" ("Natural Law"), as in "Der versetzte Himmel," Molly is very much alive for Bürger, and the poem was probably sketched out at an earlier date. It is a catalogue of his 'rights' as a human. 'Flower and fruit may I pluck for pleasure as for need.' The creatures of the field do him service; the silk worm is there to spin him satin and taffeta; even the nightingale is there to lull him to sleep or awaken him, as he pleases. Why, then, he asks, should he not be free, "compelled by love and desire" to fall into Molly's blissful embrace (literally, lap of bliss)?

The poem has something of the old fire that Bürger had lost after Molly's death, and it suggests, in content as well as in tone, a time just prior to the 'final solution' of the relationship between Bürger, Molly, and Dorette (fall, 1781). It is also slightly similar to an earlier poem, "An die Menschengesichter" (1778). "Naturrecht" is a poem couched in the form of a rhetorical question, and it provides a clear picture of Bürger, self-assured and confident in his Ptolemaic view of the universe.

"Verlust" ("My Loss") is the first of the sonnets which were clearly written after Molly's death. Reinhard suggests 1786 as a possible date, although there is no documentary evidence to support the suggestion. There is little substance to "Verlust"; it is a rather murky expression of grief at the loss of Molly, whom he had longed for and wooed so many years, and who had been so suddenly taken from him. 'Woe to me! Since you vanished./Bitterness is borne every day in my mouth./ Only in the hour of my death will I taste honey.' The force of the piece is dissipated somewhat by Bürger's use of three different, and very specific, images within the close restriction of the form. In the first quatrain Bürger portrays himself as the pilot of a ship; 'more than a hundred months, day and night, against storm and stress ("Sturm und Drang"), he has struggled toward the harbor. In the next quatrain he suddenly changes the image, and Molly becomes a cup or goblet: 'Beaker, good enough for divine tongues, Golden Jewel.' In the sestet Molly changes again from the beaker or "Chalice of nectar" to the nectar itself.

Much of the language of "Verlust" is lifeless and wooden, but the expression of sorrow in "Trauerstille" ("Quiet Sorrow") emerges original and vital. The mood of this sonnet is set at the very outset, with the slow trochaic tread, "öde, sonder Freuden-schall" ("dull, without a sound of joy"), and continues with great regularity to the end. Bürger conveys the feeling of emptiness, whether in palace or cottage, field or grove. A silence has fallen over his world and muted all sound; the intimate talk of love as well as the flutelike song of the nightingale:

> *Leere Hoffnung! Nach der Abendröte*
> *Meines Lebens einst im Ulmenhain*
> *Süß in Schlaf durch dich gelüllt zu sein!*
> *Aber nun, o milde Liebesflöte,*
> *Wecke mich beim letzten Morgenschein*
> *Lieblich, statt der schmetternden Trompete.*

(/Empty hope! After the twilight/Of my life—some time ago in the elm grove—/To be sweetly lulled to sleep by thee!/But now, O mild flute of love,/Wake me at the final dawn/Gently, instead of with the blaring trumpet./)

There is perhaps no more substance to "Trauerstille" than to several of the other sonnets, but it succeeds better than most for a number of reasons. In the first place, Bürger concentrates on ex-pressing a single basic idea and establishing a pervasive mood: the empty silence which characterizes his world. Secondly, he uses an imagery which is fresh and in keeping with the atmosphere of the poem. Virtually nothing in the entire poem suggests a sound, with the exception of the final words, "der schmetternden Trompete." Even the flute tone of the nightingale is barely audible. Thirdly, Bürger's choice of words supports the underlying mood: among the consonants, the liquids and nasals predominate, and the hooded vowels further dampen all sound. Bürger is waiting quietly, even patiently, until the final morn, when he will awaken and find eternity with Molly.

The morning that Bürger longs for in "Trauerstille" is the dawn of eternity; our temporal days with their dawns bring only a renewed grief and sorrow. In "Auf die Morgenröthe" ("To the Dawn") Bürger sees no ray of hope, but only cause for continued sadness. Unlike the mythological Tithon, the gray and withered ancient who was beloved by Aurora and who nightly greeted her afresh, Bürger will never again embrace his bride except at the "black gates of the land of shades." 'Day sank into dreary and starless darkness, when Molly was torn from this world.' The tone of the sonnet is unrelieved gloom. Where, in some of the other sonnets, there had at least been a ray of hope, here there is only darkness, and curiously enough, even the longed-for moment of his reunion with Molly will take place "an des Schattenlandes schwarzen Toren." The gloom, however, is less felt than described, and the experience seems more academic than personal. Bürger's revival of the figures of classical mythology was hardly an artistic step forward in 1789, nor was it in line with his emphatic views on *Volkspoesie*.

The last of the sonnets, "Liebe ohne Heimat" ("Love without a Home") is an analogical statement in which Bürger compares his love to a bird:

> *My Love, like the dove,*
> *Long frightened by the falcon back and forth.*
> *Joyfully believed she had reached her nest.*
> *In the branches of a bower.*

The dove has been deceived, however, for a cruel fate has no sooner shown her her home than lightning carries her off. And now she wanders aimlessly back and forth between heaven and earth, with no resting place for the burden of her wings. "For a heart, which would take pity on her,/Where she, once more, as formerly, might warm herself,/Beats for her nowhere on earth."

In addition to the sonnets, the 1789 edition contained what Bürger insistently called his "dearest, most precious song, my masterpiece,"[35] upon which he could never improve, and which he would never equal. In a rapturous tone and style Bürger gave passionate expression to his memory of Molly in "Das hohe Lied von der Einzigen, im Geist und Herzen empfangen am Altare der Vermählung." In a letter to Boie written shortly after Molly's death, he mentioned his plan to celebrate Molly in a large-scale hymn; but it was not until the winter of 1788–1789 that, under the persistent urging of A. W. Schlegel, Bürger resumed work on it and finished it. There is no single line of thought running through the poem, although it is not lacking in formal structure. Form, however, is of minor importance to Bürger in this instance, since he is principally intent upon glorifying Molly.

The first five strophes are a call to attention. In the first, he addresses his audience, "Attend! Hear of my Chosen One! Hear the most beautiful of my songs!" After his descent into the depths, the poet arises now to light and joy of spring. He has neither rank nor riches, but he will give what he has to create for Her Glory and Life, with his noblest Song of Celebration. (stanza 2). The poet, in turn, addresses Nature, "Silence, o Choir of Nightingales!" 'and everything that might disturb this song.' Finally, he addresses his song, and orders it to break forth, to be eternal (stanza 4.) From the fifth to the tenth stanza, the poet speaks of himself in the third person. He is the sufferer who at last has reached the shore of his land of bliss (stanza 5). His strength had waned, and he was about to expire, when the sky opened and, like a ray of light, She became his own (stanza 6). (Molly is not mentioned by name in the poem.) Now, however, She reigns in the fields of Paradise, where the poet projects himself into her fairy arms ("Feenarmen"), full of love, loyalty and grace (stanza 9). Can that bliss be true, or is it but a dream which dissolves with the crowing of the cock? 'Is it really She, the Glorious One, who is mine before the world and heaven?' (stanza 11). Stanzas 10 to 15 express the poet's wonder and joy that She has chosen him, and he can hardly believe it, since She could have had her choice among men, princes, and sultans, yet chose him, "withered and sick" (stanza 15).

In earlier days he had conquered with his song and with his science, but that was long ago. Beginning with stanza 16, Bürger proclaims the extent of his love for Molly for all the world to hear, "Call it out loudly, with all your soul!" (stanza 16) She was the gentlest, the loveliest, the purest; and whatever recriminations there be, "let them fall on me" (stanza 17). For She was an absolute part of himself, his heart and mind (stanza 19). In stanzas 20 through 23, Bürger views Molly in the various aspects of her physical beauty, and then in a spiritual light. She is purity and clarity itself, and her virtue, like her kiss, transcends both time and space. Bürger will hear no songs about others, so long as he can sing of her. In stanza 34 the poet begins his movement towards a conclusion and expresses his gratitude for Molly. In stanza 38 he addresses his song, as he had at the beginning (stanza 4), and directs it to celebrate her glory. He sends it forth as his son (stanza 42) "with the Master-seal of perfection on your brow," 'to proclaim your message down through the stream of time.'

The outline of the poem reveals simultaneously its nature. It is a dithyrambic eulogy in which the literal world is raised to a level of abstraction, and concrete images dissolve in a miasma of ecstacy. In its lack of concern for substance and its dependence on emotional response, it can be compared to the "Elegie," (as most critics, from A. W. Schlegel onwards, have done), but the "Elegie" was written (as noted earlier) from within the context of direct experience.

A. W. Schlegel, in a detailed and sympathetic review, noted that: "Bürger accomplished as a man, what he could not, as a youth, have accomplished for fame. This time, however, he was not writing for fame. He wanted to create a monument to the passion which had filled his life."[36] In his later consideration of Bürger's works, "Bürger 1800," Schlegel was less generous when he termed the work a "cold display piece" ("kaltes Prachtstück").[37] Schiller regarded the poem as "the most prominent piece in the collection," but accused Bürger of violating the canons of good taste and lamented that he "strays not infrequently on the borders of madness, that his fire often becomes fury."[38] Schiller's final thought on the matter was that it was only "a very excellent *occasional poem.*"[39] Even so sympathetic a critic as Barth admits that with its 420 verses, it seems, like the "Elegie," to be "too long by a good deal."[40] Undeniably, the faults of the poem have overshadowed its virtues, and, despite Bürger's conviction to the contrary, "Das hohe Lied" has not survived as his greatest monument.

"Das Blümchen Wunderhold" should not perhaps be included among the Molly Songs, but the poet's concern for Molly is so

fundamental to the poem, that this seems not an inappropriate
point at which to cite it. With stringent economy, Bürger unfolds
the story of the miraculous flower. The poem opens like a fairy tale,
"Somewhere in a quiet valley there blossoms a little flower."
Because of its beauty it is more precious than gold or jewels, and
is thus called 'Little Flower, Wondrous Grace.' The flower has
great and efficacious powers that it can work on body and mind,
for young and old, and it is greater than any secret elixir. The poet
has observed its effect with wonder and claims that whoever keeps
'Wondrous Grace,' close to his breast becomes as lovely as an
angel, and his heart is delicately tuned. By the power of 'Wondrous
Grace' the harsh becomes gentle, the rough smooth, the importun-
ate graceful, and the shrill song soft. Moreover, the flower, like a
talisman, keeps all evil elements at a distance so that they can
neither approach nor cause harm.

'This is no flower in the world of fables,' says the poet; 'no matter how hard it is to believe, 'My song is but a reflection of the
heavenly loveliness' that 'Wondrous Grace' spreads in the world.
Now the poet recalls his beloved:

> Ach! hättest du nur die gekannt,
> Die einst mein Kleinod war—
> Der Tod entriß sie meiner Hand
> Hart hinterm Traualtar—
> Dann würdest du es ganz verstehn,
> Was Wunderhold vermag,
> Und in das Licht der Wahrheit sehn
> Wie in den hellen Tag.

(/Ah, if you had only known her,/Who was once my precious jewel—/
Death tore her from my hand/So soon after the marriage altar/Then you
would quite understand/What Wondrous Grace can do/And see it in the
light of truth/As in bright daylight./)

Whenever the flower was lost, she returned it to him; to her he
owed his thanks for the blessings of the flower. But now a feeling
of impatience often snatches it from him, and he bemoans its
loss. The last stanza is a variation on the first, in which the poet
sings his praises of the flower. It is only in the final couplet that he
reveals the common name of the flower: "Thus I call it 'Little Flower,

Wondrous Grace'/Otherwise it's called, modesty (discretion) ('Bescheidenheit')."

One of the strengths of the poem is its straightforward and simple manner. Bürger was striving for the naive expression of the folk song, and to a great extent he achieved it. The elements of time and space are clouded in ambiguity, and although the marvelous powers of 'Wondrous Grace' are indicated, those who are capable of being affected remain unseen and anonymous. Thus Bürger is able to channel the energy of the poem into the one stanza (translated above) where the reference is specific. Furthermore, he attracts his audience's attention by a sudden positional change from simple narration to direct familiar address, "Ah, hadst thou but known her." The reader then moves with the poet as he recalls the 'blessings of the flower,' and moves back once again, but not quite, to the role of observer, more than participant. Not quite, since Bürger maintains his presence until the very end. The final situation resembles the beginning but does not mirror it, for Bürger has moved from the impersonal expression of the first stanza,"Therefore it is called . . ." to the "ich" of the final stanza. The impersonality of the fairy tale has been replaced by the subjective expression of the poet, and the flower has acquired a personal connotation over and above its broader symbolism.

CHAPTER 3

Epic-Lyric Poetry

THE second section of the 1789 edition of Bürger's *Gedichte* is designated "Episch-lyrisch" and contains a total of twenty-two poems, the majority of which are ballads. Many of them were carried over from the 1778 edition, and to these Bürger added at least five new ones. The earliest of the serious ballads, "Lenore" (1773) was Bürger's greatest. It is generally acknowledged to be one of the most imposing ballads in any literature and, understandably, it has been the center of much controversy.

There are two major areas of debate regarding the background of "Lenore." The first concerns its place in the history of the genre and whether Bürger did, in fact, establish a new kind of ballad. Until Bürger's time, the ballad or "Romanze" had been a relatively coarse, unsophisticated form which had its place more within the context of *Volksdichtung* than *Kunstdichtung*. Much in need of reform, it was disdained by most serious poets as a branch of the *Bänkelsang* ("Ballad-mongering" or "balladizing"). In a very significant letter addressed to Johann Heinrich Voß (April, 4, 1774), the poet Hölty (1748–1776) wrote, "I should write more ballads? Perhaps I shall write a few, but it will be very few. A ballad singer strikes me as a harlequin or a man with a peep show." ("Mir kommt ein Balladensänger wie ein Harlekin oder ein Mensch mit einem Raritätenkasten vor.")[1] The place of the ballad singer had long been in the market place, and his popularity was never greater than at executions, when in great detail he commemorated in his song the hideous deeds, the agonizing trial, and ghastly end of the condemned. It was *Moritatendichtung* in its rawest state, although in professional hands it developed into the "Schauerballade," "Schauerromanze," or "Gespensterballade" ('horror ballad,' 'horror poem,' or 'ghost ballad'), and was peopled with ghosts, apparitions, *Doppelgänger*, etc. Hölty is generally credited with establishing the (more refined) "Schauerromanze" in Germany with "Töffel und Kathe" (1771), "Adelstan und Röschen" (1772), and "Die Nonne" (1773).[2] Whether he simultaneously established the serious

"Kunstballade" is another question. Valentine Beyer, in his book, *Die Begründung der ernsten Ballade durch G. A. Bürger* (1905) convincingly argues that Bürger, not Hölty, deserves this distinction. He maintains that the "Kunstballade" or "serious ballad" depends both on the choice of material and treatment, and that Hölty could never find a suitable topic to treat in sufficiently serious a manner.[3] According to Beyer, Hölty, was primarily concerned with achieving an effect and less concerned with the larger literary or aesthetic implications.

In his book, *Die Geschichte der deutschen Ballade* (1936), Wolfgang Kayser, rejected Beyer's argument and insisted that Bürger's "Lenore" is every bit the "Schauerromanze" that any of Hölty's had been, that Hölty's "Adelstan and Röschen" and "Die Nonne" both antedate "Lenore," and that Hölty must be regarded as the true founder of the genre.[4] Kayser also cites two very well-known letters from Bürger (also quoted by Beyer), indicating that Bürger knew the Hölty pieces and competed with them. "I have now a moving Romance in the works, [and when he sees it] Hölty will go and hang himself" (April 22, 1773).[5] In the other letter, (April 19, 1773), Bürger writes that "The 'Minnelied' is dedicated to Miller; in the same fashion I shall soon write a *Romanze* for Hölty, and thus to each something in his own manner."[6] Commenting on these two statements, Kayser writes, 'Twice, therefore, Bürger acknowledges that "Lenore" was composed in competition with Hölty.'[7] (Beyer had already stated: 'In direct, explicit rivalry with these poems Bürger proceeded to work.'[8]) Kayser continues; 'Explicitly he says here that his poem is written in the manner of Hölty's pieces. It cannot be more clearly expressed that Hölty is the founder of the serious ballad in Germany.'[9] Not all critics have agreed with either Kayser's reasoning or his conclusions, and in recent years his argument has been almost entirely rejected.[10] Indeed, to many scholars they may have seemed tangential or academic in the light of Bürger's accomplishment.

Rather than debating the question of primogeniture, it is more profitable to consider the several traditions merging in Bürger's ballads. Among the earlier critics, and especially Wurzbach, it was thought that the development of the ballad, as it culminated in Bürger, derived almost entirely from the tradition begun by Gleim, who, in turn, had composed under the influence of the Spanish poet

Don Luis de Góngora (1561–1627) and the ironic romances of the French poet François Augustin de Moncrif (1687–1770). Gleim evidently believed (and falsely so) that parody was a basic quality of romance, and thereby came to equate "Romance" with *Bänkelsang*.[11]

In 1756, Gleim published three romances, the first of which bore the extraordinary title, "Traurige und betrübte Folgen der schändlichen Eifersucht, wie auch heilsamer Unterricht, daß Eltern, die ihre Kinder lieben, sie zu keiner Heirat zwingen, sondern ihnen ihren freien Willen lassen sollen, enthalten in der Geschichte Herrn Isaac Veltens, der sich am 11. April 1756 zu Berlin eigenhändig umgebracht, nachdem er seine getreue Ehegattin Marianne und derselben unschuldigen Liebhaber jämmerlich ermordet." ("The sad and grievous Consequences of infamous Jealousy, as well as the edifying Instruction, that Parents, who love their children should not compel them to a marriage, but leave them free choice, contained in the story of Herr Isaac Velten, who, on April 11, 1756 committed suicide in Berlin, after having horribly murdered his faithful wife, Marianne, and her innocent lover.")

Gleim's other two romances bore similar baroque titles, and their contents catered to the public taste for calamity—and morality, for the moral of the romance was stated explicitly at the conclusion.[12] Gleim's romances enjoyed much popularity and were widely imitated. It was in much the same vein that poets like F. W. Gotter, D. Schiebeler, and J. F. Löwen, wrote their romances, and Hölty also wrote within this broad tradition.

More recent critics who have studied the development of Bürger's ballads have not rejected the earlier theories, but have widened their base. "Bürger's serious ballad, as all writings on the origin of the *Kunstballade* set forth, is intimately bound up with Gleim's romance writings, the ironic romance, and Hölty's romances: without Gleim and Hölty, 'Lenore', in its given form, is unthinkable."[13] Lore Kaim-Kloock also stresses the influence of the *Moritaten* literature and *Bänkelsang*. "In the Moritat many characteristics of Bürger's ballad are already present in raw form, which can be seen neither in the old folk song nor in the *Salon-Bänkelsang*. Among them are: the purely material affections, the detailed, vivid presentation of cruel and dreadful happenings, the crass vacillation of mood, and an aggressive rhetoric attuned to the audience."[14] It was Bürger's achievement that he not only assimilated the various traditions but was able to endow the form with a seriousness of tone and purpose that was unprecedented.

The composition of "Lenore" occupied Bürger for at least six months during 1773. The first mention of the poem occurred in a letter to Boie, April 19, 1773 (quoted above), and is at most a very oblique reference. Three days later, Bürger again wrote to Boie enclosing "Der Raubgraf" and announcing that a "moving" (rührende") romance was in progress. The tempo of Bürger's work increased appreciably by the end of April, and in his next letter to Boie (May 6), he gives the title of his poem and tempts him with the first stanza. He intimates that the ballad is already complete, and that he is particularly proud of it; 'Until you send me something, you shall not have my most excellent ("überköstliche") Ballad: "Lenore," and a "Minnelied" that is sweeter than honey and virgin honey. Indeed! these two pieces are so grand that one can really be proud of them . . . Sir, there is a ballad for you!'

Work on "Lenore" continued through the spring into the summer, and much of the polishing that occurred at about this time must certainly have been inspired by Herder, whose "Fliegende Blätter" Bürger read early in June. 'O Boie! Boie, what rapture! when I found that a man like Herder teaches more clearly and positively about the lyric of the people and, consequently, about nature, all that I have felt and thought about for so long—but obscurely. I think "Lenore" shall correspond, in a certain measure, to Herder's teachings.'[15] It was Herder's charge that folk lyric should be purified, revitalized, and raised from the low state of comic vulgarity into which it had long since fallen. Percy's *Reliques of Ancient Poetry* and *Ossian* hovered before Herder's inner eye, and he hoped for a similar development in Germany. Perhaps no one among Herder's readers at that particular moment was in a better position to fulfill the mission he outlined.

Within the month, Bürger had read Goethe's *Götz von Berlichingen* and again took pen to paper to exclaim: "Boie! Boie! The knight with the iron hand, what a piece! . . . Emotional shudders, as only Shakespeare can evoke, I have felt down to the very marrow. Sympathy! Horror!—Shudders, cold shudders, as when the north wind blows!"[16] Quite clearly another influential factor had come into play and would make itself felt in the finished ballad. By August 12 Bürger could finally write to Boie, "Thank God, now I am finished with my immortal 'Lenore'!"[17] The poet's enthusiasm for his work could not be concealed, and he confessed that he could hardly believe that it was he who had actually written it. Nonetheless, the new Ghengis Khan of the ballad (as he called himself) had no intention of sending the finished product to Boie and allowing it to be read by someone else in his absence. The great "Condor" (as he also called himself) would come himself to read it to his friends. The Hainbund (over the signature of G. D. Miller and K. F. Cramer) rather lightheartedly attempted to clip his feathers, but Bürger was not to be cut down in midflight by the "owls, bitterns, hoopoes, and reed-buntings of the old wall, thorn bush and reed grass in Göttingen."[18] The Hain had "commanded" Bürger to appear before the assembled body on August 21 to read the ballad, but Bürger refused. Whether or not he read "Lenore" before the Hainbund remains obscure.[19] It appears from the correspondence, however, that one or several copies were circulated among the members of the Hain, and Bürger's correspondence with Boie in September reveals the extent to which the poet was involved in revising, filing, and polishing, in preparation for a definitive version. The final version seems to have been completed sometime between September 20 and 27, when Bürger wrote to Boie that he was finally feeling a bit better about the ballad and that he had given a private reading of it to his house maid, Christine.[20] It was, in fact, from this same Christine, according to A. W. Schlegel (*Neuer Teutscher Merkur* 1797; I. 392 ff.) and J. H. Voß (*Morgenblatt*, Nr. 241. October 1809), that Bürger received the stimulus for "Lenore" as well as the lines:

> *Der Mond der scheint so helle,*
> *Die Toten reiten schnelle*
> . . . .
> *Graut Liebchen auch?*

The question of the sources for "Lenore" poses a complex and controversial problem. Bürger himself claimed that he had "ferreted the material out of an ancient ballad. But what a shame, that I cannot get to the ballad itself."[21] Much later, Voß wrote, "We searched for the song in every part of Germany, but in vain."[22]

Almost from the beginning, critics and literary historians have attempted to pinpoint Bürger's source, and he has not, in fact, been spared the accusation of plagiarism.[23] It is possible that Bürger may have seen the ballad "The Suffolk Miracle," but its resemblance to "Lenore" hardly warrants the charge of plagiarism. It is also possible that Bürger could have seen a copy of Percy's *Reliques of Ancient Poetry,* since there was one in the Göttingen Library, but Beyer and others have quite convincingly shown that Bürger had little or no knowledge of Percy before 1777.[24] The number of possible sources is immense, but the number of probable ones is rather more limited. One of the most likely suggestions has been put forward by Götz Hübner, who suggests that Bürger's source was a fairy tale, rather then a ballad, and prose rather than verse (excepting a refrain).[25] Herder had very early remarked that he had known a *Märchen* similar in content to "Lenore," and Bürger's early school friend, Johann Erich Biester, also pointed to a *Märchen* source. Hübner argues for the fairy tale "Elenore," a suggestion which was also made by Bürger's contemporary, the linguist and financier, Johann Christian Christoph Rüdiger.[26] The question of sources will, in all likelihood, continue to be debated; no work of art is created in a vacuum, and it must be acknowledged that Bürger drew upon a variety of traditions, thoughts, refrains, and lines taken from here and there; but in the final analysis one should keep in mind the poet's own assertion (which seems to have been generally disregarded) concerning both his "Minnelied" and "Lenore," "Ganz von eigner Erfindung!" ("Entirely of my own invention!")[27]

"Lenore" is set at the time of the Hubertusburg Peace, which ended the Seven Years War in 1763. Many of the soldiers returning home pass through Lenore's village, and the girl eagerly and anxiously searches for and inquires about her own beloved, Wilhelm. Filled with dread, because she had not heard from him, and because he is nowhere to be found, she believes that he is dead:

> *"O Mutter, Mutter! hin ist hin!*
> *Nun fahre Welt und alles Hin!*
> *Bei Gott ist kein Erbarmen.*
> *O weh, o weh mir Armen!"*

(/"O Mother, Mother, gone is gone!/ Now let the world and everything pass away!/ With God there is no mercy./ Oh woe, Oh woe to me, poor creature!"/)

The mother urges Lenore to recite the Lord's Prayer and to have faith that all happens for the best. She suggests also that Wilhelm may have married another girl, but that, in any case, it is wiser to think of the hereafter, where the joys are greater than those of this life. Bürger propels his argument forward in a dialogue between Lenore and her mother; and Lenore, in despair, repeats her line, "With God there is no mercy." Weeping, beating her breast, and wringing her hands, Lenore retires for the night: "Und außen, horch! ging's trapp, trapp, trapp,/Als wie von Rosseshufen" ("And outside, listen! it went trapp, trapp, trapp,/ As if of horse's hoofs"). A voice asks Lenore to open the door, and then Wilhelm commands her to ride off with him: "Auf meinen Rappen hinter mich!/ Muß heut noch hundert Meilen/ Mit dir ins Brautbett eilen." ("Up, on my black horse behind me!/ [I] Must yet ride a hundred miles today/ [and] Rush with you into the bridal bed.") Reluctantly, since it is already eleven o'clock, Lenore joins her lover and the horse bounds forward in a gallop.

Wilhelm utters the refrain-like lines: "Graut Liebchen auch?—Der Mond scheint hell!/ Hurra! die Toten reiten schnell!/ Graut Liebchen auch vor Toten?" ("And are you afraid, Sweetheart?— The moon shines brightly!/ The dead ride swiftly/ And are you afraid, Sweetheart, of the dead?") Soon they pass a cortege accompanied by the mourners singing their dirge. The tempo of the ride increases with every moment, and mountains, trees, hedges, towns, and villages hurtle past—as Wilhelm repeats his lines, and his questions, "Graut Liebchen auch vor Toten?" At first confident, Lenore reveals an increasing anxiety at these questions. Finally, they reach a cemetery, inside which Wilhelm is horribly transformed:

> *Ha sieh! Ha sieh! im Augenblick,*
> *Huhu! ein gräßlich Wunder!*
> *Des Reiters Koller, Stück für Stück,*
> *Fiel ab wie mürber Zunder,*
> *Zum Schädel, ohne Zopf und Schopf,*
> *Zum nackten Schädel ward sein Kopf;*
> *Sein Körper zum Gerippe,*
> *Mit Stundenglas und Hippe.*

(/Ah look! Ah look! in that moment,/ Huhu! a ghastly wonder!/ The rider's garments, piece by piece,/ Fell off like brittle tinder./ A skull, without plait or forelock,/ His head turned to a bare skull,/ His body to a skeleton,/ With hour-glass and sickle./)

The scene of horror is accompanied by a *Totentanz* executed in the moonlight, and as Lenore sinks dying to the ground, the spirits howl,

> *"Geduld! Geduld! Wenn's Herz auch bricht!*
> *Mit Gott im Himmel hadre nicht!*
> *Des Leibes bist du ledig;*
> *Gott sei der Seele gnädig!"*

(/"Patience! Patience! Even if your heart breaks!/ Do not quarrel with God in heaven!/ You are rid of your body,/ May God have pity on your soul."/)

The immediate reception of "Lenore" among Bürger's friends was overwhelmingly favorable. Boie could report to Bürger on November 10, 1773, that wherever he had read it, in Münden, Cassel, or elsewhere, "Lenore" was greeted with enthusiasm.[28] And even more encouraging, "Goethe has talked with him (Joh. Falk) very enthusiastically about it."[29] In addition, Bürger could look with gratification at numerous excellent reviews, including one by C. F. Cramer in the *Erfurter Zeitung*.[30]

The accolades of praise were not universal, and a number of luminaries were quite cool toward "Lenore." Klopstock and Voß were not favorably inclined, and several other critics were either lukewarm or negative in their evaluation; A. G. Kästner, in the *Göttingsche Anzeigen* (1774), commented laconically on the ballad, providing only a brief resumé and expressing the thought that love, when it miscarried, generally inclined those of the gentler sex to devotion and prayer—which one might rather have expected with the daughter of such a pious mother.[31] Matthias Claudius, in the *Wandsbecker Bote*, advised Bürger to "take this excellent piece again in hand and complete it."[32] Less baffling, but considerably more irritating to Bürger was a review which appeared in the *Frauenzimmerzeitung*. An obscure Lieutenant von Hagen felt that he was showering Bürger with praise when he wrote, "Herr B. proves himself to be a not infelicitous imitator of Jacobi."[33] Bürger's letter to Boie regarding this review reveals a good deal not only about his character but also regarding his feelings about himself as a poet:

Up to now I have always thought of myself, regardless whether I might be a good or bad poet, as being, all things considered, at least a bit original, or if this word sounds too proud, as being no one other than myself. What, after all, have I in common with Jacobi? If there is someting, I shall root it out this very moment and count it as undone. Not because I dislike Jacobi's poetry unduly—on the contrary, I esteem it rather more than others—but because I would rather be anything in the world but an imitator. Rather an intolerable individual, than a fortunate, successful *(glücklicher)* imitator of any one, even if it were Summus Klopstock himself.[34]

Another aspect of the negative criticism was based on quite different assumptions. In several quarters "Lenore" was considered a most scandalous piece of blasphemy. One of the earliest remarks of this nature came from Therese Heyne (the wife of a Göttingen professor), who alleged that "Lenore" was "gotteslästerlich" ("blasphemous"), and that Bürger's other ballad, presumably "Des armen Suschens Traum," was "Quark" ("rubbish")[35]. This radical assessment found numerous and more articulate reverberations, especially among theologians and academics. Wurzbach relates that Professor Adolf Reinhard was so carried away in his charge of godlessness that he accused not only a number of professors at Göttingen, but the whole university, and thereby incurred the wrath of his Sovereign and was forced to recant and retract.[36] (The hoary legend circulating among Bürger scholars that the *Musen-Almanach,* in which "Lenore" was first published, was confiscated in Vienna, seems finally to have been laid to rest by Götz Hübner, who simply points out that after 1772 it was prohibited by law to import foreign *Kalender* into Austria.[37])

The religious aspects of "Lenore" continue to be of concern to scholars, but no longer because of any potential threat of heresy. The whole issue has expanded from a consideration of theological implications[38] into a larger question involving the function or role of religion in the ballad, and the extent to which the language and syntax have been derived from, or influenced by, the Bible and the German Protestant hymnal. The most heated (and convoluted) debate has centered on these issues, and it has involved the leading Bürger critics for nearly two decades. Albrecht Schöne, one of the most perceptive and prolific commentators on "Lenore,"[39] recognizes in the ballad a pervasive secularization of Christian ethics. Referring to Bürger, he writes, 'from this time on, his letters show an increasing separation from the strict Lutheran orthodoxy, which had determined the first twenty years of his life.'[40] Schöne also sees a secularization of Christian symbols, and compares Lenore's quarrel with God to Job's.[41] Moreover, he perceives a secularization of Biblical and hymnal speech patterns, 'a more reliable piece of evidence that the very disparately colored occasional comments about his own inner relationship is afforded by the manner in which he handles his own native religious speech patterns. Biblical words, verses of hymns and above all, liturgical formulas are liberated from their sacred codex, without any hesitation, and without any concern for their venerable . . . origin.'[42]

Such, in capsule form, was part of Schöne's argument in 1954. In 1956, Lore Kaim-Kloock, writing in the *Weimarer Beiträge*, asserted that Schöne's essay, 'attempts to restructure ("umdeuten") the religious protest in "Lenore" into a religious confession, to deprive the poem of its plebeian-revolutionary character and to present Bürger as a believing Christian.' ("den religiösen Protest in der 'Lenore' zum religiösen Bekenntnis umzudeuten, dem Gedicht den plebejisch-rebellischen Charakter zu nehmen und Bürger als gläubigen Christen hinzustellen.")[43] In 1958 Eduard Stäuble expressed the same doubts about Schöne's conclusions.[44] In the same year, Schöne vigorously rejected Kaim-Kloock's interpretation of his essay and reasserted his original position. Five years later, Kaim-Kloock, in her book, *Gottfried August Bürger. Zum Problem der Volkstümlichkeit in der Lyrik*, ignored Schöne's rebuttal and republished her earlier claims.[45] In the same year (1963), Emil Staiger joined the debate and completely agreed with Schöne regarding Bürger's use of language: 'The facts of the case are, at least as far as the language is concerned, irrefutable.'[46] Beyond that, however, Staiger regarded it as most unlikely that Bürger could have made any deliberate or consistent effort at an ethical or symbolic secularization.[47] Götz E. Hübner, one of the most recent critics to deal with "Lenore," provides an exhaustive and convincing argument for the presence of stylistically derivative, but nonrestrictive formulaic patterns.[48] Hübner sees the structural models upon which Bürger built and developed his own form of the ballad, primarily in the fairy tale and in the hymnal.

Bürger's concern for form in 'Lenore' was paralleled by his concern for both content and effect. The fundamental content of the ballad must have been determined fairly early in the creative process. The basic story is relatively uncomplicated and was probably not significantly altered once it had been established. As Staiger points out, the changes pondered during the final stages of composition concern the choice of words, good or poor images, rhymes, metrics, etc. . . .[49] In other words, Bürger's concern was with the shaping of the work, rather than with any larger questions of a theological nature. He was, after all, an eminently 'practical' poet, who wanted to create (in "Lenore" as well as in his other works) a product which would please and impress his public, and all his theories about the role of the poet and the inviolable principle of popularity confirm his practice. (There are numerous and obvious exceptions to this creed, as every critic from Schiller onward has pointed out. In broad terms, however, it applies.)

Bürger's "Lenore" fuses reality and illusion in a single shattering experience of despair, deceit, and death. Despair separates Lenore from God, and her senses deceive her into accepting illusion as reality. Her death, whether real or illusory, is as much the logical conclusion of her rejection of reality as it is the expiation of her guilt for having turned from God in despair. The entire ballad is suffused with a stifling sense of inevitability. As the natural order is displaced by a series of grotesque images and visions, the pragmatic world, with its potential for averting disaster by rational means, recedes and disappears.

The tempo of the ballad is as relentless as its conclusion is inevitable. At the very outset, Bürger establishes a driving rhythm which he maintains without interruption to the end. By constantly shifting his perspective and by the skillful use of a variety of rhetorical devices he achieves not only an aggressive pace, but extraordinary intensity as well. The combination of these qualities contributes immeasurably toward producing the staggering effect he desired.

In reading the poet's correspondence, whether on "Lenore," *Macbeth*, or the "Nachtfeier der Venus," one is struck by Bürger's insistent concern for effect ("Wirkung"). The immediate sensory effect of a work was of towering importance to him, and again and again he stresses the impact he hopes to make. In his letters to Boie

Bürger very early spoke of his intention to 'turn the flesh ice-cold'[50] or make 'the hair stand on end as in *Macbeth*.'[51] In the early stages of composition, he had read parts of "Lenore" to Frau Listn (which, given her frail mental state, he should have refrained from doing), and he reports the effect to Boie with apparent satisfaction, "It creates such an effect, that the Frau Hofrätin starts up at night in bed."[52]

To produce the spine-chilling effect was an undeniable part of Bürger's intention. With pride he quotes *Macbeth* in one of his letters to Boie, implying that this was the effect he hoped to achieve:

> *I have a tale to unfold, whose lightest word*
> *Will harrow up your souls, freeze your young blood,*
> *Make your two eyes, like stars, start from their spheres*
> *Your knotty and combined locks to part,*
> *And each particular hair to stand on end,*
> *Like quills upon the fretful porcupine.*[53]

That he may have been able to produce something of the same effect in Lenore's ride strikes Bürger as Shakesperian, "I cannot hide, that I regard them [several new strophes in 'Lenore'] as being superior, and one especially as being as sublime as Shakespeare . . . (The lines which pleased him most: 'Wie flog, was rund der Mond beschien,/ Wie flog es in die Ferne!') "Is not a ride, where it seems to one, that the whole firmament with all the stars is flying overhead; is that not a Shakespearean idea?"[54] Surely the influence of Shakespeare is evident, but perhaps even more apparent is that of Goethe's *Götz von Berlichingen*. Stäuble suggests, in fact, that Bürger envisaged "Lenore" as a '*Götz* of the ballad.'[55] According to Boie, Bürger enjoyed recounting the effect he produced reading "Lenore" to the young Graf Friedrich Leopold Stolberg.[56] At the line, "Rasch auf ein eisern Gitterthor," Bürger struck the door with his riding crop and Stolberg leapt from his chair. (This is one of the irrepressible Bürger legends, which probably had its origin in a letter to Boie, where the poet asserted that "Lenore" would make "the youngest Graf" tremble.[57])

The effect of "Lenore" was evidently a very real one, although it was not everywhere appreciated. The historian Johannes von Miller wrote to his brother, "That damned Bürger, with his 'Lenore', shattered my whole nervous system for one entire night, and when Bonstetten was reading it at about midnight and the door suddenly sprang open, he dropped the book from his hand, and his hair stood on end."[58]

Herder's experience with "Lenore" was somewhat similar and it obviously shaped his opinion of the work:

> When I read it, it took hold of me so, that that afternoon I saw naked skulls on all the church pews. The deuce of a man, to terrify people that way! Why and for what purpose? I wish some one else would sing in the same way about the devil fetching the poet.[59]

Unlike many of his contemporaries, Bürger later regarded "Lenore" as something almost on the order of an apprenticeship work. He hoped that he might follow it with a series of ballads, each one surpassing the other, until he finally won recognition as undisputed sovereign of the form. Even before he had completed "Lenore," he had sent a copy of "Der Raubgraf" ("The Robber Baron") to Boie for his opinion (April 22, 1773).[60] Boie replied that he could find no fault with the ballad, and it was published in Voß's *Musen-Almanach* for 1776.

"Der Raubgraf," as told by the coachman Matz, is a rather grim account concerning a local nobleman who plunders and thieves throughout the region. His fortress is considered impregnable and he can therefore carry out his crimes with seeming impunity. His downfall is brought about, however, through the services of an imp or sprite. The sprite was a prisoner of Master Urian and bartered her freedom by promising to bring the count down into the village where he could be captured. She changes herself into a toad, gains entrance to the Count's castle, and then changes herself into his horse. On the following morning, the Count plans his usual ride, but the sprite carries him into the town, where he is captured and placed in a cage. When he grows hungry, his keepers cut off part of his body, roast it, and serve it to him, so that, over a period of time, he entirely consumes himself. The narrator assures his audience that the cage is still to be seen and adds ominously, it is still usable.

The material for the ballad was taken from an old legend of the Harz Mountains, and harks back to a somewhat similar situation related to an incident involving Graf Albrecht von Regenstein (1323), although the historical Count managed to save his life by making sweeping concessions.[61] In presenting the tale, Bürger blends humor with horror, to the extent that the reader is not aghast at the barbaric cruelty of the Count's punishment. Wieland's review stated that "a rousing and hearty joviality and horrifying magic feeling produce a completely original 'Mittelding' [a work halfway between a ballad and a romance."[62] Bürger could not, for some time, decide whether to call it a ballad or a romance but in the end settled for ballad.

Shortly after completing "Lenore," Bürger announced to Boie (Ocober, 1773) that he was already at work on another ballad. This is the first mention of "Der wilde Jäger" with which Bürger was to occupy himself over the next five years. In the summer of 1775 he wrote to Goethe that his "Medusa is now after the Wilde Jäger," and to Boie he noted that "the longer and longer I work on it ["Der wilde Jäger"] the greater becomes my ideal of living and vital epic-lyric poetry. If I achieve it, hereafter Lenore will be my moon, but ["Der wilde Jäger"] will be my sun."[63] The ballad did not seem to progress, however, and in the same letter Bürger acknowledged that it was turning sour ("Die Geburt wird mir sehr sauer"). Two years later, with the impending publication of the collected poems, Bürger finally finished the ballad, but was unable to include it in the edition. As a consequence, it went back on his shelf, and he finally published it in the *Musen-Almanach* for 1786, or roughly thirteen years after he had begun work on it.

The plot of "Der wilde Jäger," if one can speak of one, is utterly simple. It is the tale of a Count, so consumed with a raging passion for hunting, that he rides out on the Sabbath and allows nothing to stand in his way, not God, nor man, nor beast. The ballad begins with the call to the hunt, in counterpoint to the church bells. The Hunter rides out, and he is soon joined by two strangers, one on either side. The stranger on the right warns and urges the Count to turn back, and the stranger on the left urges him on. The chase after the stag involves three episodes in which the two riders at the Count's side seek, on the one hand, to prevent and, on the other, to encourage further destruction. The farmer's pleas for his fields are brushed aside, as are those of the shepherd for his flock, and the hermit's for the sanctity of his cell. When, at last, the Hunter defies God and defiles the anchorite's hut, he is undone, and the judgment pronounced on him is that, for all eternity, he will be the hunted rather than the hunter. Immediately the forces of hell rise up and, in all their horror reach out to snag the hunter-turned-hunted. In the concluding stanza, Bürger assures his reader that the "wilde Jäger" will be hunted until the Day of Judgment, and that this is a story told by many a hunter.

Next to "Lenore," "Der wilde Jager" is undoubtedly Bürger's best-known ballad, and it, too, has been translated into several languages. Sir Walter Scott, among others, did an English version of both poems. "Der wilde Jäger" found a particularly wide audience in the final years of the eighteenth century, with its bourdon of protest against an oppressive and unconcerned nobility. The pleas of the farmer and the shepherd echo the sentiment expressed in "Der Bauer an seinen durchlauchtigen Tyrann" (1773). In addition, Bürger introduces, without imposing it, a moral and didactic element.

"Der wilde Jäger" makes an interesting companion piece to "Lenore," in so far as the two represent almost opposite viewpoints. Whereas "Lenore" is related from a feminine standpoint, "Der wilde Jäger" is a thoroughly masculine affair. In "Lenore" it is love, and in "Der wilde Jäger" the chase, which is the driving force; but instead of dying, like Lenore, the hunter is charged with eternal existence.[64]

Both ballads have an underlying concern for man's soul in the face of sin, but "Der wilde Jäger" develops almost as if Bürger were consciously trying to outdo "Lenore." Sin is compounded by crime and destruction, and to the concern of the individual is added the larger concern for social justice. "Der wilde Jäger" also has very obvious political implications. The action of both poems takes place on horseback, and Bürger employs much the same technique and many of the same devices to achieve the feeling of a relentless drive. The same iambic tetrameter occurs in both, except that in "Der wilde Jäger" the masculine endings predominate and Bürger has shortened his stanza from eight to six lines (ab, ab, cc.-m, m, f). If anything, the drive is even greater and more forceful here than in "Lenore," although it might be countered that one is also more aware of what is going on:

> *Gesagt, getan! Der Wildgraf schwang*
> *Sich übern Hagen rasch voran,*
> *Und hinterher, bei Knall und Klang,*
> *Der Troß mit Hund und Roß und Mann;*

> *Und Hund und Mann und Roß zerstampfte*
> *Die Halmen, daß der Acker dampfte.*

(/No sooner said than done! The Hunter sprang/Forward across the hedge,/ And behind, with crack and clang,/ The mob with hound and steed and man:/ And hound and man and steed trampled/ The stalks, so that the field steamed./)

In the same year that Bürger wrote to Boie that "Der wilde Jäger" would be his sun and "Lenore" his moon (1775), he composed the rather modest ballad or romance "Der Ritter und sein Liebchen." Boie had made no comment other than to say that the piece had given him pleasure. Boie called it a "poetische Schnurre" ("an amusing tale"), which is hardly a great compliment. "The Knight and his Lass" is, in fact, little more than that, and perhaps less. Told mostly in dialogue form, it concerns the poor lass who has given herself to the knight and when she innocently pleads for him to take care of himself in the war, so that he may return safe and sound, he mocks her naiveté and rides off howling with laughter. For those innocents to whom the moral may have been dim, Bürger devotes his concluding stanza, "Girls, don't trust easy knights" ("Traut, Mädchen, leichten Rittern nicht!")

In July, 1776, Bürger sent Boie "einige Kleinigkeiten" ("several trivial pieces")[65] for Voß's *Almanach*. Among them was "Die Weiber von Weinsberg," which Wurzbach calls one of Bürger's best ballads. The town of Weinsberg is under siege by the Emperor Konrad. When the town is taken, so the threat goes, deeds will be done which will give the women cause for lasting complaint. The women of the town, having taken council among themselves, send out a representative to the Emperor in order to implore his mercy. But all in vain, for the Emperor insists that he will destroy the town, and will only allow the women to take out what each can carry on her back. Next morning, lo and behold, the gates open, and each woman walks out carrying her husband in a sack on her back. The Emperor permits no interference; instead, he pardons the town and gives a great feast to celebrate the women of Weinsberg.

Derived from a very popular legend, the story goes back to the Annals of the Cloister at Hirsau, written by Johann von Tritheim, who asserts the event took place in 1140. Between Johann von Tritheim and Bürger the tale had spread all over Germany, and there were a number of towns which claimed to be the original Weinsberg. Siegmund von Birken (1626–1681) was perhaps the first to treat the legend poetically, and since Bürger, it has been set numerous times in literary form.

Bürger treats the story with broad strokes and brusque earthy humor. He establishes a mood of levity as he praises the good women of the stout little town ("wackres Städtchen") and avows that if he ever decided to go awooing, he would woo a lass from there. Even the Emperor and his siege are not matters of much gravity; the situation itself is disastrous but not serious. All is carried out in good humor; the Emperor is "mad at the good little town" ("dem guten Städtlein böse"), and his horses and men seem to spend their time running about rather than wreaking havoc and destruction. Bürger's humor comes across in the language as well as in the situation, as he indulges himself in slapstick polyglot rhymes:

> *"O weh, mir armen Korydon!*
> *O weh mir! die Pastores*
> *Schrien: Kyrie Eleison*
> *Wir gehn, wir gehn kapores!*

(/O woe to me, poor Corydon,/ O woe to me! The priests/ Lamented: Kyrie Eleison!/ We're going, we're going capores (getting busted)./)

In his comments on this poem, which he calls a "Romanze," Helmut Paustian notes that, 'the underlying characteristic of all these works is the capacity for action ("Aktionsfähigkeit") on the part of the characters portrayed; whether good or bad, they act and move, no matter whether for good or evil. Actions and events predominate, and no longer the sentimental contemplation as in the romances of Gleim.'[66]

The very short poem "Robert" is, as Bürger notes in the subtitle, "A Counterpart to Claudius's Phidile." "Robert" is simply the poetic account of an older man's recollection of a brief and lovely encounter which took place with a girl many years earlier. No names were asked, no questions, where from, where to; it all took place in a moment, and in the next she was gone. Bürger wrote the poem *ad instantiam* in June, 1775, and sent it to Goeckingk for publication in his *Almanach*. Goeckingk was clearly pleased, for in his next letter he sent Bürger "a hundred kisses for your Robert."[67] The poet's own estimate of "Robert" was somewhat less florid: he called it a trifle ("Lappalie").[68]

The desire to create an even greater ballad than "Lenore" or "Der wilde Jäger" continued to occupy Bürger's mind, and in April, 1776, he announced his masterpiece, "Lenardo und Blandine," to Boie with a grand flourish, describing it as "the queen, not only of my own, but rather of all ballads of the Holy Roman Empire, which is over 80 stanzas long and to which, according to my feelings, Lenore must yield precedence."[69]

Bürger included several stanzas to tempt Boie, and four days later sent him the complete work, 'the strongest progeny of my poetic loins' ("stärkste Ausfluß meiner poetischen Lendenkraft").[70] Apart from the first two or three stanzas, Bürger claimed to have written the entire ballad in a single day. Boie immediately wrote that "Lenardo is your masterpiece," and attributed its greatness to its having been done, in contrast to Bürger's normal creative process, in a single stretch. Friedrich Blömker calls it one of Bürger's weakest works,[71] as does Wurzbach, who regards this burst of creativity as the probable reason for its "lack of artistic perfection."[72]

The action of the ballad takes place in Burgundy, between the king's daughter, Blandine, and a servant, Lenardo. Blandine is the most beautiful of all beautiful princesses, and despite the many princes who came to pay her court and seek her hand, she wishes only for the love of Lenardo, who is not of noble birth. At a rare moment when the two are alone together outdoors, Blandine gives Lenardo an apple, 'lovely on the outside to behold, but I should wish that what is within would be ten times more lovely.' Blandine has sent Lenardo a letter avowing her love for him and asking him to meet her at midnight by the apple tree in the orchard. With much trepidation he goes to the assigned spot and is met by Blandine, who leads him through the ruins of an ancient castle along a dimly lit passage to a room, where they can share their love.

> *In Schlummer gehüllet war jedes Gesicht:*
> *Doch ach! das Verräteraug' schlummerte nicht,*
> *Lenardo! Lenardo! wie wird dir's ergehn,*
> *Noch ehe die Hähne das Morgenlied krähn?–*

Wrapped in slumber was every face:/But oh, the eye of the betrayer slumbered not./Lenardo! Lenardo! how will you fare,/Before the cock sounds his morning song?/)

The betrayer is a mighty Spanish prince, one of the many unsuccessful suitors for the hand of the princess, who is determined to stay on at the court, convinced that the situation will reverse itself. Unable to sleep, he is given to nocturnal wanderings and observes the meeting between Lenardo and Blandine. Having followed them and determined their trysting place, he rushes back to the palace to awaken the king and betray the pair. The king supposedly loves his only daughter more than his scepter and his crown. Consequently, he is reluctant to believe the Spaniard's tale, but the latter wagers his life—'Let my blood stand pawn—and may Burgundy drink it.' The two proceed to the place where Lenardo and Blandine are. The door is locked, however, and they must wait outside, listening to the whispering inside. Lenardo is plagued by fear of being found out, while Blandine attempts to reassure him. Finally, at the arrival of dawn Lenardo must return, and he leaves Blandine to sleep. Once outside the door of the room, the king and the Spanish prince attack and kill him, and the Spaniard cuts out his heart in a frenzy of rage. 'So much love, little heart? Tomorrow night you'll have more.' Blandine passes the day in anxious dreams awaiting the arrival of Lenardo at midnight, and the king temporarily disappears from the scene. At midnight, the door to the chamber opens and three young noblemen enter: the first bearing a torch and shroud, the second a golden vessel, and the third a letter. Having delivered their gifts, they bow and retire. Blandine reads the letter and becomes insane. She hallucinates, dances about in wild abandon, and finally collapses as she presses the "Blutgefäß an ihr liebendes Herz" ("the vessel of blood to her loving heart"). The cry goes up that the princess has died, and the king rushes to her, now recognizing his own mistake in heeding the word of the Spanish prince. As soon as the king sees the prince, he runs him through with his sword, but nothing can undo the death of his daughter. 'Lenardo, poor boy! Blandine, my child! Oh, Almighty Heaven, forgive me my sin.' Having been separated by rank in life, the king decrees that they shall be united in death, and he has Lenardo and Blandine laid together in a silver coffin.

As Bürger points out in his letter to Boie, the ballad is unusually long; it has 82 stanzas and goes into elaborate detail. Bürger's claim that it was entirely original did not prevent Boie from suggesting that "the little tale is also in Boccaccio, if I am not mistaken."[73] It is indeed, and occurs in the *Decamerone* (VI.1). In his study of Bürger's English influences Friedrich Blömker notes that critics have also put forth the poem, "Little Musgrave and Lady Barnhard" as a possible source.[74] Although Bürger did know the English poem, the *Decamerone* is much more likely to have been the immediate source.

In his ballad Bürger follows fairly closely the story of the Princess Ghismonda of Salerno, and her love for the noble youth Guiscardo. As in "Lenardo and Blandine," the young princess laments her rank, as it proscribes a union with her beloved. In "Lenardo and Blandine," Bürger has moved the court from Salerno to Burgundy, and he has introduced the figure of the Spanish prince. In the *Decamerone,* the father sends Guiscardo's heart to his daughter to remind her of her obligations. Whereas Blandine apparently goes mad and dies of a broken heart, Ghismonda commits suicide by taking poison. The mad scene strongly recalls Ophelia's madness in *Hamlet* and is drawn by Bürger with a lingering hand. Blömker regards it as an excess of tastelessness ("Er [Bürger] leistet sich hier das Äußerste an Unschönheiten und Geschmacklosigkeiten.")[75] In addition, Blömker points out the unmistakable resemblance between Lenardo's departure from Blandine and Romeo and Juliet's separation scene (III.5).

In reworking the Boccaccio tale, Bürger makes Lenardo a simple servant rather than a noble youth, yet at the same time he endows him with a noble spirit.

> *Der schönste der Diener trug hohes Gemüt,*
> *Obschon nicht entsprossen aus hohem Geblüt."*
> *Gott schuf ja aus Erden den Ritter und Knecht.*
> *Ein hoher Sinn adelt auch niedres Geschlecht.*

(/'The handsomest of servants had a noble disposition,/ Although not born of noble blood./ God made both knight and servant out of earth./ A noble sense also graces the lower ranks'/)

Paustian regards this change as an entirely new step in the evaluation

of the relationship between noble and middle class.[76] Bürger's
replacement of Guiscardo by Lenardo may not be quite the innova-
tion that Paustian believes, but it is very much in keeping with
the spirit of the times. More subtle, but also more consistent
in Bürger's ballads is an underlying concern for the blessing and
sanction of any union by the church. Thus while Bürger frequently
takes rather radical social and political stands, he remains essentially
conservative in his attitude towards the Church.[77] In "Lenardo
and Blandine," one of Lenardo's greatest fears is that the Church
will not bless their love: 'The bonds rent asunder, the ring of faith
shatters, where heaven does not pronounce its blessings.' At his
death, Lenardo's consuming horror is that he dies without confession, without having taken communion, and without having received absolution. Temporal constraints could be gotten round,
but spiritual concerns are inevitably to be reckoned with.

The title of Bürger's next ballad, "Der Bruder Graurock und die
Pilgerin" ("Brother Grayfrock and the Pilgrim") would seem to
indicate a central concern for religious matters, but, in fact, the
religious element is of relatively little consequence. Written in early
May, 1777, it is the first of five pieces adapted from poems in
Percy's *Reliques*. Boie called it a *Lied* (song) rather than a ballad,
which is probably a more accurate description. In a letter to Boie,
Bürger noted that there were a number of "Sujets" that he planned
to adapt from Percy, "But very freely, much more freely even than
'Bruder Graurock.'"[78]

"Bruder Graurock" is developed mainly in dialogue form. A girl
dressed in the garb of a pilgrim inquires at a monastery whether
her beloved is housed within. The friar who receives her immediately
recognizes her, but does not reveal his identity. Instead he inter-
rogates her, gives her equivocal answers, and tests her love. He
replies that her beloved has long since died and been buried. Consumed with grief, she vows that she will spend the rest of her life as a
pilgrim, although the friar advises her that "hin ist hin" ('what's gone
is gone'). After all, he suggests, perhaps her beloved was not faithful to her anyway. But nothing can console the girl, and she asks
only to be permitted to kneel at his grave before embarking on her
journey. The friar proposes that she stop for a while in the monastery, at least until the rain ceases, but to no avail:

Mag's sein, daß Regen mich befällt!

> *Wäscht Regen aus der ganzen Welt*
> *Doch meine Schuld nicht ab."*

(/It may be that rain will fall on me,/But all the rain in the world/Will not wash away my guilt./)

Immediately the Friar reveals his identity, the tone changes abruptly: "Heida! Fein's Liebchen, nun kehr um!" (Hoho! my sweetheart, just turn round!") He confesses that she has come in the nick of time; his novitiate period is about to expire (after which he would not have been able to renounce his celibacy), but now he may still leave the loneliness of the monastery ("Klostereinsamkeit"), and his beloved rejoices that nothing will ever separate them now but death.

In his version of "The Friar of Orders Gray" Bürger follows the English poem quite closely, but his ballad is an adaptation and not a translation. Minor changes occur, but there are no basic ones, as Penelope Scott, writing on Bürger's translations from the English, would have it.[79] The underlying difference is one of viewpoint. Bürger purges his poem of any languid melancholy, and eliminating the archaisms in the English, he places the dialogue firmly in the present.[80]

In "Die Entführung, oder Ritter Karl von Eichenhorst und Fraülein Gertrude von Hochburg," the second of Bürger's ballads based on a model from Percy ("The Child of Elle"), Bürger returned to the vigorous and dashing kind of material he always found so attractive and in which, for the most part, he excelled. Without giving any introduction or background whatever, Bürger plunges into his story with the sharp command, "Squire, saddle my Danish horse, . . ." and with hardly a moment's respite, the poem drives forward to its conclusion. The Knight Karl learns from her maid that his beloved, Gertrude, has agreed to accept Plump von Pommerland's suit, evidently at her father's insistence. Clearly, Gertrude is as miserable as Karl, and she sends her maid to him with a golden ring and the message that she cannot face the situation and is resolved to die. Karl asks the maid to assure her mistress that he will rescue her at all costs and will appear at midnight below her window. Having assembled his vassals and given them instructions, Karl goes to Gertrude at midnight, and after some persuasion, carries her off with him. Their conversation and flight have been overheard and observed, however, and her father, the

Reichsbaron, and Plump are soon alerted and follow in close pursuit. Plump catches up with them first, but is promptly done in by the furious abductor. When the baron arrives, both Karl and Gertrude present their case, stating that they should be allowed to marry and have her father's blessing. Whether persuaded by the number of Karl's vassals, who surround him, or by the adroitness of the lovers' argument, the father gives both consent and blessing, and all ends happily.

As Bürger had mentioned in his letter to Boie regarding "Bruder Graurock," he intended henceforth to take much more liberty with the "Sujets" he took from Percy. Later, writing to Boie regarding "Die Entführung," he noted that unless one were intimately familiar with Percy, one would be unlikely to recognize the model, ("The Child of Elle").[81] Boie evidently felt differently and suggested that Bürger should at least acknowledge his source in the table of contents, when it appeared in print. The similarity between the two is, in fact, not so remote as Bürger felt, despite all the liberties and changes. The style and character of Bürger's ballad differ greatly, however, for Bürger has transformed Percy's essentially static model into a work of action and deeds. Percy's entire prologue has been eliminated, and third person narratives or reports have been turned into direct speech. There is an extraordinary vigor throughout, and Bürger regarded the poem with some satisfaction; '"Die Entführung" comes very close to the ideal of my idea of ennobled, animate, interpretive *Volkspoesie*. With few of my poems am I so thoroughly satisfied as with this one.'[82] Boie agreed and called it a "masterpiece,"[83] but nonetheless suggested several changes Bürger might consider. Evidently Bürger was unimpressed, since he published the ballad in the 1778 edition of *Gedichte* without making any substantial revisions.

The earliest mention of "Das Lied vom braven Mann" ("The Song of the Good Man") occurs in a letter to Boie from May, 1777, but it would seem that the poem had been completed for some time. Commenting on its composition, Bürger subsequently noted that "it is one of those which poured forth in a stream, just as it stands on the page."[84] "Das Lied vom braven Mann" is a needlessly long and drab account of the rescue of a tollkeeper and his family from the roof of their house. The house stands on a bridge in the middle of a river swollen with floods, and everything is about to be swept away. The crowds watch anxiously from the shores, but no one dares to attempt a rescue. A count arrives and offers two hundred Pistolen to the man who will save these people, but no one, including the count himself, has the courage to try. Finally a stranger, a peasant, "in bearing and countenance lofty and noble," comes forward, and by making three trips out into the river saves the entire family. The count asks him to come forward to accept the reward, but the peasant declines, saying that his life is not to be bought or paid for with gold; and he suggests that the money be given to the tollkeeper who has lost everything. Thereupon he turns his back and walks away.

The story is based on an actual incident, but Bürger claimed to have it from Marmontel's *Poétique*.[85] According to Wurzbach, the event took place in 1776 on the river Etsch at Verona. The name of the count was Spolverini, and the peasant's name was Bartolomeo Rubell.[86] According to Erich Ebstein, however, the incident occurred on September 2, 1757, and the hero was a Swabian, Bartholomä Rubele.[87] Curiously, the only specific comment Boie made about the poem concerned his desire to learn the name of the hero: "In my mind, nothing seems to be wanting, but the real name of the good man."[88]

Bürger's treatment of the event is, unfortunately, cluttered with all manner of "Orgelton and Glockenklang." The poet addresses his audience, the tollkeeper in the middle of the river, the crowd of people watching from the shore, and the good man himself; exhorting, extolling, putting rhetorical questions and furnishing moral commentary. He also deliberately retards the ponderous movement of the piece by interjecting direct remarks and questions to the poem itself (as in the ninth stanza):

> *Wann klingst du, Lied vom braven Mann,*
> *Wie Ogelton und Glockenklang?*
> *Wohlan! So nenn' ihn, nenn' ihn dann!*

(/When will you sound, Song of the Good Man,/Like organ music and peal of bells?/All right, then! Name him, name him, then!/)

The physician and composer Dr. Weiss, a good friend of Bürger's, who frequently set the poet's lyrics to music, confessed he was unable to furnish a musical setting for "Der brave Mann."[89] It is not difficult to understand why.

Probably quite early in 1778 Bürger completed his only strictly religious poem, "Sankt Stephan." Boie told his friend that it was a "splendid piece," but commented that he was out of sorts ("unwürs") and not in a mood to offer criticism. Boie did give the impression that he was not altogether pleased with this relatively short poem.[90]

After an introduction, in which St. Stephen's natural faith and wisdom are praised and contrasted to the learning of scholars, Bürger describes the Saint's trial and subsequent execution by the mob. The narrative manner is restrained and the language forthright and simple, but there is almost no action or movement. We hear St. Stephen's speech at his trial; otherwise the poem is presented in the third person. As a religious lyric it lacks any strong conviction, and the figure of St. Stephen is uncharacteristically one-dimensional. His speech consists chiefly of generalities, almost as if Bürger had wished to avoid any theological involvement. Clearly, "Sankt Stephan" was more an experiment than the other poems in the collection.

If "Sankt Stephan," in its self-conscious and sober religious manner, seemed alien to Bürger's character, then "Frau Schnips," with its quasi-religious jesting, shows him much more in his element. The poem was written sometime in early summer, 1777, and in July Bürger asked anxiously for Boie's opinion.[91] The poet was obviously pleased with the piece but had some misgivings whether he should have it published under his name or not. Although his praise for the poem was impressive, Boie urged caution: "Good friend, be careful with this piece."[92] The jocular treatment of a text including biblical characters required rather delicate handling, and several people declined to publish the poem. Even Boie backed off: "Your Frau Schnips—I may not now place in the *Museum,* though even a few days ago I still intended to."[93] Bürger felt quite apprehensive about the matter and concocted an "Apologie" to follow the poem, but still no one wished to publish it. Dieterich also hedged on including it in the 1778 edition of collected poems, and it was not published until 1782, when Bürger inserted it in the *Musen-Almanach* under the pseudonym M. Jocosus Serius.

Given the prolonged agitation about "Frau Schnips," it might be expected to be more flippant than it is. Based on "The Wanton Wife of Bath" in Percy's *Reliques* (and going back to a character in Chaucer's "Tale"), it is the account of a clever and sharptongued woman, who, when she dies, wants to join the company of heaven. One biblical figure after another tries to deny her admission and exchanges words with her, but each time she skillfully turns their comments back on themselves. In the end, of course, Christ allows her to enter heaven and the poem concludes with Christ's comment that even Frau Schnips is one of his flock. She had never, as she claimed, denied Him, and therefore, He will not deny her. The apologia merely seeks to placate the implacables.

In one of his letters to Boie, Bürger complained of the trouble he was having in placing the poem: "The poor Lady! Her entry into the world is made almost as difficult as her entry into heaven."[94] When it finally appeared, it caused none of the uproar some had anticipated. Reaction on the whole, was favorable, but as Bürger grew older, his own fondness for the poem diminished, and he planned to eliminate it from his deluxe edition.

Bürger followed the English original quite faithfully, but expanded it slightly. The milieu and the characters have become thoroughly German, and the poet uses the colorful, sometimes vulgar, language of the streets. The reader is aware of a single level of speech, that of the common people and much of the comic effect is achieved by allowing the august company of Heaven to squabble with Frau Schnips on her level. Lichtenberg maintained that this was "one of the best [ballads] I have read in my life" and that "beneath the mask of frivolity it teaches a very excellent moral."[95] Wurzbach calls it "the first example of a humorous treatment of the ballad in Germany,"[96] and Penelope Scott claims that, despite its having been based on a model, it stands as "an independent German *Schwank-Ballade*" ("comic ballad").[97] In the subtitle, Bürger calls it "Ein Märlein halb lustig, halb ernsthaft, . . ." ("A Little Tale, half comic, half serious"). Goethe was neither amused nor impressed. As he commented to Eckermann: "A man, who in his thirtieth year could write a poem like 'Frau Schnips,' must have followed a path which lay in a slightly different direction from my own."[98]

In utter contradistinction to the frivolous mood of "Frau Schnips" stands the grim and fateful ballad "Des Pfarrers Tochter von Taubenhain" ("The Pastor of Taubenhain's Daughter"). As early as 1776, Bürger was apparently at work on it, since Boie inquired specifically, "How does it stand with the ballad 'Die Kindermörderin'?"[99] In 1778 Boie inquired again, but it was not until Bürger's legal involvement in an actual case of infanticide, that he was moved to take up and complete the ballad. Early in 1781 he had directed and written up the inquisitorial proceedings against "Catherine Elisabeth Erdmann von Benniehausen, an account of child murder committed in the night of 5/6 January of this year."[100] Very shortly after the trial, Bürger completed his ballad and published it in his *Musen-Almanach* for 1782, although he had originally promised it to Boie.

The ballad recounts the fate of the young pastor's daughter who is seduced by the local Junker (squire or young nobleman). Rosette is the loveliest lass in the area and accordingly has many suitors. The Junker Falkenstein sends her a letter and a ring with diamonds, enclosed in a little heart of pearls and gold. He declares his love for her and asks her to meet him (at midnight, naturally). In her innocence (and vanity?) she meets him in the garden, and Falkenstein swears to her by everything that is holy and sublime, forever to be true to her. The Junker succeeds in seducing her, and later when she can no longer conceal her condition her father beats her and turns her out of the house. She goes to plead with Falkenstein, who refuses to marry her but agrees that she may stay at the castle and offers to pay his hunter to marry her. Horrified by the suggestion, Rosette curses Falkenstein and flees. Somehow her trail takes her back to the garden of the rectory where, in the night, she delivers her child. Immediately she kills the infant and "scratched with bloody nails a grave, on the shore of the frog pond" ("Am schilfigen Unkengestade"). She is executed on the wheel, and her ghost haunts the spot by night, trying to put out the tiny flame that shines there. It is a cursed spot, where no grass will grow, and it is not wetted by dew or rain; only the dreary glimmering flame marks it and an awful draught.

In tone and execution "Des Pfarrers Tochter von Taubenhain" stands in the tradition of Bürger's "gothic" ballads, although it lacks the hurtling drive of either "Lenore" or "Der wilde Jäger." It is a framework ballad, with the first two stanzas focusing on the

locale and the miraculous tiny flame. At the end, the poet again
centers his attention on the flame. In general, the technique of this
ballad shows considerably more restraint than obtained in the
earlier ballads. The rhetorical devices have become less obvious,
and one can even forgive his matching the dove with the falcon
(Taubenhain: dovecote vs. Falkenstein: falcon-stone). On the
other hand, Bürger has lost none of his poetic skills. Quite subtly
and successfully, he uses seasonal changes to suggest both external
and internal developments: the passage of time and the decline
of Rosette. She is deflowered in early or mid-spring (i.e., when
the flowers fall and drop off), the pod expands, the fruit grows,
and the sickle cuts down the crop. As the rest of nature grows,
prospers, and flourishes, Rosette is brought closer and closer to
her fate.

Boie called the ballad a masterpiece and claimed that Bürger
was building himself an altar for the present and for posterity
with such works.[101] A. W. Schlegel was (as might be expected)
considerably less enthusiastic: "Unfortunately, we have too much
human suffering in reality for us to be bothered with it in poetry."[102]
More recently, Lore Kaim-Kloock has argued otherwise, maintaining that after "Lenore" it stands among Bürger's most significant achievements.[103]

One might also argue, though for different reasons, that "Der
Kaiser und der Abt" ("The Emperor and the Abbot") deserves
a similar place among Bürger's ballads, for it is certainly one of
his most successful humorous poems. It was probably completed
late in 1783 or early in 1784, and Bürger published it in the
1785 *Musen-Almanach*. The poet had again turned to Percy,
and used "King John and the Abbot of Canterbury" as his
model. The story is much older than the version found in Percy,
and was current both on the Continent and in England. It is a
tale wherein Mother Wit wins out over book-learning and
simultaneously brings off a victory over authority. With the briefest
of words Bürger announces that he will tell the droll tale of an Emperor, who was cantankerous, and a stately Abbot who was, alas,
less clever than his shepherd. The Emperor frequently had to live
in his armor, sleep in a tent, drink water, and eat only dry bread
and sausage, while the Abbot lived in opulent splendor and
luxury. Annoyed at this state of affairs, the Emperor decided to

put him on his mettle and bring him down a bit. Thus, at a chance meeting in the burning heat of summer, as the Emperor rode by with his squadron of warriors and saw the Abbot out for a stroll, he stopped and informed the cleric that he would give him something with which to while away his time; he wished answers to three questions. Should he be unable to answer them correctly, he would be ridden about the country astride a donkey —backwards.

The Emperor wished to know his exact worth; how long it would take, to the minute, for him to ride on his horse around the world; and what he was wrongly thinking. The Abbot has but three months to find the answers, and having turned in vain to the universities and to men of great learning, he confesses his plight to his shepherd, Hans Bendix. Hans immediately offers to rescue his spiritual shepherd, and on the appointed day he appears before the Emperor in the habit of the Abbot. To the first question, he replies that since Christ was bartered for thirty pieces of silver, the Emperor would have to be worth one less, and therefore the Emperor was worth twenty-nine ducats. To the second question, he answered that if the Emperor arose in the morning and rode in concert with the sun, he could complete the trip around the world in twenty-four hours. Finally, he tells the Emperor that "you think I am the Abbot of St. Gallen" which the Emperor admits, whereupon Hans Bendix reveals himsef as the shepherd. The Emperor wants to make Hans the Abbot, but Hans pleads his lack of learning and pleads as well that the Abbot be retained in his position, to which the Emperor accedes. All ends well, and the happy balance of order is restored.

Given A. W. Schlegel's general chariness of praise for his former mentor, it is all the more noteworthy that in this instance he finds many of Bürger's touches to be improvements over the English original.[104] Bürger did indeed make several changes; but more important, he recast the poem in a fundamentally different vein. In "King John and the Abbot of Canterbury," the situation is eminently serious and fraught with very dire consequences; if the Abbot cannot provide the correct answers, he will be killed. In the English version, the threat is real and ominous, but Bürger has radically transformed the character of the piece by changing the anger of the king to irritation, and similarly, by eliminating the threat of death. The tyrannical aspect thus gives way to sport.

In her discussion of the poem, Penelope Scott suggests that the most interesting of Bürger's changes occurs in his reworking of the third question. In the English version, King John wants to know precisely what he is thinking, but Bürger makes the question more difficult by requiring the Abbot to tell him what he is *falsely* thinking. "With this change in the third riddle the ballad becomes a proper farce ('Schwank')."[105] Miss Scott offers illuminating insights into the poem, although her statement that, 'Bürger wished to make the ballad so thoroughly German that it would become popular among the people,' should perhaps be clarified slightly.[106] Clearly, Bürger intended to make the poem pervasively German, but the story itself was already part of the heritage. In a letter to Bürger, Gerhard Anton Gramberg (1744–1817), the court physician at Oldenburg, praises the poet's work and notes: "You have recounted particularly well the farce ('Schwank') about the emperor, abbot and miller (in your version a shepherd), with which I have been familiar since my boyhood."[107] Wurzbach's assertion that Bürger's version surpassed all the others in every respect,[108] may sound excessive, but there is little doubt that Bürger could justifiably regard the poem with satisfaction.

In the same year that Bürger published "Der Kaiser und der Abt," he also published in the *Musen-Almanach* a very short narrative poem, "Die Kuh" ("The Cow"), with the notation that it was a 'true story, recast only for the requirements of poetry.' In simplest terms, it is the account of an impoverished widow who has lost her only cow and is thereby reduced to utter penury. She consumes her last bit of bread and 'extinguishes the lamp with her tears.' In the morning, after a sleepless night, the shepherd's horn reminds her of her loss afresh, and instead of praising God, she berates Him and buries her head in the pillow. Hardly has she done so than she thinks she hears the sound of lowing in the stable. Fearing that she has been delivered over to the devil, she buries her head even deeper in the pillow, but the lowing becomes an insistent bellowing. After saying a prayer, she ventures out into the stable, where she finds a splendid and beautiful cow, fresh hay, and even a shiny new pail. A note is attached to the cow's horns announcing that she is the gift of one who recognized the good widow's need. Bürger points up the moral of generosity and consideration and closes with the statement, "Thus, a Mason swore to me, did it happen."

Bürger never revealed the source of the poem, but in 1927 Erich Ebstein, one of the most distinguished Bürger scholars, offered a number of suggestions, none of which, however, could he firmly assert.[109] Lore Kaim-Kloock either rejected them or was unaware of Ebstein's article, for she maintained that in this case Bürger was composing without a model: "Bürger hat sich durch den Verzicht auf eine wirkliche Fabel um die volle Wirkung des Gedichtes gebracht, es konnte in dieser Form keine Popularität erringen." ('By foregoing any real incident [as a model] Bürger has robbed himself of the full effect of the poem; in this form it could achieve no popularity.')[110] Ebstein, on the other hand, cited M. W. Gotzinger, who in his book *Deutsche Dichter,* Part I, ranked "Die Kuh" next to "Lenore" and "Der wilde Jäger" as Bürger's most successful poem.[111] Even A. W. Schlegel conceded that Bürger had gotten out of the material all there was to be had, and that 'the entire poem is thoroughly sweet and pleasant' ("liebenswürdig und gemütlich").[112] It may well be that Bürger wrote the poem for delivery at a special meeting of his Golden Circle Lodge, the masonic order to which he had belonged since 1775; this he had also done with "Das Lied vom braven Mann."[113]

At the beginning of his article on "Die Kuh," Ebstein remarks: "We are still quite meagerly informed about the background material ("Quellengeschichte") of many of Bürger's ballads."[114] Quite correctly he cites "Das Lied vom braven Mann" and "Die Kuh," but for some of the other ballads we are quite well informed, and "Das Lied von Treue" ("The Song of Loyalty") is an extraordinary case in point. In a letter to Bürger written in December, 1778, Boie writes, "Here's a subject from the *Bibliothèque des Romans,* (April, 1776. p. 159) It is extracted from the unpublished 'Ritterroman' (chivalric romance) of Tristram and the lovely Yseult, one of the most entertaining and important of its kind. I mention the piece to you, so that if you happen to come to Göttingen, you can read the whole extract there."[115] Boie immediately proceeded to supply Bürger with a concise summary of the story, and concludes with the comment, "Nicht wahr, Freund? daraus wäre was zu machen?" ('Now then, Friend, couldn't something be made of that?').[116] Bürger did nothing with the material at the moment, but he was sufficiently impressed by it to keep it in mind, and ten years later he simply substituted German names and a German setting for the original, clothed it in verse and published it as "Das Lied von Treue" in the *Musen-Almanach* for 1789. In the execution of the poem, Bürger remains so faithful to Boie's summary that it is doubtful if he ever actually consulted the original. "Das Lied von Treue" is the account of Marschall von Holm, a great devotee of the hunt. One evening when he returns home he discovers that his wife and his two faithful dogs are gone and that the castle is empty. After searching he discovers his servant in one of the dungeons below ground and learns that his wife has been abducted by the Junker vom Steine. Von Holm rushes off in pursuit and soon overtakes the pair. He challenges vom Steine, and the two clash and struggle, but neither, it seems, can overcome the other. Finally vom Steine makes the suggestion that the Lady should decide. Von Holm, feeling secure in his wife's heart, agrees, but the poet interrupts to warn his listeners not to be too sure "that old love doesn't rust." To von Holm's surprise and dismay, his wife chooses vom Steine, and together they ride off, leaving von Holm stunned and alone, left only with his dogs. Very shortly, vom Steine reappears and somewhat shame-facedly admits that he must have the dogs too, since the Lady von Holm insists that they go with her. A second battle seems unavoidable, but von Holm, thinking quickly, suggests that they let the dogs decide. Vom Steine realizes he's been outwitted, but puts up a good show and agrees. He tries every way he knows to entice the dogs, but "Sie weichen, und springen am Marschall empor/Und weisen dem Junker die Zähne" ("they back off and jump up on the Marshall, and show their teeth to the Junker").

The movement of the ballad is strong and aggressive. It lacks the hurtling drive of Bürger's earlier ballads, but moves with a sure and convincing rhythm—a quite unusual rhythm for Bürger, as a matter of fact, in which the second line of each six-line stanza is an iambic dimeter with masculine endings, and the third a trimeter with feminine endings:

> *"Ach," wähnt er zärtlich, "sie lässt mich nie!*
> *Zu tief hat sie*
> *Den Becher der Liebe gekostet!"—*

/"Ah," he thinks tenderly, "she'll never leave me!/Too deeply has she/ Drunk of the beaker of love."/

Despite the implicit, and rather disconcerting, suggestion that dogs may be more faithful than women, Bürger seems to intend no message in the poem. The mood is light; there is no foreboding sense of harm, and von Holm even takes the loss of his wife in stride. As Boie notes, it is patently an entertaining piece, although perhaps not a great deal more than that.

Bürger's final adaptation from Percy, and the last of all his ballads, was "Graf Walter," which was based on the poem "Childe Waters." It was done in 1789 and was included in the edition of Bürger's collected poems published in that year. The theme is the familiar one of the seduction of a simple girl by the unscrupulous and cruel nobleman, except that in "Graf Walter," Percy, via Bürger, provides a happy end.

Without any introduction Bürger proceeds directly into the narrative. The decisive event has taken place some time ago, and the "schönste Maid" ('loveliest lass') is carrying the count's child. He is about to leave for Weißenstein, and when she pleads that he take her with him, he consents if she will dress as a boy and accompany him as his "Leibbursch" ('groom'). She cuts her hair, shortens her skirt, and they depart. On the way to Weißenstein the girl runs barefoot beside the count as he rides, and although she cannot swim, he forces her to ford a river. He informs her that at Weißenstein there are twelve lovely virgins, and the most beautiful is about to be his bride. Undeterred, the girl asks God's blessing on him and them. In the castle there is feasting and banqueting, but the girl is not allowed to participate. Instead, the count sends her down into the village to bring back to him the prettiest girl she can find for his night's pleasure. Her one request, to be allowed to sleep at the foot of the count's bed, is granted. An interesting but undeveloped subplot emerges when the count's sister expresses her desire to seek out the 'beautiful boy' in the stalls for her own pleasure. The count rejects his sister's suggestions, and the matter is dropped. Next morning he sends the girl out to take care of the horses, but while she is doing so she has her child in the stable. The count, alerted to the situation, goes to her, where he hears her singing a lullaby to the baby. He enters the stall and confesses that his heart is not made of ice, nor of marble. Baptism and the wedding will take place within the hour.

More than most of the ballads based on Percy, "Graf Walter" deserves to be called a translation rather than an adaptation. To be sure, Bürger expanded slightly upon the original (and advantageously so), and he altered names and places to accommodate them to the German scene; but, on the whole, he adhered quite closely to the English poem. A. W. Schlegel had very little praise for it and felt that even though it was 'only a translation, it was certainly a mannered one.' He maintained that the subject was offensive to the dignity of women, and that the language and structure were too assiduously decked out.[117] Subsequent critics have not substantially disagreed with that view.[118] It should be noted, however, that Bürger did not make the most felicitous choice in his decision to translate "Childe Waters," and that most of the problems in Bürger's version reflect the poetic weakness of the original.

Three further poems in the second section of the 1789 edition are left for comment, and two of these antedate "Lenore." The first, dating from 1770, is one of the earliest of Bürger's extant works and bears the highly baroque title:

Neue weltliche hochdeutsche Reime, enthaltend die ebentheyerliche doch wahrhaftige
Historiam
von der wunderschönen Durchlauchtigen Kaiserlichen Prinzessin Europa

etc. etc.

Also gesetzet und an das Licht gestellet durch
M. Jocosum Hilarium.

Poet. Caes. Laur.

/New secular High German rhymes, containing the adventurous yet true story of her wondrously beautiful Serene Imperial Princess Europa, etc . . . Thus composed and brought to light by M. Jocosum Hilarium, imp. poet laureate./

After a lengthy burlesque introduction, in which the poet extols his abilities as a storyteller, he relates the tale of Zeus, who, having observed a beautiful girl (Princess Europa) from his heavenly window, changes himself into a bull and grazes on the meadow near her.

The princess, believing the bull to be tame, romps with him and then playfully climbs on his back, thinking he will take her for a ride. He does—straight across the sea. When they arrive on the opposite shore, the princess collapses, and when her attention is diverted, Zeus changes himself into a dashing cavalier. The princess offers little resistance before responding to his affections, and the poet breaks off discreetly.

The title itself indicates what the innocent reader might expect to find: a jocular story quite in the typical *Bänkelsang* manner of the time and peppered throughout by Bürger's standard comic devices. The poet parades whole clusters of multilingual rhymes and constructs a variety of startling and amusing images. The language of the poem is direct and unadorned, and, indeed, is frequently quite earthy. Bürger also took delight in creating his comic effect by allusions to the "learned" world, by holding up the mirror to its habits, its mannerisms, and its speech patterns:

> *Vor alters war ein Gott,*
> *Von nicht geringem Ruhme,*
> *Im blinden Heidentume.*
> *Nun aber ist er tot.*
> *Er starb*—post Christum natum—
> *Ich weiß nicht mehr das* Datum.

/Ages ago there was a god, of no small renown, in blind heathendom. Now, however, he is dead. He died—anno Domini—I no longer know the date./

The original version of "Prinzessin Europa" was doubtless considerably shorter than the version published in 1777. In its early form, the direct, often coarse, language of the poem was probably the same, and presumably its only aim was to entertain. Bürger left the piece unfinished from 1771 until September, 1776, and when he thought of returning to it, he had to ask Boie for a copy, since he had lost his own. Between September and the end of December, Bürger reworked the poem but, in doing so, he introduced a new element, an attack on Christoph Friedrich Nicolai (1733–1811), the Berlin book dealer, author, and editor of the *Allgemeine Deutsche Bibliothek*. Bürger held Nicolai in great contempt and made only the most perfunctory attempt to conceal his feelings. He sent the revision to Boie, who refused to publish it and at the same time suggested he tone down the attack on Nicolai. Evidently Bürger was determined, for he then submitted it to his old friend Goeckingk, who later also declined to publish it. Finally, Bürger had the poem published separately by Dieterich but was adamant about not toning down his attack on Nicolai. In the course of 1777, Boie repeatedly advised Bürger on this point, and when the preparations were under way for the 1778 edition of *Gedichte,* he again urged Bürger to delete it. Bürger would not be dissuaded, however, and in the 1778 edition he devoted an entire page to the title alone, and had it set in Roman. His use of a pseudonym was no more than a gesture; everyone knew the author as soon as it appeared in print. As a simple *Bänkelsang,* it would have been harmless and amusing, but as a cloak to cover the poet's attack on Nicolai it became ostentatious. Bürger won few friends by it, and Boie did not soon forget the incident.

At the time when Bürger may have had his first thoughts about "Lenore" (March, 1773) he sent off a short poem, "Des armen Suschens Traum" ("Poor Suschen's Dream"), to ask Boie's opinion of it. Bürger called it a ballad,[119] but he later changed his mind and came to regard it as an example of a "true lyric Romance."[120] Wurzbach regarded it as a preliminary exercise or trial run for "Lenore."[121] It is a narrative poem, told by the girl from her own experience. She describes how her false lover came to her in a dream, took off and broke her ring, and threw her a strand of pearls instead. When the girl goes out into her garden to see her myrtle bush (from which she had hoped to weave herself a wreath), the strand of pearls breaks and scatters the pearls all over the ground. Search as she may, she cannot find a one, and the myrtle bush is turned to rosemary. The ring is gone, the pearls are tears, and she can only weave herself a funeral wreath from the rosemary.

The success of the poem lies in its economy of form, structure, and content. The whole poem consists of eight quatrain stanzas, and it focuses on the depiction of one sentiment. To be sure, it is the retelling of a dream, but it has none of the shadowy qualities of a dream; the girl says, 'I would almost swear that I was wide awake,/So clearly did I see him.' The girl reacts not so much to the objects as to their symbolic significance, and as the ring (union—perfection) is replaced by the strand of pearls (tears), the myrtle is replaced by the rosemary. There is no pretension in the poem, and the language and syntax are utterly simple. Friedrich Leopold Stolberg wrote to Bürger that the poem was as dear to him as "Lenore."[122]

Three years after completing "Des armen Suschens Traum," in February, 1776, Bürger sent Boie his most recent product, "Schön Suschen." Shortly before he had read it to Boie in prose, but now had reworked it in verse and appeared quite satisfied with it: "O how many golden arrows I now have in my quiver."[123] Boie expressed complete delight in the poem and told Bürger that he was becoming ever more popular, precise and polished.[124] Bürger published the poem in the March, 1776, issue of the *Deutsche Museum*.

Like "Des armen Suschens Traum," "Schön Suschen" is very brief and consists of six eight-line stanzas. It is not Schön Suschen who speaks here, but her lover; and the poem is not so much a narrative as it is an inquiry into the capricious ways of the heart. The poet has known Schön Suschen for some time and recognizes her beauty as well as her virtue:

> *Ich kam und ging, ich ging und kam*
> *Wie Ebb' und Flut zur See,*
> *Ganz wohl mir tat es, wann ich kam,*
> *Doch, wann ich ging, nicht weh.*

(/I came and went, I went and came,/Like the ebb and flow at sea./I was happy when I came,/But when I left, not sad./)

In the course of time, the lad discovers that he loves Suschen very much; and thus when he leaves, he is very sad. Later still he finds that he has grown indifferent toward her, and again, he is happy when he arrives, but not sad at leaving. How, he wonders, does one know what the heart will do? Alas, there is no answer;

> *Drum, Lieb' ist wohl wie Wind im Meer:*
> *Sein Sausen ihr wohl hört,*
> *Allein ihr wisset nicht, woher?*
> *Wißt nicht, wohin er fährt?*

(/For love is like the wind at sea:/You hear its whistling well,/Except you do not know from where/ Or whither it doth blow./)

CHAPTER 4

Miscellaneous Poetry and Poems after 1789

THE third section of poems in the 1789 edition, entitled "Vermischte Gedichte," is by far the shortest. A few figures may give some idea of its composition: there are forty-nine titles in the space of twenty-four pages (of normal print); of these, ten titles were taken over from the 1778 edition (covering twelve pages), and twenty-nine titles (covering six pages) are epigrammatic in character. The immediate conclusion to be drawn from these figures is, first of all, that there are only ten new poems here, and secondly, that Bürger was no longer writing any poems of more than modest length. Strictly speaking, the second point would be more an assumption than a conclusion, but in any case it is correct.

The ten poems retained from the 1778 edition of the *Gedichte* are of relatively minor importance. They include the very early encomium "An Arist," (1770), the title of which was suggested by Boie, who also believed that it was addressed to Bürger's youthful friend, Biester.[1] "Das Dörfchen," which was an adaptation of a poem by the French poet Pierre Joseph Bernard (1710–1755) praises the land and country about the village, although bestowing the greatest praise upon Elise, whose presence and love raise the situation from idyllic to paradisiac. Written in iambic dimeter, it moves rapidly, but its length tends to weaken the effect of the meter. Gleim's response to the piece was vigorously enthusiastic; 'A thousand times, my dearest Herr Bürger, since reading your "Dörfchen," I have wished to live in such a village . . . ."[2] "Zum Spatz" ("To the Sparrow") addresses a sparrow which has flown in through the poet's window. Although the sparrow may be a prince in his own realm, which is outside in the free air, he is now a captive and at the mercy of man; all of which gives Bürger an opportunity to reflect upon the advantage of freedom over enslavement. "Mamsell La Regle" ("Mistress Rule") is an occasional poem in praise of a governess. The two poems, "Notgedrungene Epistel des berühmten Schneiders Johannes Schere an Seinen großgünstigen Mäcen" ("Necessary Epistle of the Famous Tailor Johannes Schere

[Shears] to his Most Gracious Patron"), and "Der Hund aus der Pfennigschenke" ("The Dog from the Penny Pub"), are both bitter and contentious, and are oblique complaints proffered by the poet himself. In the former, the great tailor receives little or no pay for his work, although he needs money far more than posthumous fame. While his patron goes about in the finest attire, his own coat is full of holes and open to the elements. The second poem is aimed at Bürger's critics, and Bürger recognizes the futility of creating an uproar by striking back at them: "Dies Fabelchen führt Gold im Munde:/ Weicht aus dem Rezensentenhunde" ("This little fable is worth its weight in gold: keep out of the way of canine critics"). Bürger never took his own advice, and over the years he spent considerable time on poetic retaliation against his critics.

The four remaining poems are two exchanges of verse letters, the first with Goeckingk, and the second with Stolberg. The Goeckingk-Bürger letters date from 1776. Goeckingk's letter to Bürger is a friendly, whimsical one deploring in mock fashion their lives as poets; no matter what one achieves poetically, the realities of life cannot be escaped. Bürger's reply is equally buoyant, as he (literally) advises against throwing out the baby with the bath water and stoutly defends the role of the poet. No matter that critics and scholars may pick at it:

> *Dort preist man unsere Opera*
> *Durch Commentationen*
> *Inaugural-Programmata*
> *Und Dissertationen.*

The day will come, Bürger maintains, when students will memorize lines and words from the poet's works. And it will be worth it.

The correspondence with Stolberg stands in sharp contrast with the exchange between Bürger and Goeckingk and is written in full seriousness of purpose. In the mid and late 1770's, Bürger was intermittently at work on his translation of Homer and was stunned to learn that Friedrich von Stolberg was to publish the twentieth Book of the *Iliad* in the November, 1776, issue of the *Deutsches Museum*. Bürger hurriedly wrote a poetic charge to Stolberg, which was published in the next issue. Bürger was outraged at the competition, and infuriated that Stolberg had chosen the twentieth Book. "It is one of the grandest, and I, doughty codger, chose one of the dullest."[3] Bürger's poem is done in iambic pentameter (the same meter he had chosen for his translation of the *Iliad*), and Stolberg's reply was, appropriately enough, in hexameters. Bürger's challenge is in the manner of a battle cry: "Sieg gilt es oder Tod!" ("To victory or death!") Stolberg's reply, however, is moderate and conciliatory, but he declares he will proceed: "For see, the Muse motions me; I follow the beckoning goddess." Wurzbach regards the confrontation as a peaceful, friendly competition: "It is here a matter more of peaceable endeavor ("friedliches Streben") towards the same goal, than of a hostile struggle."[4] A cursory glance at Bürger's correspondence at the time suffices to disabuse one of that opinion. Wurzbach cites a friendly letter from Stolberg supporting his [Wurzbach's] claim, but Bürger neither answered it nor wrote again to Stolberg until 1787[5], and then, at least partially, to ask him if he could help him find a different position.

Among the new poems in the "Vermischte Gedichte" there are three occasional ones: the "Prolog zu Sprickmann's Eulalia," "Als Elise sich ohne Lebewohl entfernt hatte" ("When Elise went away without saying Good-bye"), and "An die blinde Virtuosin, Mlle. Paradies." The first of these poems was composed late in 1779 for a private performance by a student group in Göttingen.[6] Writing in iambic pentameter (the meter of the drama), the poet addresses his audience and in somber language comments on the grim action about to take place upon the stage. The second poem, "Als Elise. . . .", was written, as Bürger notes just below the title, at nine o'clock on the morning of November 22, 1784 in Göttingen. The Elise to whom it is addressed was Elise von der Recke, a well-known writer and luminary of the period. She had met Bürger during a visit to Göttingen. In rather moving language the poet urges himself to rally and not be so downcast at her departure, for surely they will see each other again: "Sie ist nicht fort, das glaube mir!/ Denn— Abschied hat sie nicht genommen." (/She has not gone, believe me!/ For she did not take leave./) Elise's reply came almost immediately: "Ich bin nicht fort von Ihnen, Bürger! ("I haven't left you, Bürger!")[7] The friendship thus begun continued until Bürger's death.

It was evidently not Bürger's intention to place all of his occasional poems among the "Vermischte Gedichte," and a number of them are scattered among the lyrics in the first section. Bürger also included there the two abysmal pieces written for the celebration of the fiftieth anniversary of the University of Göttingen ("Gesang am heiligen Vorabend des Fünfzigjährigen Jubelfestes der Georgia Augusta" and "Ode der fünfzigjährigen Jubelfeier der Georgia Augusta am 17. Sept. 1787"), several *Stammbuchblätter* (entries in guest or autograph books), and the memorial to his grandfather, "Bei dem Grabe meines guten Großvaters Jakob Bauers," written in 1773. The elder Bauer had not always been the most gracious or tractable of men, but he had been immensely generous when Bürger had needed him, and the poet acknowledged that debt:

> *Ach! Er war mein treuer Pfleger,*
> *Von dem Wiegenalter an.*
> *Was ich bin und was ich habe,*
> *Gab der Mann in diesem Grabe,*
> *Alles dank' ich dir, du guter Mann!*

(/Ah, he was my faithful guardian,/ From the cradle on./ What I am and what I have,/ All I owe to you, thou good man./)

The sentiment of the piece is unquestionably greater than its poetic worth, but Bürger did not intend a florid memorial: "Prunk der Poesie ist nicht drinn, aber was ich drinnen sage, ist wahr und geht mir von Herzen. Es sollte auch nur sein Lob und meine Empfindung ganz simpel drinn ausgedrückt sein." ("There is no poetic virtuosity in it, but what I have said in it is true and comes from my heart. It is only supposed to express quite simply his praise and my feeling.")[8] The poem accomplished the purpose Bürger intended for it. The poet had it privately printed in one hundred copies for distribution among his friends and relatives in Aschersleben.

In addition to occasional poems and those carried over from the earlier edition, the "Vermischte Gedichte" contain two rather clever, but minor poems, "Der kluge Held" ("The clever Hero"), and "Die Schatzgräber" ("The Treasure Diggers"). Both are quite short, and much of their success derives from their brevity. In the former piece, the young hero decides, on the day before the battle, that it is pointless to fight and be killed for nothing. The king has no care for him. He therefore goes to his chief and tells him that he has received word that his father is about to die and that it is his duty to be at the deathbed to receive his father's dying kiss. The permission is granted, and the chief wishes him safe journey. The poem is a vignette, sketched with bold and incisive lines. Bürger does not enter the scene, but his familiar attitudes about the inhumanity and callousness of the nobility move visibly on, or just below, the surface. The point of the poem emerges at the end, in the words of the chief, who recognizes the true intent of the young hero and, in giving him permission to go, ironically suggests that his father's kiss is essential for his well-being and a long life.

"Die Schatzgräber" also contains an ironic twist and is told with strength and humor. The old vintner, in dying, tells his children that, "in unserm Weinberg liegt ein Schatz:/Grabt nur darnach" ("In our vineyard lies a treasure;/ Dig for it"). When the old man dies, the children rush into the vineyard and dig everywhere, even putting the dirt through a sieve, but they find no treasure and give up. The following spring the vines bear three times the number of branches, and the sons recognize the meaning of their father's words. The movement is lively and the language clear, precise, and sharp. Syntactically, this is the kind of poem with which Bürger had the least difficulties; it is straight narrative, unencumbered with abstract or symbolic meanings, and the allegory is rudimentary.

The final pages of the 1789 edition suggest both that Bürger had used up his material and had to resort to "fillers," and that he was no longer able to sustain length in a poem. The final twenty-nine poems, which are almost exclusively epigrams, are pervaded with bitterness and reveal a depressing dependence on sarcasm and irony. The titles themselves indicate the poet's weary and contentious frame of mind: "Auf einen literarischen Händelsucher" ("To a Literary Quarreler"), "Gänsegeschrei und Gänsekiele" ("Goose Screech and Goose Quills"), "Herr von Gänsewitz zum Kammerdiener" ("Sir Goosewit to his Servant"), etc. All his life, Bürger was fragiley sensitive to criticism, and many of these epigrams are unveiled attacks on his critics: "Kritik betreffend" ("Concerning Criticism"), "An die Splitterrichter" ("To the Faultfinders"). In many of them,

the poet's anger is roused because of a mistake or error that has been
pointed out to him, as in "Schnick und Schnack," in which we
are told that the best of deeds could be placed before these characters
without their noticing it; but make *one* weak stroke ("*einen*
schwachen Streich"), even, as it were, "in the cellar, deep in the
night of the earth" ("im Keller gleich,/ Tief in der Nacht der Erde"),
and with the cunning of a fox, the nose of a bloodhound, the
eyes of a lynx, and the ears of a hare, they will ferret it out, and
mercilessly attack like vultures. Another, "Trost" ("Consolation")
reads:

> *Wann dich die Lästerzunge sticht,*
> *So laß dir dies zum Troste sagen:*
> *Die schlechtsten Früchte sind es nicht,*
> *Woran die Wespen nagen.*

(/When the slanderer's tongue stings you/ Take this as consolation:/ The
worst fruits are not those/ On which the wasps suck./)

It was not only the critics, however, who attracted Bürger's ire,
but he turned his attention to sermons ("An Stentor unter der
Predigt"—"To Stentor during the Sermon"), merchants ("Ein
casus Anatomicus"—"An Anatomical Case"), where the merchant
Harpax dies and an autopsy is performed on him: "So kam man
auch aufs Herz, und sieh! er hatte keins:/ Da, wo sonst dieses
schlägt, fand man das Einmaleins." ("Then they came to the heart,
and behold, he had none/ There where it usually beats, they found
the multiplication table."), lawyers ("Advokatenprahlerei"—"Lawyers' Boastings"), and inevitably, the scorn for high social station,
as in "Auf das Adeln der Gelehrten" ("On Making Scholars
Nobles") and "Der Edelmann und der Bauer" ("The Nobleman
and the Peasant"):

> *"Das schwör' ich dir, bei meinem hohen Namen,*
> *Mein guter Claus, ich bin aus altem Samen!"*
> *"Das ist nicht gut," erwidert Claus,*
> *"Oft artet alter Samen aus."*

(/"This I swear to you by my high name,/ My good Claus, I come from
ancient seed!"/ "That is not good," replied Claus,/ "Old seed often
degenerates."/)

There is little doubt that these epigrams are sharp and clever, but in their thought as well as in their execution they indicate the distance Bürger had traveled since the early 1770's. The poet of "Lenore" had been heaven-storming and aggressive; the poet of the epigrams was tired, harassed, and defensive, and the voice of his muse had become almost inaudible.

In the years between 1789 and 1794, the year of his death, Bürger was still active as a poet, but on an increasingly smaller scale. There were no great sweeping poems left in him, and after Schiller published his review in 1791, Bürger's self-confidence was so shaken that he found it almost impossible to write. Instead, he took out his earlier poems and pathetically tried to file them into a form which would satisfy Schiller. The prolix "Rechenscharft über die Veränderungen in der Nachtfeier der Venus" is but a single instance of the numerous justifications he felt impelled to offer. His critical notes to the poems which he was revising for the envisioned *Luxus* edition are little short of embarrassing. "Das Mädel, das ich meine" had become "Die Holde, die ich meine," and "Mollys Werth" was rewritten to accommodate Schiller. "Das Blümchen Wunderhold" underwent the same kind of surgery, as did numerous others, yet almost without exception, Bürger's changes weakened the poems he was trying to improve. In sum, then, Bürger's final years were spent reworking earlier poems rather than creating new ones.

Much of the poetry produced after 1789 was published in the *Musen-Almanach,* although a great deal of material appeared only posthumously in the edition prepared by Karl Reinhard in 1796. Since the contents of the 1796 edition were selected "nach eigener Prüfung und nach eigenem Geschmacke" ("according to my own tests and tastes"), many poems did not appear until the later edition by Bohtz in 1835 or even later.

Among the poetry written in the final years there are several *Lieder,* some occasional poetry, some humorous or sportive pieces, the lyric addressed to Elise Hahn (the "Schwabenmädchen"), the defensive polemics against Schiller, and a few serious poems of reflection and contemplation.

Several of the songs have a strongly political, nationalistic, or even martial quality. In the "Straflied" ("Song of Reprimand"), written after the unsuccessful post-revolutionary uprising in France (1792), Bürger reminds his audience that he "who cannot die for

freedom deserves chains," and that the deeds of tigers are not
accomplished by the timid in heart. Bürger was much interested in
politics at the time and followed the events of the French Revolution with great interest.[9] "Für wen, du gutes deutsches Volk"
("For whom, thou good German people") is a fragment deploring
German intervention in the French Revolution, and Bürger implicitly suggests that the cause to fight and die for is at home. The glory
in death for the fatherland is the theme of the "Feldjägerlied"
("Courier's Song"), in which the poet hails the bravery and perse-
verance of the courier. It is a rousing song, ending on a note of militant patriotism:

> *Und färbet gleich auch unser Blut*
> *Das Feld des Krieges rot:*
> *So wandelt Furcht uns doch nicht an;*
> *Denn nimmer scheut ein braver Mann*
> *Fürs Vaterland den Tod.*

(/And even if our blood/ Colors the battlefield red:/ Fear never seizes us
/For an honorable man is never afraid/ To die for the fatherland./)

The themes of death for the fatherland and death for the cause
of freedom played an increasingly important role in Bürger's thinking
in the years surrounding the French Revolution, and in "Die
Tode" ("Death"), he reflects upon the causes for which a man
should die. The solemn mood of the poem is set immediately by
the slow moving and dignified iambic hexameter:

Für Tugend, Menschenrecht und Menschenfreiheit sterben
Ist höchst erhabener Mut, ist Welterlösertod

(/To die for virtue, human rights and human freedom/ Is most sublime
courage, is the death of the savior of the world./)

Death which comes in the service of a good prince may also be
regarded as death for "Volk und Vaterland," and death for friend
or wife or child is similarly noble. Whoever regards dying for majesty
alone or for tyrants, however, errs; such death is not heroic, but
is like the execution of murderers and thieves. Bürger retains his
slow, measured pace throughout the poem, and both language
and style correspond to the seriousness of the topic.

Quite a different mood pervades the two songs, "Hummellied" ("Song of the Bumble Bee") and the simple "Lied." The first likens young men to bumble bees who swarm about in spring and never lose their taste for honey ("Die Unschuld ist dem Honig gleich"— 'Innocence is like honey'). Bürger draws the analogy of the bumble bees attracted to the honey they find in the flowers (girls). The bumble bee, however, flies here and there, and flowers are cautioned to be wary. The piece is written in a light manner, although it is rather unusual to find Bürger feeling the need to warn the girls about young men. The "Lied" (based on Wm. Congreve's song, "Pious Selinda goes to Prayers")[10] moves quite directly without any analogical overtones, and the poet admits his bewilderment at the reaction of his sweetheart: if he is too demanding, she moves away, but if he is less aggressive, she thinks he doesn't love her. If love cannot turn him, in both heart and mind, into a saint, then may she, as a sinner, attend the sinner's wish. These are pleasant poems, but not of great distinction.

Most of Bürger's occasional poetry was published posthumously, and there is very little of more than passing interest. The odes to the Hannoverian Princes and the Duke of York are unfortunate products of a command performance, and August Barth was correct when he wrote, "Der Dichter . . . hat auf dem Gebiet der Oden . . . vollständig versagt." ('In the field of the ode the poet has failed completely.')[11] The Easter Cantata does not rise much higher, and the personal occasional poems, such as "An Demoiselle Wagemann," "Impromptu," "Zu Julchens Geburtstag," etc., fall much below Bürger's earlier standards.

In the last few years of his life, Bürger had little reason to be witty or amusing, but several poems have survived which indicate that he had not entirely lost his sense of humor. In some of these poems, he demonstrates a tendency to revert to the coarse vulgarity of some of his earliest efforts, as in "Veit Ehrenwort"; but even when he resists that inclination, his humor is now invariably tinged with bitterness, and most of it is expressed in epigrammatic form. From the late 1780's on, Bürger turned more and more to that form as best suited for the particular kind of terse, acerbic statement he wished to make. In "Mittel gegen Agrypnie" ("Remedy for Insomnia") the speaker complains of insomnia and leaves for church in the hope of falling asleep during the sermon. "Ein kleiner Schlag"

("A Minor Point") explores the difference that can occur in the meaning of a word simply by changing a letter: "balzen" (to woo or court) to "walzen" (tramp).[12] In "Die Esel und die Nachtigallen" ("The Donkeys and the Nightingales") Bürger remarks upon the importance of native talent:

> *Es gibt der Esel welche wollen,*
> *Daß Nachtigallen hin und her*
> *Des Müllers Säcke tragen sollen.*
> *Ob's recht? fällt mir zu sagen schwer.*
> *Das weiß ich: Nachtigallen wollen*
> *Nicht, daß die Esel singen sollen.*

(/There are donkeys who wish/ That nightingales should carry the miller's sacks back and forth./ Whether that is right is difficult for me to say./ This I know: nightingales do not wish that donkeys should sing./)

Bürger's disastrous courtship of Elise Hahn had been launched by one of her poems published in a Stuttgart journal and subsequently forwarded to Bürger. The poet could not suppress either his curiosity or his desire, and he replied in kind. In "An .. Y .." (generally referred to as "Das Schwabenmädchen"—"The Girl from Swabia"), Bürger answered Elise's poem and asked her to step out of the shadows (she had published her poem anonymously):

> *Denn ach! die Liebesgötter wallen*
> *In meinem Herzen. wie zu allen,*
> *Durch Auge lieber als durchs Ohr.*

(/Now, see! The gods of love travel/ Into my heart as into every one else's,/ Preferably through the eye rather than through the ear./)

Bürger tries to persuade her to identify herself: it is not necessary for her to be extraordinarily beautiful: "Denn ich bin selbst nicht jung und schön" ("For I myself am not young or handsome"). Very shortly Bürger discovered for himself Elise's full name and indicated that he knew it in a riddle sent to Marianne Ehrmann, wife of the editor of the Stuttgart journal:

> *Führt dich der Reim auf rechte Bahn*

> *Triffst du des Holden Namen an.*
> *Mich lobt und liebt E . . . H . . .*

(/If the rhyme leads you on the right track, you'll get the fair one's name.
I'm praised and loved by E . . . H . . ./)

Two main elements predominate in the poetry written to Elise.
The first of these is the element of play; of guessing games, and hide
and seek, and poetic tricks. The second is a persistent tendency
to try to "win the Schwabenmädchen."[13] The poems to Elise have
an obvious utilitarian purpose: they are persuasive, not profound.
Bürger's personal relationship with Elise may well have attained
a modest depth, but the poetry she inspired him to write never
went much below the surface.

One of the major poetic catalysts in Bürger's last years was
Friedrich Schiller. Unfortunately, but quite naturally, it was a
thoroughly negative catalyst, and the poems and epigrams aimed at
Schiller invariably bear the mark of unquenchable rage. Bürger had
realized his mistake in replying immediately to Schiller's critique,
and two years later he composed the carefully reasoned fragment
"Über mich und meine Werke." In verse, however, Bürger never
felt constrained in expressing his feelings about Schiller, and he
leveled his attacks with abandon. The result is anything but great
poetry, although it does furnish an insight into the depths of
Bürger's fury. Such efforts as "Unterschied" ("The Difference"),
"Anti-Kritik" or "Über die Dichterregel" ("On Poetic Rule"),
with their insatiable appetite for vengeance, deserve to be passed
over in silence. Of all the broadsides directed against Schiller, perhaps the only one requiring comment is "Der Vogel Urselbst, seine
Rezensenten und der Genius. Eine Fabel in Burkard Waldis'
Manier" ("The 'Beyourself' Bird, His Reviewers, and the Genius.
A Fable in the manner of Burkard Waldis").[14]

It is the story of the strange and curious bird called "Original"
(or "Beyourself"), or in German "Urselbst." He had no mate and
therefore flew alone, but he could fly very high and far in both time
and space. He was the favorite of Genius, and was shocked to hear
someone say that his flight was not beautiful to see or hear. Thus
spoke a sick owl who called out to him from the ruins and
rubbish of Troy. The owl's cry was taken up by the parrot, then the
hens, the geese, and all the barnyard fowl. Anxious to solve the

problem, Urselbst flies to the owl and asks its advice. The owl recommends that Urselbst tear out some of his feathers. The owl next urges Urselbst to seek out the bird Ideal and deck himself out in Ideal's feathers. Of course, the owl does not know what Ideal looks like, nor can he demonstrate the kind of beautiful flight he urges Urselbst to strive for. Gradually, Urselbst begins to think the owl may not know exactly what he is talking about, but the owl thunders,

> *Ich habe recht, recht, recht, recht, recht;*
> *Halt's Maul vor mir, du loser Knecht!*

(/I'm right, right, right, right, right;/ Hold your tongue in my presence, you wanton knave./)

Urselbst flies off to seek the advice of the parrot, who recommends that he tear out more of his feathers and replace them with flowers. Hapless Urselbst follows the advice of the parrot, but finds his power of flight appreciably reduced. Next, he flies to the "Gick und Gackgeschlecht" ("chatterboxes" or "magpies") who advise him to tear out all his feathers and stay with them. By now, Urselbst is totally confused, and in despair he tears out all his feathers, only to find that he can no longer fly. Realizing his folly, he appeals to his sublime patron, Genius, who, after reprimanding him for being so foolish as to listen to a sick owl, a parrot, and other fowl, restores his wings to him on the condition that, henceforth, Urselbst listen only to the voice of Genius.

The intent of the poem is abundantly clear. It is quite simply a diatribe against Schiller saturated with allusions to him and his works.[15] Most of the references were to Schiller's review, but Bürger also incorporated allusions to Schiller's classical interests, his poetry, and even to "Die Räuber." All in all, it is a very clever "fable" and Bürger was enormously pleased with it. He anticipated that its publication in the *Musen-Almanach* (1793) would arouse something of a clamor[16] but to all appearances there was little or no reaction, and even Schiller, against whom the barbs were directed, remained impervious.[17]

Despite his passionate animadversion for Schiller, Bürger did not entirely neglect to turn his hostile energies in other directions, and he commemorated several other contemporaries with some animosity. The vehicle closest at hand was the epigram, and among those whom Bürger celebrated in that form were the novelist Karl Große (1761-?) in "Karl der Große als Dichter" ("Charlemagne as a Poet"), August von Kotzebue (1761-1819) in "An einen Gewissen nicht leicht zu errathenden" ("To a Certain Person, not easily Guessed"), and Gottlob Benedikt von Schirach (1743-1804), the editor of the *Magazin der schönen Kritik,* in "Fragment eines 13. kleinen Propheten Eschechirach am toten Meer" ("Fragment of a 13th minor Prophet Eschechirach by the Dead Sea"). Bürger evidently felt particularly venomous towards Leopold Aloys Hoffman (1748-1804), the editor of the *Wiener Zeitschrift* and a militant campaigner against the Enlightenment. "Auf einen Zeitschriftsteller" ("On a Journalist") is a collection of twelve epigrams, one for each month of the year. Bürger called it his "Jahrgang der Epigrammen."[18]

Fortunately, Bürger was not solely preoccupied with polemics during his final years, and many of his late lyrics are eminently serious in character. Bürger had always had divided poetic loyalties, and in his early years he had vacillated between being the popular, sometimes coarse, poet of the people and the intellectual, academic poet of the literary aristocracy. Schiller had pointed out the two vastly different audiences for whom Bürger wrote, "By no means are they the same readers who read the 'Nachtfeier' and 'Frau Schnips'."[19] As Bürger grew older, however, that side of his character so dedicated to *Volkspoesie* became less insistent as he sought a more formal means of poetic expression. Simultaneously, as his poetry became more formal, it grew increasingly sober and reflective, and an elegiac tone runs through almost all of the serious poetry of the 1790's.

Two sonnets written in 1789 indicate the direction Bürger's serious lyric was taking. "Der Entfernten" ("To the Absent One") is a pair of sonnets written to the wife of Professor Dr. Kaulfuß (of Göttingen) after her departure from Göttingen. In the first, the poet expresses his sorrow at her absence, but the memory of her final words, "Mann, du wohnest ewig mir im Herzen" ("Friend, thou dwellest forever in my heart"), buoys him, and he realizes that he need not name her to his heart; for his heart will recognize her by her voice. The sonnet moves smoothly enough, but the thought is somewhat obscured by the convoluted relationships between the poet, his heart, his beloved, and his song. The second sonnet articulates a more direct experience: the poet grieves at the absence of his beloved and wishes that she were with him. Although the central concern of the sonnet is ostensibly his beloved, the entire poem moves from a perspective which focuses primarily on the poet and *his* plight.[20] Indeed, it appears that his beloved was specifically created only to love him, and that that is the whole purpose of her existence:

> *Du, mein Heil, mein Leben, meine Seele!*
> *Süßes Wesen, von des Himmels Macht*
> *Darum, dünkt mir nur hervorgebracht,*
> *Daß dich Liebe ganz mir anvermähle!*

(/Thou, my weal, my life, my soul!/ Sweet being, brought forth by the power of heaven/ Only, so it seems to me,/ That love should wed you wholly to me./)

Having established himself as the center of gravity in the poem, Bürger cannot comprehend why she is not with him, "O warum erquickt sie mich denn nicht?" ("O why does she not revive me?") Both sonnets are written in trochaic pentameter, a rather unusual meter for Bürger.

One of the more attractive poems of Bürger's late period is "An Madame B., geb. M" (1789). Critics are divided as to the identity of the lady so honored, but when the poem appeared in the *Musen-Almanach* for the following year it was quite favorably received. C. G. Lenz, a student of Bürger's and quondam poet, called it a "Sinngedicht im altgriechischen Sinn" ("Epigram in the Ancient Greek sense").[21] The poet addresses his "friend" directly and asks her to consider the 'blossoms of fortune which criss-cross the disordered course of our existence; blossoms which do not bloom for every pilgrim.' But even they, like the flowers of May, fade and wither. When they drop off, they yield to the developing fruit, and "Memory" is the name of the fruit—sour at first, then sweet. Now Bürger addresses himself to his phantasy, asking for that fruit to assuage his thirsting heart, and leading to the final couplet,

> *Reiche sie reif und süß im Weidenkörbchen, durchflochten*
> *Mit Vergißmeinnicht, kummerverlächelnd ihm dar!*

(/Offer it ripe and sweet in its woven basket, interstrewn/ With forget-me-nots, and smiling cares away./)

In the dignified and measured pace imposed by the hexameters Bürger develops his poem organically, so that, structurally, it is in accord with the underlying thought, that friendship, like the plant, is an organic development. In the same way, the "blossoms of fortune which criss-cross the disordered course of our life" (second line) reappear in the penultimate line as the now fully developed fruit, which "criss-crosses the wearying course of our life." Bürger's felicitous handling of language and syntax provides for an exceptionally smooth flow, and the imagery is consistent with the theme of growth. Grimm notes that the word "kummerverlächelnd" in the final line is a new coinage.

Two poems stand out as the final expression of Bürger's genius; the sonnet "An das Herz" ("To My Heart"), and "Resignation." The former was written in 1792 and published in the *Musen-Almanach* the following year. The poet's divorce from Elise had been decreed early in 1792, and the experience had not only embittered him, but had left him in failing health and alone. The possibility of yet another love seemed now remote, indeed, and yet, Bürger could not suppress the "hangen und verlangen," the eternal longing of his heart:

> *"Lang schon in manchem Sturm und Drange*
> *Wandeln meine Füße durch die Welt.*
> *Bald, den Lebensmüden beigesellt,*
> *Ruh' ich aus von meinem Pilgergange.*
> *Leise sinkend faltet sich die Wange;*
> *Jede meiner Blüthen welkt und fällt.*
> *Herz, ich muß Dich fragen: Was erhält*
> *Dich in Kraft und Fülle noch so lange?*
> *Trotz der Zeit Despoten-Allgewalt*
> *Fährst Du fort, wie in des Lenzes Tagen,*
> *Liebend wie die Nachtigall zu schlagen.*
> *Aber ach! Aurora hört es kalt,*
> *Was ihr Tithons Lippen Holdes sagen.—*
> *Herz, ich wollte, Du auch würdest alt!"*

(/Long now in many a storm and stress,/My feet have wandered through the world;/Soon, joining those weary of life,/I shall rest from my pilgrimage./Gently sinking, my cheeks wrinkle;/Each of my blossoms fades and falls./Heart, I must ask thee: what retains/Thee in power and fullness yet so long?/Despite the despotic tyranny of time,/Thou goest on beating, as in the days of spring,/Loving like the nightingale./But oh! Aurora listens coldly/To what Tithon's lips tell her of loveliness.—/Heart, I wish thou, too, might grow old./)

Almost echoing Goethe's lines, "Warte nur, balde ruhest du auch" ('Wait but a little; soon thou too shall rest'),[22] Bürger sees himself approaching the end of his pilgrimage. The sense of age weighs upon him, and while his other faculties forsake him one by one, his heart refuses to recognize his physical decline. Tangible and intangible find their confluence in the heart, but now, frail beyond his years, Bürger no longer has the strength to endure the inevitable ordeal that love again would bring. Stiefel writes of this poem; "The poet gives his most personal destiny utterance in the broader frame of general human destiny, in one of the most moving poems of modern German lyric overall.[23]

"Resignation" (1793) expresses in broader terms than "An das Herz" the sense of finality and the poet's retirement from life and the world around him. Not only his body, but now his heart too has lost its pulse. The poet sees life as a burden and the pleasance of the world as an illusion:

> *Mich täuschet ferner kein Vertrauen*
> *Auf dieser Welt. Beim nahen Schauen*
> *Ist jedes Glück der Erde Wahn;*
> *Kein Weiser bleibt ihm zugetan.*

(/No confidence in this world deceives me any longer. On a close look every good fortune on earth is an illusion; no wise man remains devoted to it./)

CHAPTER 5

Critical and Creative Prose

IN the Introduction to the second edition of his *Gedichte,* Bürger repeated an assertion he had often made before, that 'poetry is an art, which must be practiced by scholars ("Gelehrte"), but is not necessarily for scholars, but for the people.'[1] The point of interest here is his insistence that poetry be written by scholars, and since he regarded himself as a poet, the conclusion is syllogistically inescapable. It is, in fact, true that Bürger thought of himself as something of a scholar, and many of his friends, including Goethe, urged him to find a place somewhere on a university faculty. In the traditional sense of the word, however, Bürger was not a scholar, and one of the reasons for his inacceptability to the faculty at Göttingen was his lack of credentials. Moreover, Bürger lacked the frame of mind characteristic of the scholar, if it is possible to speak of such a thing. He was not a systematic or abstract thinker, and except at the most primitive level he was not a theorist. Bürger's world was the immediate, tangible, visible world, and within that context, he was eminently capable. He was gifted with a fertile imagination and a capacity for sound, practical, and sometimes brilliant ideas. In addition, he was innovative in his suggestions, and although he sometimes tended towards oversimplification and a one-dimensional view of literature, he had essential grasp of it and urged constructive reform. It is quite true, as Lore Kaim-Kloock states, that 'Bürger was as little capable of developing a comprehensive aesthetic system as he was of constructing a philosophical one.'[2]

Bürger's thoughts about the nature and function of poetry, and the role of the poet, are contained in a number of essays, which, considered in toto, form a collection of reactions and practical suggestions. The earliest of these essays, "Aus Daniel Wunderlichs Buch," was written in 1776 and published that same year in the *Teutsches Museum.* The extract—for that is what it was intended to be—consists of an Introduction and two essays, "Von der Einteilung des Schauspiels" ("On the Classification of Drama"), and "Herzens-ausguß über Volks-Poesie" ("Outpourings of the Heart of Folk Poetry"). The two essays are quite disparate in length as well as content. In his Introduction, Bürger explains the approach he intends to follow and indicates roughly what his concerns are. Above all, it is to be unambiguously subjective. Much is intuitive and tantalizingly ineffable: 'And yet, it seems to me as though I knew many a thing that not everyone knows, as though I felt the elasticity of spirit . . ., the courage and strength to seize a thing, hold it, swing it, and hurl it up into the air; it seems to me as if a light surrounded me that illuminated things, near and far, etc.'[3] The outpourings of his heart that Bürger had promised for the second essay is already abundantly in evidence in the Introduction, where he also announces that "I wrote without any other books, out of my own head and heart." The reader is fully and explicitly warned, therefore, as to the technique and approach applied to the material that follows. Bürger concludes this dithyrambic introduction with the ecstatic exclamation that what he seeks is 'Truth! Inscrutable, eternal Godhead! Towards thee are my glances directed.' ("Wahrheit! Unerforschliche, ewige Gottheit! Nach dir gehen meine Blicke aus.")

The first of the essays, "On the Classification of Drama," is a counterpart to Reinhold Michael Lenz's "Anmerkungen über das Theater." Bürger reveals his inclination to see certain issues in oversimplified terms. He urges that the various designations of drama, such as tragedy, comedy, farce, etc., are a pointless fragmentation, which has been imposed by scholars and critics, but which, in effect, contributes nothing to our understanding of a play. "Schauspiel ist—Schauspiel, und damit gut!" ("A play is a—play, and that's that."). Bürger reasons that all emotions are part of a greater whole, that tears and laughter, like pain and pleasure are closely bound together, and that classifications beyond "Schauspiel" are, therefore, gratuitous.

The second essay, on folk poetry, is somewhat less phrenetic than the Introduction and provides the only substantive argument of the whole work. Moreover, Bürger introduces in this essay the nearest thing to a formal program that he ever evolved, and all of his subsequent writings on the subject have their germ in this essay. The argument itself is not at all complex; it is an appeal for German as a language, simplicity in expression, and realism in style.

There is no reason, Bürger maintains, that poetry should be

by and for the gods alone, nor should it have to be consistently elevated and sublime. Far better, he suggests, for poets to shed their heavenly raiments, don the garb of men, and leave the groves of Arcadia. The poet regrets that Germans are known for their learning but not their wisdom, and he ascribes Germany's failure to produce great poets (or great poetry) to a compulsion to learn and know ("weil wir so tief und hoch gelährt sind"). Learning has become an end in itself, and it is all "todtes Kapital" ("idle capital"). When learning suppresses poetic expression, it should be repulsed, and Bürger sees the best remedy in Nature and the real world. 'Let one come to know the people thoroughly, let one explore one's imagination and sensibilities, in order to furnish the former with appropriate images and for the latter to strike the right tone.' Successfully pursued, this approach will produce poetry which will appeal and speak simultaneously to all levels of society. 'This is the proper *non plus ultra* of all poetry.'

The second half of the essay is a consideration of lyric and epic-lyric genres. The magic wand of epic poetry is a rare gift, but in its quintessential form it may be observed in the folk song. Bürger sees the ancient folk songs as offering even the most mature poet an insight into natural poetic art, particularly for the lyric and epic-lyric genres. In the evenings Bürger went about listening to the common people singing their ballads, and he never ceased to be instructed. '. . . The recitation of ballad and romance or of the lyric and epic-lyric poetry—for both are one!—and all lyric and epic-lyric poetry may be said to be ballad or folk song, is glorious and instructive.' Ultimately, the study of these forms will lead the poet back among the people, where he will achieve 'popularity.'[4] More specifically, he stated that 'Through popularity . . . poetry should once again become that for which God created it and laid it in the souls of chosen men.' It should be noted that Bürger by no means regarded everyone as a potential poet. Quite the opposite, his use of "auserwählte" ("selected" or "chosen") indicates a strong conviction of his high view of the poet; of the poet as priest, one might say.

For Bürger the Muse of the ballad and romance held the touchstone of great poetry, and with disarming innocence (though in tones reminiscent of Herder) he proclaimed his theory that the ballad was the venerable progenitor of the major epics: *'Orlando Furioso, . . .* Fingal, Timora, and, is one to believe it?—the *Iliad* and *Odyssey* too? That's the truth! ("Wahrhaftig!") All these poems were to the people who sang them nothing but ballads, romances, and folk songs.'[5]

Bürger complains that, until recently, *Volkspoesie* had been held in low esteem, and that any poetaster felt he could concoct a ballad or romance simply by following a recipe. Take the first fable within reach without any final purpose or interest at all, grind it into boring, utterly miserable stanzas, here and there foolishly sprinkle in archaic words or phrases, etc.,' and label it "Ballad" or "Romance." 'No life stirs there, no breath!... No vital surge, etc.' Take heed, Bürger declares, and do not be misled: '*Volkspoesie*, just because it is the *non plus ultra* of the art, is the most difficult of all." The poet expresses his hope for a German 'Percy' who will collect the ancient songs of the German-speaking peoples and publish them. Having extolled the virtues of forthright, unadorned simplicity—and that at the expense of the learned and scholarly element of his society, it is rather ironic to find Bürger's earnest wish for "So eine Sammlung von einem Kunstverständigen, mit Anmerkungen versehen!" ("Such a collection, provided with footnotes by an expert!").[6]

The reforms Bürger called for were both reasonable and refreshing, although his was neither a new nor a solitary voice in the wilderness. Herder was saying very much the same thing at about the same time—in fact somewhat earlier. Herder had called for a collection of German folk songs in his essay, "Über Ossian und die Lieder alter Völker," written in 1771 and published in 1773. Bürger had read Herder's essay in the year it appeared and had written to Boie: "Der [Ton], den Herder auferweckt hat, der schon lange auch in meiner Seele auftönte, hat nun dieselbe ganz erfüllt . . ." ('The tone which Herder has awakened, which for so long has sounded in my soul, has now filled it entirely.').[7]

"Aus Daniel Wunderlichs Buch" did not go unnoticed by the critics, and among the writers of the slightly older generation caused something of a stir, particularly with Bodmer, Ramler, and Nicolai. Nicolai's satirical reply in "Ein feyner kleyner ALMANACH" took the Enlightenment position that the poet could not operate from the basis of the *Volk* without descending to it. He also pointed out a lack of critical discernment in judging *Volkspoesie*, since even there, in his opinion, there had to be some distinction between good

and bad. In a letter to Justus Möser, Nicolai stated his purpose
with the ALMANACH, 'My intention is to give our self-styled
Geniuses, who do all sorts of mischief, a little nip on the ear, to
prod them to rescue from obscurity such folk songs as have genuine
"naiveté." '[8]

Bürger's reply to Nicolai makes up the third essay of "Daniel
Wunderlichs Buch" and was written in 1777. It focuses on Nicolai's
challenge of the use of extra-natural or supernatural phenomena
in literature. In making his argument Bürger relies chiefly on Shakespeare as his authority, and he points out that even the English
poet employed witches and ghosts, although today one looks a-
skance at them. The underlying point of Bürger's essay is his reluctance to reject out of hand what we have no knowledge of (i.e., the
supernatural world), and that ultimately, "des Menschen Herz
ist stärker als seine Vernunft" ("Man's heart is stronger than his
reason").

Bürger's Introduction to the 1778 edition of his collected poems
may, in part, be considered an extension of several of the ideas
first expressed in "Aus Daniel Wunderlichs Buch." The Introduction is not a cohesive essay, but at least in two respects it points
up the continued line of Bürger's thinking and his ideas about the
German language. It is also fundamental to Bürger's image of himself and his role as a poet. He expresses the hope that his poems
will appeal to people "aus allen Klassen" ("from all classes,") and
goes on to ask rhetorically:

... warum sollte es mich nicht freuen, daß es ... mir gelungen ist, zu
bestätigen die Wahrheit des Artikels, woran ich festiglich glaube, und
welcher die Achse ist, woherum meine ganze Poetik sich dreht: Alle dar-
stellende Bildnerei kann und soll volksmäßig sein. Denn das ist das Siegel
ihrer Vollkommenheit. ...[9]

(/ ... why should it not please me, that I have succeeded in confirming the
truth of the article [of faith] in which I firmly believe, and which is the axis
about which my whole poetic revolves: all art can and should be popular.
For that is the seal of its perfection./)

Bürger proceeds to acclaim *Volkspoesie,* "die ich als die einzige
wahre anerkenne und über alles andere poetische Machwerk erhebe"
("which I recognize as the only true kind and raise above all other
poetic clutter"). The true *Volksdichter*—and he considers himself
one—must accordingly write for "das Volk—worunter ich mit

nichten den Pöbel allein verstehe" ('the people—whereby I do not mean the rabble alone'). With minor variations the phrase and the distinction will recur frequently in Bürger's writings.

The other aspect of Bürger's introductory essay evidences his concern for language per se and for orthography, both themes to which he would often return. After several general remarks on the disordered state of German orthography, he makes a number of practical suggestions for the standardization of the language. His observations have clearly come from personal experience, and like so many of his other recommendations for reform, these are thoroughly practical and reasonable.

At some point in the interval between the publication of the *Gedichte* (1778) and "Über Anweisung zur deutschen Sprache" (1787) Bürger once again set down his thoughts on popularity in "Von der Popularität der Poesie." Bohtz first published it in his edition (1835) with the notation, "from the manuscript," and Wurzbach dates it 1784, although Sauer, in his chronology, assigns no date to the piece. The essay consists of a dozen individual statements, ranging from a single sentence to several paragraphs in length and although each statement is separate, there is a discernible chain of thought.

Bürger begins by pointing out that the German word "Dichtkunst" ("poetry") does not correspond to the Greek *poiesis* and suggests instead "Bildnerei" ("depiction"). He then proceeds to relate depiction to the concept of "Gestalt" ("figure" or "shape"), and from there he goes on to consider the depiction or representation of an object. Nature presents an object, but the poet can only re-present it ("Nachbildnerei"). Not everything should be represented, however, and "Geschmack" ("human taste") enters as the second governing factor. Thus Nature and human taste are the ultimate arbiters in poetry, with Nature as the "Monarchin." Bürger's argument leads him to a rather belated altercation with the theories of the French rhetorician and critic, the Abbé Charles Batteux (1713–1780). Batteux had argued that art only has beauty by its truth, and that its truth derives from the imitation of Nature. Bürger rejected such qualifications and instead, insisted on realism and immediacy in poetry. In the eleventh and twelfth sections, Bürger takes up the question of popularity in poetry and reiterates the by now familiar phrases, "Unter Volk verstehe ich nicht Pöbel" and "Die größten, unsterblichsten Dichter aller Nationen sind *populäre* Dichter gewesen" ("The greatest, most immortal [!] poets of all nations have been *popular* poets"). He urges German poets to seek their subjects at home and not in foreign models, since in portraying what is familiar, they can achieve a true and genuine popularity ("echte und wahre Popularität").

It should be pointed out that some of Bürger's ideas in this essay, as elsewhere, are rather ambiguously stated. In certain cases the ambiguity in expression may reflect an ambiguity in the poet's mind regarding what he wishes to define or describe. In the final paragraph of this essay, Bürger deplores the fact that his utterances on *Volkspoesie* have had so little affect, and he complains that he has not been understood:

Alles das überzeugt mich, daß wenige, ja wohl niemand verstehen, was ich meine. Gleichwohl, was ich auch diesen Gegenstand schon erwogen habe und noch immer erwäge, so wird doch der Satz meinem Geiste stets gewisser: Alle Poesie soll volksmäßig sein, denn das ist . . .[10]
(/All that convinces me that few, indeed probably no one understands what I mean. Nevertheless, after what thoughts I have devoted to the object and shall continue to ponder, that sentence grows ever more certain in my mind: all poetry should be popular, for that is . . . /)

When the second edition of the *Gedichte* appeared in 1789, Bürger pursued in the Introduction several of the themes he had taken up in "Aus Daniel Wunderlichs Buch," the Introduction to the first edition, and "Von der Popularität der Poesie." The poet's central theme and concern, however, was to elucidate again his thoughts about *Volkspoesie* and to buttress his claim as a true *Volksdichter.* Initially, the tone of the Introduction is conciliatory and modest, as Bürger makes a plea for reason and good will: "Denn je mehr Verstand, Herz und Geschmack: desto mehr Gerechtigkeit, Toleranz und Bescheidenheit" ("For the more understanding, good will, and taste, the more justice, tolerance, and discretion").[11] He expresses his desire to bring honor to his *Vaterland* and his hope that the present collection may be found to have some poetic merit.

When Bürger comes to discuss his ideas on *Volkspoesie* and his role as *Volksdichter* he moves much less timidly. He discounts any suggestion that he should be called a *Volksdichter* because of the "Hopp, Hopp, Hurre, Hurre, Huhu, etc.," since these are merely forceful expressions that he may have blundered onto, but which hardly justify his being called *Volksdichter,* no more so than his versification of a few *Volksmärchen.* Bürger enumerates the specific qualities he strives for—and which, he maintains, define his claim to the title *Volksdichter:*

Bestreben nach Zusammenklang der Gedanken und Bilder; nach Wahrheit, Natur und Einfalt der Empfindungen; nach dem eigentümlichsten und treffendsten, nicht eben aus der toten Schrift-, sondern mitten aus der lebendigsten Mundsprache aufgegriffenen Ausdrücke derselben; nach der pünktlichsten grammatischen Richtigkeit, nach einem leichten ungezwungenen, wohlklingenden Rein- und Versbau. . . .[12]

(/Striving for clarity, precision, polish, order and harmony of thoughts and images; for truth, nature, and simplicity of the sensibilities; for the most characteristic and precise expressions of the same, not just drawn from the fossilized literary language, but rather from the most vital current language; for the most minute grammatical accuracy, for a light, but not forced, euphonious structure of rhyme and verse. . . .)

In order to achieve these goals Bürger wishes to provide the reader immediate access to his poetry, in which everything, stripped of all confusion and obfuscation, will emerge sharply and clearly before the mind's eye.[13]

There are very few new theoretical insights in the 1789 Introduction; Bürger repeats that he is writing for "unser ganzes gebildetes Volk!—Volk! nicht Pöbel!" and he incorporates the phrase he had used in the Introduction to the first edition, "Die Popularität eines poetischen Werkes ist das Siegel seiner Vollkommenheit." He continues to insist that poetry is an art that must be practiced by scholars, etc. It is not easy to discern in Bürger's statements in the 1789 Introduction any signs of substantive growth, development, or even change, from his statements a decade earlier.

Bürger's reply to Schiller's review has been considered a mistake by everyone from Bürger and Schiller on down to the present day. Understandably outraged, Bürger rushed immediately into print with his "Vorläufige Antikritik und Anzeige" ("Provisional Counter-Critique and Denouncement"). The reply was written in the heat of anger, is saturated with irony and sarcasm, does not reply to Schiller's criticisms, and was altogether unworthy of Bürger. Schiller recognized the thoroughgoing weakness of Bürger's reply and noticeably sharpened his language and his attack.

Bürger was invariably more successful when addressing himself

to practical rather than theoretical issues, as in "Über Anweisung
zur deutsche Sprache und Schreibart auf Universitäten. Einladungs-
blätter zu seinen Vorlesungen" ("On Instruction of the German
Language and Style at Universities. Notification and Invitation
to His Lectures.") Written and published as a separate document
in 1787, it is an extraordinary manifesto, praising the art of language
and style, vehemently at times, arguing that language and style,
and competency in them, are the alpha and omega of wisdom,
taste, and culture; and that mastery of language and style lies at
the very heart of the educated man. The poet admits that probably
little of what he says is new, scholarly or profound; but he believes
that it is worth repeating and calls his essay a "populäre Predigt"
("a popular sermon") with the emphasis on "Energie."

Bürger declares that the Germans have always felt they have
two distinct languages: the common, everyday speech and a kind
of Sunday language. The latter unfortunately suffers from the
widespread belief that it reflects preciosity or fanciness. Facility
with language and style is indispensable for the educated man,
however, and if it were only preciosity of fanciful adornment, it
would not warrant the time and energy required to master it. And
it does require diligent study to master one's own language. Most
people have learned what they know about style by trial and error,
i.e., pragmatically, and are quite ignorant of the structure or grammar of their native tongue. Language, Bürger maintains, is the
most expedient and explicit means for the expression of thought,
and he arrives at the natural and justifiable conclusion that 'the
more perfectly one understands his own language, the richer he is
in the conception of things and their manifold facets. . . . To have
mastery over one's language is nothing more than having mastery
over all the forces of one's spirit and the entire warehouse of thought
which language transcribes.'[14]

As Bürger warms to his subject, his own prose style increases in
heat and intensity and he addresses his audience in an impassioned
speech, which sets linguistic achievement, rhetoric, and style at
the very peak of human achievement:

'Menschen, die ihr Sinn für Menschenrecht und Menschenadel habt, laßt
den Tyrannen Festungen über Festungen bauen, laßt ihn seine stehenden
Heere bis zu Millionen vermehren! Werbet ihr dagegen die Künste des

Geistes, vornehmlich die Redekünste an, und laßt sie um Freiheit und Eigentum ihre Wagenburg schlagen! Es ist nicht wahr, daß Kanonen mehr vermögen als Gedanken und Worte, wie bisweilen gepaß wird. Wenn wir Sklaven sind, so sind wir's wahrlich nicht durch jene Stein-, Eisen-, Blei- und Fleischmaßen der Tyrannen, denen wir nicht ähnliche Maßen entgegenzustellen haben: sondern darum sind wir's, weil wir die kraft-, tat-, und siegreichsten Künste des Geistes, die Künste zu reden und zu schreiben, vernachlässigen. Die Körper herrschen nicht über die Geister; sondern die Geister herrschen über die Körper. Und was sind die Evolutionen der Körper gegen die Evolutionen der Geister?'[15]

(/People, you who have a mind for human rights and human nobility, let the tyrant build fortress on fortress, let him increase his standing armies to millions! Recruit, instead, the arts of the spirit, especially rhetoric, and let them set up their barricades in the cause of freedom and property! It is not true that cannons can do more than thoughts and words, as now and then has happened. If we are slaves, then truly, we are not so because of those stone, iron, lead, and human masses of the tyrants, to which we cannot oppose similar masses: rather we are slaves because we neglect the powerful, creative victorious arts of the spirit, the arts of speaking and writing. Bodies do not rule over spirits; but spirits rule over bodies. And what are the evolutions of the bodies against the evolutions of the mind?/)

Having soared to such rarefied and rapturous heights, it is something of a letdown for the reader to find himself suddenly back in the academic world of hours and fees:

Meinen hiesigen Freunden mache ich hiedurch nur noch bekannt, daß ich künftigen Winter die allgemeine Theorie der Schreibert Nachmittags um 4 Uhr wöchentlich in fünf Stunden vortragen werde.... Auch bin ich zu praktischem Unterrichte im Style privatissime erbötig.[16]

(/To my local friends I herewith announce that in the coming winter I shall lecture on stylistics weekly at four o'clock in the afternoon in five sessions ... I am also available privately for private tutoring in style./)

Shortly after its publication Bürger forwarded copies of the essay to several friends and officials, including Hofrat Brandes and President von Hardenberg-Reventlow.[17] In both cases he spoke of the essay as simply the "Vorrede" ('Introduction') to a larger work, although the larger work was never written. In his cover letter to the historian Johannes von Müller, he commented modestly that "es ist freilich nur leichte Speise" ('It is, to be sure, rather bland fare.')[18] While it would be difficult to defend the length of the essay—or some of the less restrained panegyrics—it does propound in basic terms an enlightened and wholly valid attitude towards language and style.

Several years after the first edition of his *Gedichte,* perhaps in 1782,[19] Bürger returned to his concern for German orthography as he took up the theme again in several very brief essays. In "Vorschlag zu einem deutschen Rechtschreibungsvereine" ("Proposal for an Association for German Orthography"), he repeats in far more concise terms much of the argument he had set forth in the Introduction to the *Gedichte* (1778), and the essay abounds in practical suggestions. One of the chief concerns in 1778 had been the letter "ß" which Bürger called, "ein höchst alberner Buchstabe" ("an utterly silly letter"), but in the "Vorschlag" he addressed himself to numerous letters of the alphabet individually. Almost without exception his suggestions have been subsequently adopted and are reflected in modern German: 'Do away with the "h" in *Thräne, Thal,* and *Thor;* eliminate the "b" in *Ambt* and *darumb.*' Bürger laments the fact that no two people in Germany write or spell alike. On the other hand, he simply wishes these to be regarded as suggestions: "Ich will nicht Gesetze geben und aufdringen, sondern nur Vorschläge tun..." ("I don't intend to establish and impose rules, but only to make suggestions...").[20]

Another essay, "Über die Rechtschreibung" ("On Orthography"), is dedicated to the philosopher Lichtenberg and responds to the latter's call for someone to treat the question of German orthography with insight and tolerance. Bürger doubts that any single person could terminate the prevailing anarchy in language (and style), but he is willing to submit several basic points for consideration; such as derivation, pronunciation, etc.[21]

The strongly national character of the essay for Lichtenberg is, if anything, more pronounced in "Über deutsche Sprache" which was addressed to Johann Christoph Adelung (1732–1806), one of the leading German grammarians of the day. Written in 1783, it focuses attention on German grammar: 'I could more gladly forgive any sin but a grammatical one'[22] It is Bürger's greatest wish to serve truth and his *Vaterland,* and he proposes a correspondence with Adelung (to be published in the latter's journal) on questions of German grammar. Bürger wanders somewhat from a consideration of grammar to a consideration of taste, which as he says, comes to us exclusively through the medium of language: "Taste is the ability to discern beauty."[23] The tone of the essay does not entirely conceal Bürger's animosity towards Adelung, and it was evidently part of Bürger's plan to attack and overthrow him. As he wrote to Dieterich, "I intend to take the field against him. I intend, moreover, to arm myself better than his former antagonists, who in their short night shirts have sallied forth against the man in full armor."[24] Despite the bravado, there is no indication that Bürger's essay ever came to Adelung's attention. As in so many cases, Bürger's intentions were not realized.

Bürger wrote four other short essays on style, but they were not published until Bohtz incorporated them in his edition of 1835, where he took them, as he noted, "from the manuscript." The first of the three, "Wider die majestätische Länge," was motivated by an article in Schlözer's *Staats Anzeigen* and inveighs against prolixity. The other three are so short that they hardly qualify as essays, and all treat various aspects of style: "Wissenschaft des Styls" ("Science of Style"), "Geschäfts-Styl" ("Business Style"), and "Vollkommenheit des Styls" ("Perfection of Style"). None of the three is more than the kernel of an idea that Bürger might have developed at a later point, but never did. In 1826 Karl Reinhard assembled Bürger's notes for his lectures on language, grammar, and style at Göttingen and published them in the *Lehrbuch des deutschen Styls* (Berlin.)[25]

The question of style occupied Bürger sporadically throughout his life, and after assuming the editorship of the *Göttinger Musen-Almanach,* the issue became a very urgent one. In the "Notgedrungene Nachrede zum Musenalmanach" ("Necessary postscript to the Musen-Almanach"), 1782, Bürger, the editor, addresses himself to his readers and prospective contributors, at least in part on the matter of style. Some of the works submitted to him demonstrate that numerous authors cannot write correct German. It had quite evidently been a hard week, and Bürger makes little effort to hide his annoyance. "Mein Gott! sperren denn die Herren gar die Augen nicht auf, um wahrzunehmen, wie unsere rechtlichen Schriftsteller sowohl in Prosa als Versen machen?" ('My God! Don't these gentlemen open their eyes to perceive how our proper authors use prose or verse?')[26] The essay is not written either to win favor or attract students and is an utterly forthright statement of Bürger's position and attitudes. It is also an entirely practical affair, and Bürger offers his contributors some sound and sensible advice, particularly the younger fledgling poets, whom he councils to 'stay away from love poems, for they require the skill of a master, not a novice. They must be able to convey the sense of love and feeling tastefully and convincingly to someone who is *not* in love. Writing love lyrics demands much more than repeating the phrase, "I love you," over and over!'[27]

Writing to A. W. Schlegel in October, 1791, Bürger noted that his "Reimkunst in der Nuß" was finished.[28] The full title of the work is "Hübnerus redivivus. Das ist: Kurze Theorie der Reimkunst für Dilettanten" ("Hübner Revisited. That is: Short Theory of Versification for Amateurs.") The 'Hübner' of the title was Tobias Hübner (1577–1636), to whom the development of versification by accented syllables in German is generally attributed. Although completed in 1791, it was not published until 1797–1798, when it appeared in the *Akademie der schönen Redekünste*.

The essay is divided into two major parts, "Von der Richtigkeit" ("On Correctness") and "Vom Wohlklange" ("On Euphony"), and each half consists of several subdivisions. While the external structure is relatively obvious, the internal structure is less apparent. The essay is quite discursive and subjective in its approach and is essentially a personal expression of Bürger's tastes, attitudes, and prejudices, written in a conversationally didactic tone. Characteristic of the general orientation are Bürger's concluding remarks on "reicher Reim" ("full rhyme"), which he obviously didn't care for, and apparently had given little thought to: "Warum er der *reiche* Reim heißt, das mag der Himmel wissen. Ich würde ihn lieber den *armseligen* heißen." ("Why it is called 'full rhyme,' heaven only knows. I should rather call it 'impoverished.' ")[29] For a supposed textbook, presumably written for pedagogical purposes, the piece leaves the disconcerting impression that *poeta nascitur non fit*. Wurzbach saw the same problem elsewhere as well, "sie leidet an dem Fehler aller derartigen Werke, ihr Studium kann die natürlichen Anlagen zur Poesie nicht ersetzen, und wenn die letzteren bei jemandem vorhanden sind, kann er derselben entraten" ('it suffers from the error of all such works, its study cannot replace the natural talent for poetry, and if the latter is present in a person, he can work it out himself.')[30]

In the same year that Bürger completed his "Hübnerus redivivus" he was asked to act as arbiter in a poetic competition, and two years later (1793) he published his findings under the impressive title, "Aktenstücke über einen poetischen Wettstreit. Geschlichtet auf dem deutschen Parnaß ("Documents regarding a Poetic Contest. Arbitrated on the German Parnassus").

Three gentlemen, Regierungsrat von Wildungen, Freiherr von Wülknitz, and a Dr. Bunsen had agreed upon a competition or wager, to compose a poetic New Year's Greeting for a mutual friend, who was also to judge the poems. The three poems were to be written in free style, except that the end rhymes of each line were prescribed. (Bürger himself had engaged in this sport on at least two occasions.[31]) The poems were submitted anonymously, and when the decision was made by Geheimer Justizrat Erxleben (the recipient of the New Year's Greetings) first prize had been awarded to Dr. Bunsen. Evidently, the other gentlemen were not happy at Erxleben's decision, and they approached Bürger with the request that he review it.

The work is divided into nine sections, all formally numbered, labeled, and indexed ("Rotulus Actorum") in the manner of a legal document. The various documents are supplied, including the end rhymes, the three poems, etc., and the language of the whole is mock-legal and determinedly pompous.[32] There are appropriate and inappropriate citations from Homer, Kant, Horace, Eschenburg, and the letters of Lady Wortley Montague, all documented with footnotes. Finally, when Bürger made his judgment, he awarded the prize to Von Wildungen. In his reply, he attempted to imitate the ponderous legal style, but admitted that he was incapable of using that kind of language, although he generously sprinkled his commentary with Latin phrases.

Bürger's letter, in which he discusses each of the three poems separately, is not a theoretical essay, but it affords one more insight into those qualities upon which he placed a strong emphasis. The several aspects of form, order, content, execution of the idea, strength and clarity of expression, and proportion are stressed to varying degrees. Bürger also comments deductively on the manner in which the two poems were composed. (He had eliminated one of the poems at the outset.) By their content he suggested that one of the authors had pondered the end rhymes for some time and had conceptually structured the poem as a whole before putting pen to paper, whereas the other man had worked at it from one end rhyme to the next. The entire affair provides a welcome sense of relief to Bürger's more oblique essays, and it demonstrates that even after the Schiller catastrophe he still possessed a vein of humor.

In the same way that the "Aktenstücke" illuminate Bürger's thoughts about poetry and poetic composition, his reviews of other authors are informative about what he looked for in their works. Between 1786 and 1789, Bürger wrote perhaps four or five reviews for either the *Allgemeine deutsche Bibliothek* or the *Allgemeine Literaturzeitung*. Among these is the torso of what was planned to be a comprehensive critical study of Blumauer's poems (*Gedichte,* Vienna, 1787. 2 vols.) Bürger admits that he was not the first to comment critically on Blumauer's poetic achievements, but if well-meaning and honest judgments are supposed to assist an artist in his attempts to improve, then Bürger's time and effort will have been well spent. Bürger agrees with the many critics who rank Blumauer among the leading poets of the nation, and he indicates those qualities which he regards as most important and on which he places the greatest emphasis, such as "seinen lebhaft funkelnden Witz . . . die komische Kraft . . ." ("his lively, sparkling wit . . . the comic power . . ."). At the same time, Bürger feels that Blumauer's sense of inventiveness and creativity is not capable of a broad, cohesively structured vision. Bürger regarded Blumauer's poetry as more of an 'aggregate' than a work produced under a compelling sense of order and unity. Delightful thoughts, images, and ideas are bound together with wit and rhyme, but Bürger complains that Blumauer is not always lucid, and that his thoughts are not so much part of a tightly knit whole as they are a "Perlenschnur" ("string of pearls").[33]

Bürger also reviewed the *Portrait de Philippe II, Roi d'Espagne* ("Portrait of Phillip II, King of Spain"), published in 1785 in Amsterdam, which was written in dramatic form, but not intended for the stage. Bürger questions whether this combination of history and poetry is a deliberate attempt to create a third form, yet he rejects the piece on the grounds that is satisfies neither an historical curiosity nor our aesthetic sense. Drama requires real people, speaking in the first person singular, present tense, but the historian chronicles past events from a third-person point of view. In the work under consideration the vital give-and-take of dialogue succumbs to the necessity of conveying historical information, and although it is not satisfying, it is not without interest. The approach is objective and nonpartisan, and Bürger discusses the work with considerable insight.

The *Gedichte* of Levin Adolf Moller received considerably less favorable treatment, but there is nothing in the review which throws any further light on Bürger's ideas on poetry. He complains, in passing, about Moller's orthography. Two further reviews of the *Gedichte* of Zacharias Werner and the *Gedichte* of Karl Theodor Beck, in the *Allgemeine Literatur Zeitung* (August, 1789) were probably, but not certainly, written by Bürger.

At the request of Professor C. G. Heyne, one of Bürger's strongest supporters at Göttingen, the poet reluctantly agreed to compose an Introduction to K. G. Bock's translation of Virgil's *Georgics*. In his letter to Heyne, Bürger fulminated that Bock didn't have the 'slightest sense of rhythm, harmony, or melody, not to mention other deficiencies in style. The most unholy of all demons has prompted him to concoct a "Mischmasch" of true and false—so-called Kleistian hexameters, . . . '[34] It was to Bürger's credit and ingenuity that his completed Introduction (1790) revealed none of his feelings; it is a brilliant noncomittal essay, as Heyne readily acknowledged. The poet duly notes the existence of the translation by Voß, but maintains that there is always room for another good translation. Bürger does not commend Bock over Voß but declares that all translations, if they are well done, will offer new insights, and the best way to get at a work in a foreign tongue, if one doesn't read it, is to read several translations and compare them.

Among Bürger's non-theoretical prose works must be counted the Freemason addresses he delivered before his lodge in Göttingen. Bürger was a member of the Golden Circle Lodge from 1775 until its dissolution in 1793. After 1777 (excluding 1783–1786), he held the honorary title of Brother Speaker ("Bruder Redner") and apparently gave numerous addresses on special occasions. With the exception of three speeches and "Das Lied vom braven Mann," which he delivered before the Lodge on St. John's Day (June 24) 1777, all of the texts have been lost, although the titles of many are known.[35] The three texts which have been preserved are "Über die Zufriedenheit" ("On Contentment"—1788), "Ermunterung zur Freiheit" ("Encouragement to Freedom"—1790), and "Über den moralischen Mut" ("On Moral Courage"—1791). As the titles of these pieces (and those which have been lost) indicate, they are heavily didactic. In the address on Contentment, Bürger admonishes his audience to eschew envy, for envy contains the poison which can ruin contentment. What we should seek to cultivate in ourselves is envy of wisdom, virtue, and grace. Finally, we should foster within ourselves the sense of confidence that all is ordained for the welfare of man. The 'content' man believes and knows that everything God does is well done ("alles, was Gott tut, sei wohlgetan"). The content man trusts God.

The "Encouragement to Freedom" is bolder in its implications. Bürger reminds his listeners of America and their 'black brothers, whose humanity has been crushed under foot.'[36] Primarily, however, Bürger's glance is focused on the French Revolution and implicitly he urges his audience to consider it as an example. Explicitly, he urges his brothers to learn the power of the pen ("Schreib- und Redekünste"). The third of the addresses, "On Moral Courage," is less cohesive, but, essentially, Bürger calls on his fellow Masons to live by the laws of reason and morality, rather than according to the prejudices of appearance and habit.

All three essays make it apparent that Bürger had never forgotten his upbringing in a parsonage, nor the fact that he himself had once studied for the clergy and had, on occasion, preached in one or another of the small parish churches in the neighborhood of Göttingen. The style is consistently and vigorously homiletical, suggesting that Bürger was still strongly attracted to 'pulpit German,' and, secondly, it reinforces the impression that he greatly enjoyed the role of speaker, in which he could be the focus of attention. His language is sweeping and impassioned as he calls his audience to moral and intellectual renewal, and exhorts them to break the chains of slavery for freedom. In their totality, the Freemason speeches attest once more to Bürger's passionate nature, but they shed little new light on his poetic talent.

Finally, there are three miniature works of creative prose, the fables. The first of these, "Der Maulwurf und der Gärtner" ("The Mole and the Gardener"), was included among the poems in the *Gedichte* (1789). The second, "Das Magnetengebirge. Eine Allegorie oder Fabel" ("The Magnetic Mountains. An Allegory or Fable"), probably written about 1792, was published the following year in the *Musen-Almanach*. The third, "Der Mensch und der

Kranich" ("Man and the Crane"), was not published until 1858, is not included in any edition of Bürger's works, and has generally gone unnoticed.[37]

The first of the fables concerns the mole which has devastated the garden. The gardener lies in wait, captures the mole and is about to kill him when the mole speaks up and begs for mercy, saying that 'he eats the grubs and other insects which destroy the garden, and is therefore not entirely without value.' 'The devil take you,' replies the gardener, 'to counterbalance virtue with vice,' and thereupon dispatches the mole.

"Das Magnetengebirge" consists of two parts: the first tells of a magnetic mountain range in the middle of the ocean, which attracts everything made of iron and steel; the ships' joints all split, and the ocean is littered with wrecks. Now shipbuilders have taken to building their ships of silver and gold, and a new age of shipping has begun. The second half of the fable tells of a mighty "Magnatenburg" ("Magnate's Fortress") surrounded by many smaller "Magnatenbürgen" ("Magnates' Fortresses") standing in a great plain which is dotted with cottages. The castles of the magnates ("Das Magnatengebürge") attract everything containing gold and silver, and all the gold and silver is drawn out of the cottages to the castles, leaving the plain littered with ruins of the cottages. Then every one rebuilds with iron and steel, and a new form of architecture is developed. The fable concludes: "I don't know where the 'Magnetengebirge' lie or lay, but every one knows where the 'Magnatengebürge' are."

The third fable is simpler in plot, but more convoluted in thought. In the autumn of the year a grandfather sits surrounded by his children and grandchildren and contemplates the cranes flying south overhead. He compares man's life to the flight of the cranes: when the harvest is gathered, and the snowflakes settle on his head, and the chill of age comes upon him, "dann stillt der ernste Engel des Todes die Sehnsucht des Menschen; er nimmt ihn auf in seine dunkeln Fittiche und trägt den Schlummernden still über die Wässer der Zeit in das heimatliche Land voll Paradiesbäume und Sonnen." ('Then the earnest angel of death stills the longing of man; he takes him up in his dark wings and bears the slumberer quietly across the waters of time into his native land of paradise trees and sun.')

Of the three fables, the second is most representative of Bürger's style and manner. His pleasure in words and his delight in exploring the outer boundaries of language with puns and neologisms exhibit both inventiveness and humor. Simultaneously, he uses the sport of word play in order to assail an oppressive political or social system which centralizes wealth and spreads poverty. The third fable is less characteristic of Bürger's manner of thinking and expression, although it contains one or two characteristic turns of phrase. If, in fact, Bürger was the author of the third piece, then it affords a unique insight into his interest and capacity for writing parables.

CHAPTER 6

Translations and Adaptations

TO an extraordinary degree, Bürger's Muse was activated by
external stimuli, and their effect on his work was substantial.
No poet is ever entirely immune to outside influences, but Bürger
was probably more susceptible than most. The shades of Klopstock,
Shakespeare, Herder, Ossian, for instance, are undisguisedly present
in Bürger's work, but beyond that, Bürger sought his inspiration in a
number of specific literary models. From his earliest days as a
student of Klotz's at Halle, he had taken singular pleasure in the
adaption, recasting, and reshaping of an already extant work, to
the point where it took on the unmistakable stamp of his own
poetic genius. The case of "Christus in Gethsemane" (now lost) is a
case of influence (Klopstock); the "Nachtfeier der Venus," one of
adaptation. Throughout his life, Bürger was almost always at work
on the adaptation of one or the other work, and at least in an indirect,
circuitous way, the course of his literary career is reflected in the
types of models he chose and the manner in which he adapted them
—from the fragile but deceptive grace of the "pervigilium Veneris"
to the Rococo delicacy of "La Reine de Golconde," to the prosaic
translation of Benjamin Franklin's autobiography (and the "Republik England"). To the middle years belong Ossian and Shakespeare,
but no major work ever occupied Bürger over so long a period as
did Homer.

Like the "Nachtfeier der Venus," the *Iliad* held a deep and
lasting fascination for Bürger, although all his efforts over a period
of some seventeen years only yielded a torso of the epic in translation. During the years 1767–1784 Bürger worked intermittently on
his translation, and ultimately, he produced a considerable volume
of material, primarily from the first six books. Many of the selections he translated twice, the first time in iambics and the second
time in hexameters. During the same years, Bürger devoted an
almost equal amount of time to commenting on the work and the
metrical treatment he felt it demanded.

Bürger's early interest in the *Iliad* dates from the time he was a

166

student of Klotz, probably late in 1768. In his essay "Etwas über eine deutsche Übersetzung des Homers" ("Thoughts regarding a German Translation of Homer"), which he submitted as part of his application for admission to membership in the Deutsche Gesellschaft in Göttingen (1769), Bürger presented his earliest thoughts on a translation of the *Iliad*. He stressed the importance of establishing the illusion that the past was vital and immediate, and that the reader should not have the impression that he was reading a translation. At the same time, the reader should have a sense of antiquity, and the translator should avail himself of certain archaisms—not those which are unknown, but those which are familiar and convey the flavor of the past.

The choice between prose and verse was a difficult one, and Bürger acknowledged that some of the best critics (Riedel and Klotz (!)) had maintained that Homer should either be translated in prose or not at all, but he maintained his own position and noted that this is a point, "dem ich doch im ganzen nicht beistimme" ("with which I don't entirely agree").[1] Bürger did agree with Klotz in rejecting a translation in hexameters, unless it could be done by a poet with the gift or greatness of a Denis (the Austrian translator of *Ossian*) or Pope. Indeed, a translation in prose, for all its faults, would be preferable to a translation into hexameters: "Eine langweilige Monotonie werden sie [die Hexameter] verursachen" ('hexameters will give rise to a dreary monotony').[2]

Two years later (1771), Bürger published his essay "Gedanken über die Beschaffenheit einer deutschen Übersetzung des Homer, nebst einigen Probefragmenten" ('Thoughts on the Nature of a German Translation of Homer, together with a few Samples'). The essay reiterated much of what Bürger had said earlier. It recognized the universal desire to have a "German Homer" and expressed the hope that a man of such genius and knowledge might appear, one who could step between the factions with a translation, over which might be written, "Sacred to Posterity and Eternity."[3] Bürger regarded it as a patriotic duty to make Homer available and accesible to Germany.

Bürger stresses, as he had before, the need of creating the illusion that Homer had been an ancient German who had sung in German,[4] and that the translator should use archaic words, not because they are better, but *"weil sie alt sind"* ("because they are old").[5] The purpose is to create a Homeric *Iliad* and not a reflection thereof; and Bürger asserts that Pope created an *Iliad*, but "Homers *Iliade* ist es nicht" ("Homer's *Iliad* it is not").[6]

The essay contains two new ideas, which were to become basic to Bürger's general thoughts on translation, and which serve to mark his adaptations as works singularly his own: in the first place, he urges the translator to ennoble or elevate, "Ich glaube, man wird größtenteils wohltun, wenn man den homerischen Ausdruck, der uns lächerlich und unedel klingt, zu adeln sucht" ("I believe one will, for the most part, do well if one seeks to ennoble the Homeric expression which sounds comic or base to us").[7] Bürger gives himself considerable latitude in this regard as he does in the matter of actual translation: 'No one should attempt to translate simply according to the dictionary; that certainly is not translating, and the result would be laughable.'[8] Appropriately, Bürger insists that the translator must discover the proper German expression to fit the thought of the original.

When Bürger turned his attention to the question of meter, his argument was fundamentally the same as before. The translator must compose for his German audience, and that does not mean translating into hexameter. To support his stand, Bürger looked to Herder, who also rejected translation from the Greek into hexameters. For Bürger the obvious and ideal meter for a German *Iliad* was the iambic. In his insistence on iambs, he was challenging the hegemony of Klopstock and the hexameter, although Cramer managed to win a reluctant nod of approval from Klopstock when he read him part of Bürger's translation in April, 1773.

Bürger had hoped to create something of a stir with his samples, but there was little response, and the translation was put aside until 1776, when the first three hundred lines or so of the Fifth Book were published. It was this translation that attracted Goethe's attention and prompted the gift of the 65 Louis d'or. Bürger then submitted the entire Sixth Book, which was published in Wieland's *Teutscher Merkur* (1776). Until this time, Bürger's militance regarding iambs had elicited little reaction, but now, with Goethe's open support, the matter took on a different character, and Klopstock and other writers set about opposing Bürger's position. The latter replied with his "Bürger an einen Freund über seine deutsche Ilias" (Bürger to a Friend about His German *Iliad*"—1776), in which he once again stoutly defended his stance. The letter offers almost nothing that is new to Bürger's original argument, but it is of considerable interest in demonstrating his ability to construct original dramatic dialogue. The give and take is surprisingly real and the conversation flows with extraordinary ease. The tempo is rapid, the exchanges are interrupted, the language is vital and realistic, and the whole is both lively and engaging.

One enlightening point which may throw some light on Bürger's almost intransigent position, emerges from the letter-essay-dialogue, and that is the suggestion that a German *Iliad* in iambs would be more popular and attract a larger audience, that it might be, "nicht für den Gelehrten allein, sondern fürs ganze Volk" ("not simply for the scholar, but for all the people").[9] In other words, it might sell better.

Bürger's opposition was of two kinds: the theoretical (Klopstock, Bodmer, et al.) and the practical; and in the long run, the effect of the latter was more telling. In his *Deutsches Museum* Boie published Stolberg's hexameter translation of the Twentieth Book, and Bürger began to read the handwriting on the wall. He had already begun to lose interest in the project, and work was progressing slowly. What he had *promised* to do, others were actively doing, and doing it in hexameters. Despite Bürger's flamboyant pronouncements, he set his translation aside once more and did not take it up again until 1783. In 1781 Stolberg's translation went into its second edition and Voß's version of the *Odyssey* appeared, as did Wobeser's *Iliad*. Prodded into action by these external stimuli Bürger (as might have been expected) finally returned to his translation in 1783, and with blithe insouciance he announced his intention to publish his translation of the *Iliad* in Goeckingk's *Journal von und für Deutschland*—in hexameters. In the course of 1784, Bürger did, in fact, bring out in hexameters the fragments he had earlier rendered in iambs, but the enthusiastic response he had anticipated failed to materialize, and with that Bürger finally lost all interest in the *Iliad*. Goethe, presumably, did not even raise an eyebrow.

Given the inordinate amount of time Bürger devoted to his work on the *Iliad,* it seems appropriate to cite at least half a dozen lines in order to give some idea of what he was trying to do. The two versions—in iambs and in hexameters—may then be compared

with Voß's version. The selection is taken from the beginning of the
First Book:

> *Iambs:*
> *Sing, Göttin, den unsel 'gen Groll Achills,*
> *Des Sohnes Peleus, welcher tausend Weh'*
> *Auf die Achaeer lud, ins Todtenreich*
> *So vieler Starken tapfere Seelen trieb*
> *Und ihre Leichen hin, ein Raubmal, warf*
> *Den Hunden und den Aaren allzumal.*

(/Sing, Goddess, the unholy rage of Achilles, the son of Peleus, who brought
a thousand woes upon the Achaeans, drove so many strong ones, brave
souls forth into the realms of the dead, and cast their bodies, a feast of
prey to the dogs and the eagles together./)

> *Hexameters:*
> *Göttin, singe den Zorn des Peleiden Achilleus,*
> *Jenen verderblichen, welcher den Griechen unnennbares Weh schuf,*
> *Viele tapfere Seelen der Helden dem Aides zustieß,*
> *Ihre Leichnam' aber den Hunden und allem Gevögel*
> *Dar zum Raubmahl bot. So ward Zeus Wille vollendet;*

(/Goddess, sing the rage of the Peleidian Achilles, /That despoiler, who
created for the Greeks unnamable woe,/ Thrust many brave souls of the
heroes to Hades/ Proffered their bodies to the dogs and all manner of birds/
For feast of prey. Thus was the will of Zeus accomplished./)

> Voß

> *Singe, o Göttin, den Zorn des Peleiaden Achilleus,*
> *Ihn, der entbrannt den Achaiern unnennbaren Jammer erregte,*
> *Und viel tapfere Seelen der Heldensöhne zum Ais*
> *Sendete, aber sie selber zum Raub ausstreckte den Hunden*
> *Und dem Gevögel umher: so ward Zeus Wille vollendet.*

(/Sing, O Goddess, the rage of the Peleidian Achilles,/ Him who, enraged,
caused the Achaeans unnamable misery/ And sent many brave souls of the
heroes' sons to Hades/ But [their bodies] he offered as prey to the dogs,/
And all manner of birds about: thus was Zeus' will accomplished./)

Bürger later confided that he could have spent his time better, and unfortunately, his efforts have not been accorded a significant place among the many German versions of Homer. Moreover, there were sizable gaps in Bürger's knowledge of Greek, which did not make his task easier. As Gleim later said, "Einem Genius, wie Sie, konnte nicht schwerer seyn, ein Original zu werden, als ein Copist. Mich wundert's nicht wenig, daß ein Bürger zu so saurer und undanckbarer Arbeit sich entschlossen hat." ("It could not be more difficult for a genius like you to become an original poet than to become a copyist. I am not a little astonished that a Bürger embarked upon such a sour and thankless task.")[10] Wurzbach concluded that the scholarly value of Bürger's *Iliad* is even less than its poetic worth.'[11] Not all critics have been quite so harsh, however; A. W. Schlegel, Michael Bernays, and Siegfried Kadner all agree that Burger's *Iliad* was his only truly successful translation. It was the one time when Bürger was able, "sich dem Geist des Originals zu fügen" ("to fit himself into the spirit of the original").[12]

By the time Bürger finally put away his work on the *Iliad,* he had spent some fifteen years on it. His project to produce a German *Ossian,* however, only covered a brief span of some six months—between November, 1778, and early summer, 1779— though, during that short time, the flames of his enthusiasm burned with characteristic heat. Bürger's original acquaintance with *Ossian* dated from the early 1770s, though whether he had actually read the works or had only heard about them cannot be firmly established.[13] By 1775 he must surely have read *Ossian,* both Denis's translation and Hahn's translation of "Carric—thura" (which appeared in the *Deutsches Museum* in March of that year). In 1776 a list of his favorite authors included Shakespeare—"the Bible of poets"—Ossian, and Ariosto.[14] Although Bürger was apparently enraptured with *Ossian,* the first mention of his intention to produce his own translation came in early November, 1778.[15] Boie advised strongly against the plan, maintaining that there were too many translations already, but Bürger had been inspired, and it was too late to redirect his energies—as Boie tried vainly to do by suggesting a new volume of poems.[16]

At some point between December 3, 1778 and January 14, 1779, Bürger managed to persuade the Berlin publisher Christian Friedrich Himburg to bring out the *Ossian,* and moreover, to pay Bürger the very handsome sum of 100 ducats. The first part of 1779 was almost entirely taken up with work on *Ossian,* although for some unfathomable reason Bürger was having difficulty making up his mind to sign the contract with Himburg. "Himburg oder Limburg," wrote Goeckingk in March, "for 100 ducats you can't afford not to sign."[17] Boie's advice was essentially the same. "Wenn du 100 Ducaten oder mehr bekommen kannst, so übersetz in Gottes Namen den Ossian, zumal es dir nicht sauer wird" ("If you can get 100 or more ducats, then, for God's sake, translate Ossian, especially since it is easy for you").[18] The contract was never signed, however, and in May, 1779, Bürger wrote to Dieterich that they should discuss publication of *Ossian.*[19] His comments throbbed with excitement for the project, but he had already lost interest, and when Boie inquired early in September about progress with the translation (even offering, with Stolberg, to contribute to it), Bürger replied laconically, "Mein Ossian hat eine Zeitlang geruhet" ("My Ossian has been resting for a while").[20] Thus ended Bürger's plan to translate the "König der Lieder." Boie published "Carric-thura" in the *Deutsches Museum* in July, 1779, but Bürger took no notice of it.

Bürger contended that the available German versions of *Ossian* were inadequate or faulty, or both, and he proposed to furnish a translation that "for the next fifty or hundred years will take the wind out of the sails of any Christian who thinks he can do a better job."[21] Like so many of the translation projects, it was never completed, but Bürger did complete three sections, "Carric-thura," "Komala," and "Kath-Loda." These three were done in prose, and a very short "Klage um Karthon" ("Lament for Karthon") was done in verse.

Bürger approached his task with a fairly clear view of what he intended to do, and, in contrast to many of his other adaptations, he realized that with *Ossian* he would be translating from a translation. Like his contemporaries, he believed that he was dealing with genuine Celtic songs which Macpherson had laboriously and meticulously translated into English, and that it was imperative to reprouce these songs as faithfully as possible, that they should not be contaminated in the process. As a consequence, Bürger's treatment of *Ossian* adheres much more closely to the original than many of his other translations.[22]

For "Carric-thura" Bürger translated and supplied the "Argument" ("Inhalt"), but he did not do so for either of the other two sections.

It was not terribly missed for "Komala," which is a dramatic poem and relatively self-contained, but the lack of an "Argument" for the "Kath-Loda" places a considerable strain on the uninitiated reader. Bürger also supplied explanatory footnotes, signing them "B", but almost without exception they are taken verbatim, and without acknowledgment, from Macpherson's own footnotes.

Macpherson first published *Fingal, An Ancient Epic Poem, in Six Books, with other Lesser Poems* in 1762. Immediately it attracted widespread attention, but the critical response was sharply divided. Moreover, it soon became clear that the central issue was not the poetic merit of the work, but its provenance and authenticity. Several of the London literati branded it a hoax,[23] and Dr. Johnson, who was never favorable to the literary efforts of the "barbarous north," maintained (in his *Journey to the Western Islands*) that "the poems of Ossian never existed in any other form than that which we have seen," and that "the editor or author never could show the original, nor can it be shewn by any other." Some years later (in 1807) the Highland Society of London did, in fact, publish the Gaelic originals, but by then the question had become almost academic. As for Macpherson, he was little moved by the arguments, either pro or con; he flourished and prospered; and when he died in 1796 he was buried in Westminster Abbey.

Macpherson maintained that *Ossian* had survived in an oral tradition, and that his task had been to listen to, transcribe, compile, and finally to edit the material for publication. Inevitably, much editing had to be done, but Macpherson refrained almost entirely from superimposing his own broad classical education on the work and from introducing any classical allusions or images into it. Classical influences on *Ossian* have been considerably overemphasized and specifically the influence of Homer. On close examination, moreover, it is clear that the underlying spirit of the two works differ markedly: Homer is filled with the vitality of life and animacy of Nature; Ossian, on the other hand, always projects a slightly melancholy attitude towards life and Nature.[24]

In additon to classical influences the Bible has also been cited for its influence on *Ossian* but again, the differences are basic. *Ossian* is purportedly the product of a very primitive culture. As such it depicts a stage in the development of civilization anterior to that of the Bible. Macpherson himself pointed out that there are no divine beings worshiped by his heroes, but beyond that, there are numerous differences. The orchards, the well-cared-for fields, and the spices, so common in the Bible, as well as the cities with their markets and temples, are nowhere to be found in *Ossian*. *Ossian* represents a less advanced era when man was still quasi-nomadic in his habits. It was a hunt-oriented society rather than agrarian, and the needs and outlooks of the two differ significantly. Finally, the Bible is the product of a thoroughly southern climate, whereas *Ossian* depicts the roaring winds and blazing hearths of a harsh and rugged northern climate.

It is not surprising, in view of the many social and environmental differences, that the literary style of *Ossian* differs from both Homer and the Bible. One of the many characteristic features which distinguish *Ossian* is a heavy reliance on genitives, and Bürger's attempts to carry them over into German were manful, but not altogether successful:

The moon came forth in the east. Fingal returned in the gleam of his arms. The joy of his youth was great, their souls settled, as a sea from a storm. Ullin raised the song of gladness. The hills of Inistore rejoiced. The flame of the oak arose; and the tales of heroes are told.[25]

Bürger: Der Mond ging im Osten hervor. In blinkender Rüstung kam Fingal zurück. Groß war die Wonne der Seinen. Ihre Seelen beruhigten sich, wie nach dem Sturme das Meer. Ullin stimmte ein Freudenlied an. Die Hügel von Init-Tore frohlockten. Die Flamme der Eiche wuchs an, und Heldensagen wurden erzählt.

For the most part, Bürger retains original compounds: soft-rolling eyes ("sanft rollende Augen") or car-borne Annir ("des erlauchten Annir"). In general he also resists his natural inclination for using expletives. Syntactically, Bürger demonstrates great adroitness and grace:

Frothal heard the words of Fingal, and saw the rising maid: they stood in silence, in their beauty: like two young trees of the plain, when the shower of spring is on their leaves, and the loud winds are laid.

Bürger: Frothal hörte Fingals Worte und sah das empor sich raffende Mädchen. Schweigend standen beide jetzt in ihrer Schönheit da, wie zwei junge Bäume der Aue, wenn ihr Laub von Frühlingsregen trieft und der laute Sturm nun schweigt.

At the time Bürger took up the task of translating *Ossian,* a number of translations were already available, as Boie noted, including versions by Baron Edmund de Harold, Lenz, and Hahn, in addition to Denis, who remained the most popular at the time. Bürger's version, despite the fact that it remained incomplete, is a successful blend of linguistic skill and poetic gift. As Horstmeyer puts it,

Wenn Bürgers Übersetzung auch nicht die Schönheit und Ausgeglichenheit der Goetheschen "Lieder von Selma" [in *Werther*] erreicht, so darf sie doch —nächst der Goetheschen—für die beste ossianische Prosadichtung des 18. Jahrhunderts gelten.[26]

(/If Bürger's adaptation does not quite achieve the beauty and smoothness of Goethe's "Songs of Selma," it may, nonetheless, be regarded—next to Goethe's adaptation—as the best Ossianiac prose of the eighteenth century./)

Of the many translations and adaptations that Bürger made during the course of his career, none offers more points for discussion, debate, and speculation than *Macbeth.* The situation is complicated, however, by the fact that one of the basic texts from which Bürger worked (the translation-qua-adaptation by F. L. Schröder), has never been published and exists only in a single manuscript in the Mannheim Theater Archive.[27] Bürger's heavy reliance on Schröder was detailed in a dissertation by Kurt Kauenhowen (Königsberg, 1915), and since that time all scholarship on Bürger's *Macbeth* has depended on that study. At the same time, it appears that no more recent research has been undertaken with the Schröder Manuscript.

The origin of Bürger's involvement with *Macbeth* may be traced to his profound admiration for Shakespeare in general and, more specifically, to a letter from Boie written at the beginning of 1776, which conveys Schröder's request for an adaptation of the Witches' scenes.[28] Schröder had performed *Hamlet* with much success in Hannover and was planning a performance of *Macbeth;* both he and Boie felt that the inclusion of a really excellent adaptation of the Witches' scenes would add immeasurably to the success of the performance. Bürger was intrigued with the idea and within three days sent off to Boie the scenes requested. Encouraged by Bürger's (uncharacteristic) promptness, Boie and Schröder now suggested that Bürger prepare a full-scale version of the drama, which Schröder would use in lieu of his own. Schröder envisaged putting it into rehearsal almost immediately. Bürger's response was somewhat less enthusiastic, but he agreed and set to work. In his earlier correspondence with Boie he had expressed some dissatisfaction with the Eschenburg translation (1776), but now he had also Schröder's translation to work from. He found it generally satisfactory structurally, but less so linguistically. He also had Wieland's translation at hand, and Professor Heyne had sent him a copy of Bell's Edition of *Shakespeare's Plays* (London, 1774). In spite of the abundance of texts to work from—or perhaps because of them —Bürger's interest flagged, and work on the project came to a halt. Schröder had hoped to perform the work in the spring of 1777, yet on January 1, 1778, Boie brought up the question with some trepidation: "Nach dem *Macbeth* darf ich wohl nicht fragen" ("I probably shouldn't ask about *Macbeth*").[29] Indeed, he should not have. The whole matter had become a sore point with Bürger, who replied caustically that it was proceeding as it should, which, of course, it was not. A year later, in January, 1779, Schröder was still waiting, but he complained that, having acted on Bürger's recent assurances, he had costumes, sets, and music in a state of readiness, but not a single line of the drama itself. Even Bürger had little to reply to that. There the matter stood[30] until 1782. In February of that year, Bürger finally completed the adaptation and sent it off to his publisher, Dieterich, with the comment that "Ich muß jetzt meine Talente zu Gelde machen" ("I now have to turn my talents to cash").[31] Evidently no cash was forthcoming,[32] but *Macbeth* went through two editions within as many years (1783, 1784).

In preparing his adaptation, Bürger adhered to the broad outlines of Shakespeare's drama, but followed his general practice of expanding or condensing, supposedly in order to achieve a greater dramatic effect. Some of the changes found in the earlier parts of Bürger's version, such as the encounter between the King's Halberdier and the Soldier (I.2), were compromises worked out with Schröder for economic reasons. Schröder's budget simply would not allow a wholly uncut stage performance. The changes which occur later in the play, however, were introduced at Bürger's pleasure. As he replied to one of Boie's inquiries: "Indessen ist schon vieles dran geschehen. Außer Sprache, Form und Weglassungen habe ich hie und da eine neue Scene hinzugethan. . . . die Lady stirbt im Shakespeare so kurz weg. Ich habe sie erst ein bischen zappeln lassen, daß einem die Haare zu Berge stehen." ('In the meantime, a lot has happened to it [*Macbeth*]. Besides language, form, and deletions, I have introduced here and there a new scene. . . . Lady Macbeth dies too abruptly in Shakespeare. I let her thrash about a bit first, so that your hair will stand on end.')[33]

The drama opens with the Witches' scene and conveys the same atmosphere of mystery and fatefulness as Shakespeare's second scene. However, with its rather large cast, including Malcolm, Duncan, Donalbain, and Lenox, Schröder regarded it as an unnecessary expense, and he tried to persuade Bürger to tie Shakespeare's first and third scenes together. Bürger balked, and the exchange between the Halberdier and Soldier was apparently the compromise agreed upon. The scene could be (and probably was originally) played on a bare stage, the only stage direction being "Sounds of the Battle from the rear," and the two actors approach each other from opposite sides of the stage. Upon inquiry about the progress of the battle, the Soldier replies that it is too late for any help. To the former's cry of distress, however, he proclaims that the battle has been won, not lost; but as the Halberdier is about to rush back to inform the King, the Soldier claims that it was all a lie. The suggestion of a lie turns out to have been a ruse to detain the Halberdier, so that the Soldier can give an account of the battle. With much condensation, Bürger then returns and picks up the description of the battle by the soldier in Shakespeare, I.2. Perhaps in order to give the Soldier more character or identity, Bürger has him ask that the news of the victory be forwarded to the king from "Harold, who, though no General, has done his part." Scene Three returns to the Witches and ends with their chorus in unison. Macbeth and Banquo enter the stage (Scene Four), and the Witches' predictions are faithfully rendered. Macbeth is hailed as Thane of Glamis, Thane of Cawdor, and future king, while Banquo is greeted as less than Macbeth, but greater; less fortunate, but happier; a progenitor of kings, but not himself a king. As they speculate on the meaning of these sayings, Rosse and his retinue (Bürger elimi-

nated Angus entirely) arrive from a meeting with the King, who has
heard the news of Macbeth's heroism in gaining the victory and
has named him Thane of Cawdor. The First Act (Scene Six) concludes with a return to the Witches, who comment ominously
on Macbeth's reaction (Bürger's invention):

> Fischchen lockt der Angelbissen
> Gold und Hoheit das Gewissen

(/The bait lures the little fish; gold and grandeur lures the conscience./)

The first scene of Act II follows roughly the fifth scene of Act
I and is a conversation between Macbeth and Lady Macbeth,
who has learned of the prophecy and is determined to make it come
true. The speeches are partly Shakespeare's and partly Bürger's, but
their sequence runs almost directly counter to the original, although
the intent of the original scene is approximated. It is, in effect, a
composite of Shakespeare and Bürger, where one hears and recalls
numerous familiar strains. Lady Macbeth plots evil and drives her
husband into complicity, though she has misgivings:

> Ich fürchte, ich fürchte deine milchichte Gemütsart.
> Sie is zu voll von menschlicher Güte.

(/I fear, I fear, thy milky disposition. It is too full of human goodness./)

Shakespeare: Yet I do fear thy nature;/ It is too full o' the milk of human
kindness.

Shakespeare's Lady Macbeth is hardly drawn as an attractive
figure, but Bürger borrows an additional negative quality from
Eschenburg (who rarely indulged in interpolation) by allowing her
to make the stipulation, "Das mußt du tun, wenn du mich haben
willst!" ("That thou must do, if thou wouldst have me!")

The second scene of Act II is a combination of Shakespeare's
I.4 and I.6. It takes place in a park in front of Macbeth's palace
(in the day rather than at night) and begins with an exchange between
Banko and Rosse (instead of Shakespeare's Duncan and Banquo,
respectively). With Banko's remark that Duncan has named
Malcolm heir to the throne, the scene has reverted to Shakespeare's

I.4, the conversation between Duncan and Macbeth. (Bürger eliminated Duncan entirely from the play, possibly at Schröder's behest.) Act II, Scene Three, follows rather more faithfully the events of Shakespeare's I. 7. Macbeth, having absented himself from table and being in a state of near despair, is interrupted in his morose reflections by Lady Macbeth, who will hear nothing of hesitation or doubt, though her scathing demand (in Shakespeare) that he "screw [his] courage to the sticking place" is hardly matched by Bürger's appropriation of Eschenburg's limp rendering, ". . . nur muthig gerad' auf das Ziel, so kann's nicht mißlingen!" ('. . . just courageously straight on to the target, thus it cannot fail').

Lady Macbeth finally succeeds in rousing her husband, and with his announcement, "I am settled . . .," Shakespeare ends Act I. Bürger, however, is in the middle of his own Act II, and before proceeding to Shakespeare's Act II, he interjects a monologue by Banko (II.4). At the conclusion of Bürger's II.2, Banko had announced his intention of spending the night outside, and now he awakens from a troubled sleep and comments on the apprehension his dreams have aroused in him. The Witches' prophecies weigh heavily on him, and implicitly he expresses the fear that others may 'assist' Nature in bringing about their fulfillment. The scene seems to have been inspired by Eschenburg's footnote to Shakespeare's I.1: "Man sieht aus dem Folgenden, daß Banquo in einem Traume aufgemuntert war, etwa zur Erfüllung der Weissagung der Hexen zu unternehmen, wovor er sich beim Wachen entsetzte; und Shakespeare macht hier zwischen seinem und Macbeth's Charakter einen sehr schönen Kontrast."[34]

Bürger's invention of this scene and his insertion of it directly before that which contains Macbeth's "Is this a dagger I see before me? . . . and wicked dreams abuse/ The curtain'd sleeper," would suggest Bürger's intent to stress the contrast between the characters of Banquo and Macbeth as suggested by Eschenburg. Such a contrast is, in fact, achieved, since Bürger's vocabulary in Banko's monologue anticipates Macbeth's speech in the following scene. The vocabulary is much the same in both speeches, but used in very different contexts. At the conclusion of Banko's monologue, he can again lie down to pleasant dreams, whereas Macbeth will soon claim he has murdered sleep. The sixth scene of Bürger's version (Shakespeare II.1) is, to all intents and purposes, simply

Macbeth's monologue: "Is this a dagger . . .?" The German text
is quite straightforward in following the original, but Bürger
attempts to heighten the dramatic effect by including expletives,
"Hahhh!, Bei Gott!" etc. The remainder of Bürger's Act II covers,
in general, the material in Shakespeare's II.2 and II.3, with
inclusions from II.2 and II.4. The dialogue between Macduff and
Lenox in Shakespeare (II.3) takes place between Macduff and
Banko, however, since Lenox had been deleted.

The action advances through the assassination of Duncan, the
discovery of the corpse by Macduff, Lady Macbeth's fainting, and
the announcement of the flight of the Princes. The King's gift of a
diamond to Lady Macbeth (Shakespeare II.1) is recalled in the
dialogue between Macduff and Banko. The incidents, dialogues, and
individual speeches, however, are culled from all four of Shakespeare's scenes without any concern for their original sequence. Jux-
taposition, deletion, and invention abound; direct address becomes
indirect speech, and vice versa; characters are substituted for those
Bürger had deleted (Banko for Lenox, Malcolm for Donalbain) or
simply replaced for the sake of the action. The opening of Bürger's
II.7 characterizes the kind of freedom taken in the adaptation. It
approximates Shakespeare's II.2:

BÜRGER:

(Ein Diener mit einer brennenden Fackel geht über die Bühne nach der
Seite, wo geklopft wird. Macduff und Banko treten auf.)

    Macduff.   Gingt ihr so spät zu Bette, Freund, daß ihr so lange
schlaft?
    Diener.   Wahrhaftig, Sir, wir schwärmten bis zum zweiten Hahnschrei.
    Macduff.   Ist dein Herr noch nicht bei der Hand?
    Diener.   Ich will ihn wecken. (Ab.)
    Banko.   Das war mir eine gräßliche Nacht! Von fünfzig Jahren her
kann ich mich noch wohl besinnen, und in dieser langen Zeit habe ich
fürchterliche Stunden und seltsame Dinge erlebt; aber diese Nacht hat Alles,
was ich vormals kannte, zu Kleinigkeiten gemacht.
    Macduff.   Wenn sie hier haben schlafen können, so segne Gott ihren
gesunden Schlaf. Auf dem Flügel, wo ich lag, stürmte es den Schorn-
stein herunter, und wie der Wächter sagt, hörte man Wimmern in der Luft,
und gräßliches Todtengeheul. Er ist ein alter, eisgrauer Kriegsknecht,
der sich rühmt, viel erfahren zu haben, und sich auf die Deutung solcher

Dinge zu verstehen. Er ließe sich rädern, daß es Vorläute blutiger Begeben-
heiten und gräßlicher Verheerungen sind.

Banko.   Der Uhu heulte die ganze Nacht durch, und mich dünkt, die
Erde selbts hat im Fieberschauer gezittert. (Macbeth kommt.) Seht, da
kommt unser Wirth. Guten Morgen, Lieber!

Macbeth.   Guten Morgen, meine Freunde!

Macduff.   Rührt sich der König noch nicht?

Macbeth.   Noch nicht.

Macduff.   Er befahl mir, ihn frühzeitig zu wecken. Beinahe hab' ich
die Stunde schon versäumt.

Macbeth.   Ich will Euch zu ihm führen.

Macduff.   Ich weiß, es wäre Euch eine angenehme Mühe. Aber Mühe
bleibt es doch immer.

Macbeth.   Angenehme Arbeit versüßt die Mühe. Hier ist die Tür.

Macduff.   Ich will so dreist sein, zu rufen; denn ist's mir befohlen.
(Ab.)

Banko.   Reist der König heut wieder ab?

Macbeth.   Bestellt hat er es wenigstens so.

Banko.   Er ist gestern abend außerordentlich fröhlich gewesen, und
hat deine Hausbedienten ansehnlich beschenkt. Diesen prächtigen Diamant
befahl er mir deiner Gemahlin für ihre so freundliche Bewirthung heut zu
geben, und ging ausnehmend vergnügt in sein Schlafgemach.

(A servant carrying a burning torch goes across the stage to the side, where
there has been a knocking. Macduff and Banko enter.)

Macduff.   Did you go to bed so late, Friend, that you sleep so long?

Servant.   Faith, Sir, we carried on until the second cry of the cock.

Macduff.   Is your Master not yet about?

Servant.   I'll waken him. (Exit.)

Banko.   That was a terrible night for me. A span of fifty years I can
recall with accuracy, and in this long time I have experienced fearful
hours and strange things; but this night has turned everything I
formerly knew to trifles.

Macduff.   If they have been able to sleep here, then God bless their
healthy sleep. In the wing where I was, the chimney blew down, and as the
watchman says, one heard moans in the air and dreadfully mournful
howling. He is an old, ice-gray warrior, who prides himself on having
lived through many things, on having learned much and who understands
the significance of such things. He would stake his life on it, that these
are forecasts of bloody happenings and dreadful devastation.

Banko.   The owl howled all night long, and methinks, the earth itself

shivered as in a fever chill. (Macbeth enters) See, here comes our host.
Good morning, Old Friend.

Macbeth.   Good morning, my friends.

Macduff.   Has the King not stirred yet?

Macbeth.   Not yet.

Macduff.   He commanded me to awaken him early. I have nearly missed
the hour.

Macbeth.   I will take you to him.

Macduff.   I know it would be a pleasant task, but a task it remains all
the same.

Macbeth.   A pleasant task makes the effort sweet. Here is the door.

Macduff.   I shall be so bold as to call; for thus I have been commanded.
(Exit.)

Banko.   Is the King leaving today?

Macbeth.   He has arranged to, at least.

Banko.   He was extraordinarily happy last evening, and was munifi-
cent in bestowing gifts on your household staff. This superb diamond he
ordered me to give to your wife today for her most gracious hospitality, and
then, exceedingly contented, he went to his bed chamber.

A close examination of this passage reveals Bürger's general
approach and technique in adapting *Macbeth* for his German
audience. He consistently sought to electrify or horrify his audience,
'to make their hair stand on end.' The repeated use of words like
"gräßlich" and "Fieberschauer" almost inevitably calls to mind the
vocabulary of "Der wilde Jäger" or "Lenore." Whether for
economic or aesthetic reasons, Bürger's liberties with the original
were considerable.

The final scene of Act II returns to a barren region with thunder
and lightning. Bürger composed the scene specifically to reintro-
duce the Witches and conclude the act on a highly dramatic note.
The three Witches comment on the murder of Duncan and the
further consequences which that deed will have:

Alle.

> Königsblut soll seinen Rachen
> Unersättlich lüstern machen.
> Blut erhitzt des Räd'rers Wuth,
> Reitzt den Durst nach frischem Blut
> Dolch und Hand wird blutig bleiben,
> Trotz dem Waschen, trotz dem Reiben.

(/Royal blood shall make its revenge/Insatiably tempting./Blood fires up the executioner's wrath,/ Whets the thirst for more blood./ Dagger and hand will remain bloody/ Despite the washing or the rubbing.)

Each of the Witches sings a stanza, followed by the choral refrain and dance:

> *Lust in Unlust, das ist Lust!*
> *Kraut und kitzelt uns die Brust.*

(/Pleasure in aversion, that is pleasure!/ Scratches and tickles our breast!/)

In comparison with the draconic changes introduced by Bürger into the first two acts, the final three acts seem to follow Shakespeare's original more closely. It might be reasonable to speculate in this regard that some time may have elapsed between the completion of Acts I and II, and Acts III – V. The final acts may have been completed some time late in 1781 or early in 1782, shortly before Bürger sent the finished manuscript to Dieterich (March, 1782).

Bürger's Act III opens with Banko's monologue, and is followed by Macbeth's appearance with his wife and company, at which time the invitation to the banquet is issued. The interview with the two murderers is only slightly changed. The banquet follows, and the guests are thrown into confusion and consternation by Macbeth's behavior, when he sees Banko's ghost. The final scene of the act takes place on the heath with the three Witches and the elder Witch. A "Hexenfrau" has replaced Hekate.

Bürger concluded Act III with the Witches' scene on the heath, and the scene with which Shakespeare ended Act III, the "exchange between Lenox and another Lord," is moved to Act IV, where it follows Macbeth's announcement to Rosse (Lenox) of his intention to slay Macduff's family. As in Shakespeare the act had begun with the Witches' scene, and Macbeth's conversation with the Witches is a relatively faithful rendering. In the scene with Lady Macduff, her son, and Rosse, Bürger remains close to Shakespeare, but has Rosse explicitly warn Lady Macduff to flee: "Ihr Gemahl ist edel, weise, bedächtlich, und weiß am besten, was die Zeit erfordert. Wäre ich Sie, ich—reiste ihm auf dem Fuß nach. Viel mehr darf ich nicht sagen." ("Your husband is noble, wise, careful, and knows best what the times demand. If I were you, I—should follow close after him. Much more I dare not say.") Apparently Bürger felt that such a remark would heighten the dramatic effect, and the same doubtless holds true for Rosse's parting from Lady Macduff, where Bürger has him disclose: "Mein Alles habe ich gewagt, mich hieher zu stehlen, und nur so viel zu sagen" ("I have dared my all to steal here, and only say that much"). Again Rosse gives the warning: "Was ich Ihnen rieth, Lady/ die Kinder mitgenommer.! Gott sei mit Ihnen!" ("Remember what I have advised you, My Lady, take the children with you! God be with you!")

In the original, Lady Macduff has neither time nor opportunity for escape, and Shakespeare brings the assassins on stage, where they murder the son and pursue the terrified mother as she makes her exit. Bürger revised the original and eliminated both the assassins' appearance and the murder. The murders are accomplished, however, before the dialogue between Rosse and Macduff takes place at the end of the following scene. The beginning of the scene, enacted between Malcolm and Macduff, is Bürger's equivalent to Shakespeare's IV.3, but in fairly jumbled fashion, with speeches expanded, contracted, and generally rearranged. Bürger omits the doctor and moves directly into the Rosse episode. Rosse's report and the remainder of the scene follow the original fairly closely, but, unfortunately, Bürger deleted the final sentence of the act: "Receive what cheer you may;/ The night is long that never finds the day." Presumably, he felt that " . . . and the powers above/ Put on their instruments" (which Bürger translates as "Die Schnitter dort oben greifen schon nach den Sicheln" – "The reapers above reach already for their scythes"), was a stronger statement with which to conclude the scene, and simultaneously, that it pointed to the action of Act V.

In terms of structure and sequence, Act V remains fairly close to Shakespeare. The second, fourth, and sixth scenes (the country near Dunsinane and the plain before the castle) may have seemed unnecessary to Bürger, and he deleted them. The contents of the two scenes are simply reported, instead. The death of Lady Macbeth, while also reported, is quite another matter. Although Bürger had displayed some delicacy in deleting the actual murder of Banko and Fleance, and the murder of Macduff's son, he showed no such hesitation in the case of Lady Macbeth. Rather he gave the audience ample opportunity for catharsis. The third scene is entirely of his own composition and includes a graphic description of the Queen's malady:

Das war ein Aufruhr in ihrem Bette! Wie mit halb erdrosselter Kehle rief sie: Hilfe! Hilfe! Dann gab's Ach und Krach. Als ich herzu lief, zuckte, röchelte und schnappte sie zum letzten Male. Was für Klauen ihr das Gesicht auf den Rücken gedreht, und die blauen Flecken gekniffen haben, mag der allmächtige Gott wissen.

(/There was a commotion in her bed. As with a half-strangled throat she cried, Help! Help! Then there was a terrible din. When I [the maid] came running up, she was having convulsions, gagging and gasping for air for the last time. What kind of claws have distorted her face, and pinched her black and blue—God only knows!/)

Fortunately, the scene is not prolonged, and the doctor leaves to inform Macbeth of his intention to attend the Queen. Macbeth, however, anticipates her death, and Bürger here weaves in Macbeth's "She would have died another time. There would have come a time for this report. Tomorrow and tomorrow and tomorrow . . . "

Seyton reports briefly on the state of affairs (the events of V.4), and Bürger moves directly into the fifth scene. The "cry of women" and Macbeth's "I have almost forgot the taste of fear" have been moved up by Bürger to precede the announcement of the Queen's seizure. Thus the movement proceeds from the speech, "Hang out our banners on the outward walls," directly to the last line of the scene. Bürger's fifth scene picks up in the middle of Shakespeare's V.7 (Macduff and the soldiers), then moves back to the beginning of V.7 with Macbeth appearing alone:

Sie haben mich gestellt wie einen Eber. Entfliehen kann ich nicht; ich muß fechten. Das will ich! bis mir das Fleisch von den Knochen abgehackt ist. Warum soll ich den tragischen Narren spielen, und in mein eigenes Schwert fallen? Nein!

(/They have cornered me like a boar. I cannot flee; I must fight. That I will do, until the flesh is hacked from my bones. Why should I play the tragic fool and fall upon my own sword? No!/)

Young Siward is portrayed anonymously, simply as an English Officer, but Bürger includes the duel between him and Macbeth, with the original outcome. Bürger then brings Macduff and Macbeth together in the eighth scene and introduces their dialogue with the lines directly following Shakespeare's "Why should I play the Roman fool?" Shakespeare's directions read, "Exeunt fighting," but this is too great an opportunity for Bürger to forego, and he has the duel take place on stage, with Macbeth falling, Macduff claiming victory and leaving, and then a final death scene for Macbeth:

Macbeth. (Sterbend) Ist das die Erfüllung?—Entsetzlich! O Hölle, daß ich mich von deinem Doppelsinne täuschen lassen mußte!—Meinen Ohren hast du Wort gehalten, nicht meinen Hoffnungen.—Verfluchter Ehrgeiz!—Nun ist's aus, das bunte Gaukelspiel! Der Vorhang rauscht! —Die Lichter verlöschen;—und ich erwache in dicker Finsternis, kalt angeweht von dem Grausen der Hölle.—Meine Seele watet im Blut! Im Blute der Unschuldigen!—Der Strom schwillt.—schwillt—hebt mich empor. —Ich kann mich nicht mehr halten.—Seufzer und Flüche brausen mir nach wie Stürme,—sie treiben,—sie wälzen,—mich wälzen die Wogen hinunter,—hinunter,—hinunter zieht mich die Hölle.—Oh!—Verloren bin ich. Auf ewig verloren!—Oh!—(Stirbt.)

(/Is that the fulfillment? Hideous! O Hell, that I had to let myself be deceived by thy double meaning! You've kept your word to my ears, but not to my hopes.—Accursed ambition! Now it's finished, the colorful spectacle! the curtain rustles! The lights go out;—and I awake in deep darkness, chilled by the horror of hell. My soul wades in blood!—In the blood of the innocent! —The river swells,—swells,—raises me up.—I can hold on no longer.—Sighs and curses thunder toward me like storms,—they drive me,—they toss me— they drag me under the waves,—down it draws me, to hell. Oh!—I am lost! Lost for all eternity!—Oh!—(Dies.))

With the arrival of Macduff, Malcolm, Rosse, Noblemen and Soldiers, the drama is swiftly, indeed abruptly, brought to a conclusion with three short speeches, almost entirely of Bürger's own making. Macduff points to Macbeth's corpse and tells Macduff: "Ihr Thron ist frei" ("Your throne is free"), roughly similar to Shakespeare's "the time is free." Malcolm acknowledges the greeting with a vow to pour balsam into the wounds of his shattered fatherland in order to heal the wounds caused by Macbeth. Macduff acclaims Malcolm's speech, and the entire cast responds, "Long live the King of Scotland," whereupon the curtain falls amidst the sounds of trumpets.

Bürger's involvement with *Macbeth* spanned a period of some six to seven years, and predictably, the quality of the work is uneven. As he acknowledged in the oft-quoted letter to his publisher, his many debts and personal problems forced him to turn his talents to money, and the nearly complete translation of *Macbeth* probably lay near at hand. By the time Bürger finished *Macbeth* it was long after Schröder had any need of it (the relationship between the two had cooled perceptibly), and Bürger dedicated the work to his childhood friend Johann Erich Biester, who became Royal Librarian in Berlin the following year (1784).

The first performance of Bürger's *Macbeth* took place in the Königliche National-Theater in Berlin in 1787 with Fleck in the title role and Karoline Döbbelin as Lady Macbeth. Over the next twenty years, it was performed some forty times, until eventually it was superseded by Schiller's version, which, in turn, succumbed to the Schlegel-Tieck translation. As with *Hamlet* and *Lear*, *Macbeth* was then billed as a "Schauspiel," and like them, was fitted with a conciliatory ending.[35]

To a very great extent, Bürger relied heavily on the translations by Wieland (1756) and Eschenburg (1775), and probably even more so on Schröder's adaptation. Bürger had looked at the translation by H. L. Wagner (1779), and he was at least aware of the translation (adaptation) by the Austrian poet Stephanie the Younger (1772), although he did not know Stephanie by name. While it is known that Bürger had a copy of Bell's *Shakespeare* and had access to the Pope-Warburton and Johnson editions, it is doubtful that (excepting the Witches' scenes) he based his own work, to any large degree, upon the English editions. A close examination of Bürger's version— compared line by line with the Wieland and Eschenburg translations —confirms his dependence on his German predecessors, including Schröder, who, according to Bürger's preface to his own work, also relied on Wieland and Eschenburg. Interestingly enough, in Bürger's IV.6 (equivalent to Shakespeare's IV.3) there are several echoes of Stephanie, though his influence elsewhere in Bürger's version is not discernible. The lineage would appear to be: Shakespeare—Wieland —(Stephanie)—Eschenburg—Bürger. Ultimately, both Eschenburg and Schröder were much in Wieland's debt, and it is not surprising, therefore, to find long passages in Bürger's version which run parallel to either Wieland or Eschenburg.

More important perhaps than determining Bürger's sources and appropriations is the need to establish in what respect Bürger's was an independent and original effort. What did he contribute? First and foremost in importance is his adaptation of the Witches' scenes, and these lay, as Bürger noted in his Introduction, at the very heart of his work. Wieland had gamely attempted a verse translation of the two scenes in Act I, but had entirely abandoned the attempt in III. 6 and IV.1. He paraphrased them and asserted in a footnote that they were impossible to translate into any language. Eschenburg, in turn, sought to render a more accurate version, but his prose is lifeless and awkward. It remained for Bürger to apply his linguistic and rhythmic virtuosity to the problem: "His love of strong rhythms and vigorous speech found a ready outlet in the Witches' incantations; and the grotesque as well as the fantastic elements clearly held a strong appeal for the poet who had already exploited such elements in ballad form."[36] Such lines as, "Double, double toil and trouble:/ Fire burn, and cauldron bubble," gave Bürger unique opportunity to let his genius erupt in that area where he could give his fantasy freest reign—at the semantic edges of language. What he achieved was a tour de force, seldom, if ever, equaled. Even so unsympathetic a critic as Friedrich Gundolf, who regarded Bürger with virtual disdain, conceded that, "wirklich produktiv war er hier auch in sprachlicher Hinsicht. Derbe Fülle und Saft kann man diesen Szenen nicht absprechen . . . " ("he was truly productive here also in a linguistic sense. The rough pith and marrow cannot be denied . . . ")[37] Simply in the lines, "Lodre, brodle, daß sich's modle,/ Lodre, Lohe, Kessel brodle!"—Bürger's translation of the above lines—there was the built-in invitation to match parallelism with parallelism, assonance with assonance; the Witches' scenes had a natural and irresistible appeal for Bürger; but the translation of the rest of the drama was drudgery.

The immediate reaction to Bürger's *Macbeth* was reassuringly favorable. Lichtenberg called it "vortrefflich" ("excellent"),[39] and Goeckingk was thrilled by the portions Bürger had read to him.[40] Other critics, both contemporary and posthumous, have been less generous, and A. W. Schlegel evidently had little hesitation about terming it, "das mißlungenste" ("the greatest failure") of all Bürger's works.[41]

Seven years after completing his adaptation of *Macbeth*, Bürger was once again encouraged to consider a Shakespearean translation. In the fall of 1789 he was persuaded by his young protégé, A. W. Schlegel, to begin a joint effort to translate *A Midsummer Night's Dream.* It was the first of Schlegel's translations, and one has the impression that he, not Bürger, was the moving force behind the effort. The play had not been popular with the *Stürmer und Dränger,* and its delicate character was difficult to transfer into German. Bürger's share in the work was minimal, although Michael Bernays maintained that it was his manner that established the overall tone of the work ("bestimmte seine Manier den Stil des Ganzen").[42]

The sum of Bürger's contribution totals less than 150 lines, and consists of six separate fragments taken from Acts II and III. Bürger avoided the lyric sections and confined himself almost entirely to the scenes involving Puck and his company. Many of the same liberties he had taken with *Macbeth,* he also took with *A Midsummer Night's Dream.* Generally, he expanded upon the original and introduced elements he must have felt added to the effectiveness of the work. Among other things, Bürger liked concrete images, and he introduced them whenever possible; thus the "mad spirit" (III.2) became "du Aff' der Affen" ("ape of apes") or "How now mad spirit!/ What night rule now?" (II.4) became "Du Arme, mit dem wärmsten Triebe" ("Thou poor girl with the strongest drives") or, the from the same scene, Oberon's "Wake, when some vile thing is near" (II.2) was expanded to "Sähest du doch beim Erwachen,/ Gleich den häßlichsten der Drachen" ("If thou shouldst see on waking,/ Straight off the ugliest of dragons").

Another liberty Bürger allowed himself was the "Germanization" of several of Shakespeare's names. In making these changes, Bürger showed little feeling for Shakespeare's underlying intentions. Puck became Droll, the Hobgoblin became "mein süßes Drollchen," but least successful was the change from Robin Goodfellow to Hans Haberschnack. Shakespeare's Peaseblossom, Cobweb, Moth, and Mustardseed all disappear or are fused into "Fee" ("Fairy"). Similarly, Shakespeare's "dewberries" (III.1) increase and multiply to "Melonen und Ananas" ("melons and pineapples") [!].

Bürger's translation of thirty-seven lines from II.1 was published in November, 1797, in the *Allgemeine Literatur Zeitung* (# 347) and a sampling of these lines affords a general picture of what Bürger was attempting:

Puck.   *And sometimes lurk I in a gossip's bowl,*
               In very likeness of a roasted crab.
               And, when she drinks against her lips I bob
               And on her withered dewlap pour the ale.
               The wisest aunt, telling the saddest tale,
               Sometime for three-foot stool mistaketh me;
               Then slip I from her bum down topples she, . . .

Droll.   *Bisweilen stehl' ich mich, mit schadenfrohem Sinn,*
               Ins liebe Buttelchen der Frau Gevatterin,
               Da lausch' ich in Gestalt der rothgebrühten Krabbe,
               Und fahr' ihr, wenn sie trinkt, auf einmal an die Labbe.
               Versprudelt wird alsdann das teure Cordial
               Auf's platte Außenwerk. Gibt wohl ein andermal
               Die hochwohlweise Bas' den hochgeehrten Gästen
               Ein Mordgeschichtchen ernst und andachtsvoll zum Besten,
               So stell' ich dreigebeint und ähnlich auf ein Haar
               Als ihren Sessel mich im nächsten Winkel dar.
               Bedächtig setzt sie—husch! vor den hochgeehrten
               Entschlüpf' ich ihr, und plumps! liegt sie auf ihrem Werthen.

(/Sometimes I steal with a mean mind,/ Into the nice little bottle of my
Mistress Neighbor,/ And there I lurk in the form of a boiled red crab,/
And when she drinks, I touch her on the lips,/ The precious cordial showers
then/ On her astonished face; Another time,/ Our high and learned friend
recites to her honored guests,/ A tale of murder seriously and solemnly,/
And then I place myself three-legged,—and just like it to a hair/ As her perch
in the nearest corner./ Prudently she sits down, and hush, before the honored
guests/ I slip out from under her, and bump! she's lying on her backside./)

Despite the unrewarding experience of a translation of a translation, the above passage reveals Bürger's general approach and
technique in his work on the *Sommernachtstraum*. These lines
were published as part of an announcement of Schlegel's own
translation. Presumably the writer of the article in the *Allgemeine
Literatur Zeitung* had gotten the fragment from Schlegel, "for
whom a comparison with the work of his famous predecessor
and mentor could only turn out to be highly advantageous."[43]
Like the other fragments, the few lines published reveal that
the spirit of Shakerpeare's play was simply alien to Bürger's
character, and that, in the final analysis, he could not grasp it. More-

over, they demonstrate Bürger's unfortunate and, doubtless, unintentional error in transforming a buoyant original into a rather crass and ponderous German, more suggestive of Hans Sachs than Shakespeare.

The completed *Macbeth* and the fragmentary portions of *A Midsummer Night's Dream* are all that have survived of Bürger's adaptations of Shakespeare. From his correspondence it appears that he either worked on or planned two other translations as well. In a letter to Boie from the end of June, 1775, Bürger writes that he has almost finished "Der wilde Jäger" and "Timon ['s Monologue]" —"Das sollen ein Paar Stücke werden—doch ich sage nichts." ("These should be a couple of [real] pieces—but I'm not saying a word").[44] In January of the following year, he may have sent Goethe a copy of the monologue, since he asks him how he likes it.[45] Goethe made no response, and the only other mention of the monologue came from Boie, who in March, 1778, inquired how it was progressing.[46]

It is difficult to determine exactly which speech in Shakespeare's *Timon of Athens* Bürger was working on, but in the letter to Goethe, in which he refers to Timon as "Gifftmichel" he also comments on the "ogres" who 'sniff and eat the flesh of children.' From that, it may be possible to assume that Bürger had in mind Timon's speech in IV.3, with the lines, "Engendered the black toad and adder blue,/ The gilded newt and eyeless venomed worm."

The only other Shakespearean work that Bürger expressed an even veiled interest in translating was *King Lear*—one of the most popular of Shakespeare's dramas in Germany during the latter part of the eighteenth century. The only reference to a possible plan for *King Lear* occurs in a letter to Boie written in January, 1777 (at a time when Bürger was fully involved with his work on *Macbeth*). With rare modesty Bürger doubted that he could do justice to *King Lear* and expressed the fear that it would be like robbing the church and that his version would be but copper to Shakespeare's gold.[47] Boie replied with his usual strong encouragement, but Bürger dropped the idea and never revived it.

It is one of the sad ironies of Bürger's fate that the one work, which is perhaps more widely known even than "Lenore," is almost never associated with his name except in academic circles. That work is the *Wunderbare Reisen zu Wasser und zu Lande,*

*Feldzüge und lustige Abenteuer des Freiherrn von Münchhausen,
wie er dieselben bei der Flasche im Zirkel seiner Freunde zu
erzählen pflegt. (The Marvelous Travels at Sea and on Land, the
Campaigns and Charming Adventures of Baron von Münchhausen,
as He Enjoys Telling Them—over a Bottle—in the Company of His
Friends.)*: The tales of Baron von Münchhausen was one of Bürger's
major efforts in translation, but he added so much of himself, and
so successfully, that it can almost be considered his own work.

In 1781 the Eighth Volume of the *Vade Mecum für lustige Leute
enthaltend eine Sammlung angenehmer Scherze, witziger Einfälle
und spaßhafter kurzer Historien, aus den besten Schriftstellern
zusammengetragen (Vade Mecum for Jolly People, Containing a
Collection of Pleasant Jests, Clever Thoughts, and Amusing Short
Stories, Compiled from the Best Authors)* was published by August
Mylius in Berlin and contained sixteen stories under the title
M-h-s-nsche Geschichten." In the Ninth Volume (1783) these
were followed by "Noch zwei M.-------Lügen" ("Two More
M--------- Lies"). In 1785 all these tales, but one, were translated into
English by the author, adventurer and sometime Professor
Rudolph Erich Raspe (1737–1794), under the title, *Baron Mun-
chausen's Narrative of his Marvellous Travels and Campaigns in
Russia,* and published at the end of 1785 or beginning of 1786.[48]
Very shortly afterwards (in 1786), two more editions followed, and
it was from the second (Schweizer says, "eigentlich dritte") of these
that Bürger made his first German adaptation, which was published
in 1786 by Dieterich in Göttingen, but bore the false imprint London
on the title page. There is a copy of the second English edition
(1786) in the Göttingen University Library, which may be the copy
Bürger used. The work evidently proved to be popular, and two years
later (1788) Dieterich published a second enlarged edition (still with
London on the title page). For this edition Bürger used the 5th
London edition (1787), which was considerably enlarged over
the preceding ones.

For some years it was thought that Bürger had been the author of
the English edition as well as of the German; in other words, that the
tales of Baron von Münchhausen were his own creation. Meusel, in
his *Gelehrten-Lexikon* (1811), indicates, however, that he knew Raspe had done the translation into English.[49] The historical evidence
linking Bürger to the Münchhausen affair hangs by the merest—but

surest—thread. The only mention ever made by Bürger in his correspondence of his association with the Münchhausen project occurs in passing in a letter to Dieterich, in which he complained that he had never received any payment for either *Macbeth* or *Münchhausen*.[50] The letter was not published until 1872, and until that time there was no documented link between Bürger and Münchhausen, excepting a statement by Reinhard made in 1824.[51]

In making his translation, Bürger followed his usual approach and allowed himself substantial liberties with the structure or format, although he remained relatively close to the language of the English original, when he followed it. He juxtaposed numerous adventures and situations; he omitted what he felt would not adapt well to a German audience; and he introduced some fifteen wholly new adventures or incidents in addition to lacing the work with his own remarks and asides.

The hero of the work was an historical figure, Baron Karl Friederich Hieronymus von Münchhausen (1720–1797), known during his lifetime, among other things, for his extraordinary prowess as a teller of tall tales. He had been a page at the court of Duke Anton Ulrich at Branschweig, then spent nine years in the *Kürassierregiment* in Riga. He served with distinction under Czar Peter II and the Czarinas Anna and Elisabeth in the wars against the Turks, and returned in 1760 to his family estates in Germany. There were also strong ties of the Von Münchhausen family with Göttingen. The University had been founded by Gerlach Adolf von Münchhausen (1688–1770), who had also been its first Curator.[52] It is at least possible that Bürger may have met Baron Karl Friederich, but he evidently was acquainted with Baron Carl Ludwig August Heino (1759–1836), since two letters from him to Bürger have been preserved plus a poem dedicated to him.

The work itself consists of two parts of unequal length. The first part contains the Baron's tales of his campaigns and adventures. In the first German edition (1786) Bürger added to Raspe's seventeen tales another six of his own in the section on Russian adventures and two dealing with sea adventures. When he prepared the second edition (1788) he worked from the much enlarged fifth English edition (1787) and added another seven incidents, thus giving the work its final form.[53]

The two parts of the book are not linked in any internal way other than by the presence of the hero himself, and they differ considerably in outlook and style. The first or original section, which covers slightly less than a third of the entire work, is a good deal more modest in scope. Presented as a single continuous narrative, it relates the Baron's adventures while on military duty in Russia. The tales center on the pleasures of the hunt and of the board, but incidents of gallantry and battle also occur. There is even a brief sojourn to the moon. The account is marked by the manner in which the Baron combines wit, skill, and strength to extricate himself from uncomfortable and sometimes perilous situations.

The second part of the book, the "Sea Adventures," is more contrived, since Von Münchhausen had had no personal experience at sea, and his personality, which was so integral to the first part, had to be incorporated into the compilation of tales fabricated to provide the sequence. The absence of a coherent narrative makes itself also felt in the division of the second part into separate chapters or "Adventures." There are a total of eight adventures concluding with the "Reise durch die Welt" ("Journey Through and Around the World"), and each adventure is, itself, a compilation of numerous incidents. The sixth adventure is introduced by a narrator, and the seventh (in which the Baron is not present), is narrated entirely by a third person, who gives a brief account of the Baron's personal history. At the conclusion of his account, the narrator identifies himself, for no apparent reason, as the natural son of Pope Clement XIV.

The scope of the second part is far greater than the first, and the Baron's adventures carry him to the exotic parts of the world—to Ceylon, Constantinople, and Cairo—and out into the universe (for a second trip to the moon via a cyclone or hurricane), and finally into the interior of the earth (which he reaches by leaping with his horse into the crater of Mt. Aetna). Moreover, the Baron is propelled into a quasi socio-political existence which brings him into contact with major public figures, such as the Grand Sultan of Cairo and General Elliot, the Defender of Gibraltar. The first part of the book had accomplished its end by simply narrating, in an unadorned fashion, the incredible but charming escapades of the Baron—without the distraction of other personalities. Very few of the characters in the first section are given names and the full attention of the audience is focused on the Baron. The second part, however, is clearly a sequel, in which the basic rhythm, although constant, carries a far more complex contrapuntal superstructure. The result is that the first part may be viewed as a whole consisting of numerous parts, whereas the second part gives the impression of many parts assembled to produce a whole.

The collection of adventures is, in a sense, a set of idealized memoirs, set off against the social background provided by the Baron's nobility and his position in the military aristocracy of the period. The Baron takes an obvious pride in his achievements, but the individual incidents are presented in a matter-of-fact manner. There is no suggestion that the rules of logic or natural law have been suspended, and it is left for the reader to conjure to himself the immensity of the deeds:

Ein anderes Mal wollte ich über einen Morast setzen, der mir anfänglich nicht so breit vorkam, als ich ihn fand, da ich mitten im Sprunge war. Schwebend in der Luft wendete ich daher wieder um, wo ich hergekommen war, um einen größeren Anlauf zu nehmen. Gleichwohl sprang ich auch zum zweiten Male zu kurz und fiel nicht weit vom anderen Ufer bis an den Hals in den Morast. Hier hätte ich unfehlbar umkommen müssen, wenn nicht die Stärke meines eigenen Armes mich an meinem eigenen Haarzopfe, samt dem Pferde, welches ich fest zwischen meine Kniee schloß, wieder herausgezogen hätte.

(/Another time I wanted to cross a morass, which did not initially seem to me so broad as I found it to be when I was in the midst of my leap. Hovering in the air, I turned around to where I had come from, in order to take a longer running start. Even so, on the second time I again leapt too short and fell not far from the opposite bank up to my neck into the crevasse. Here I would certainly have been killed, had I not, with the strength of my own arm, drawn myself up by my own pigtail—together with my horse, which I held tightly clasped between my knees./)

The style is developed through the personality of the Baron, and his manner is that of the ideal urbane raconteur, who, by association, glides smoothly from one anecdote to the next without the slightest hint of interruption—as it were, all in a single breath. The transitions are accomplished with such skill that the reader is unaware of the rapid sequence of events. Each proceeds naturally to the next, suggesting an organic development and resulting in an evenly sustained narrative. Werner Schweizer, in his recent study of the Münchhausen tradition, maintained that Bürger's "bedeutendstes

Verdienst liegt in der stilistischen Fassung, womit er den Deutschen den 'Münchhausen' mundgerecht, anziehend und zum Volksbuch-machte" ("most significant contribution lies in the stylistic manner, by which he made 'Münchhausen' palatable, and attractive to the Germans and made it into a Volksbuch").[54]Bürger could not have wished to do more.

In 1770, at about the time Bürger was working on his translation of Homer, he had also turned his attention to one of the minor Greek romances by Xenophon of Ephesus. The story of Anthia and Abrocomas was presumably written in the second century A.D. and consists, in its present form, of five books, which are probably a condensation from an original ten, which Suidas (c. 970 A.D.) knew as the *Ephesiaca*. The version which has survived exists in a single manuscript in the Laurentian Library and was first published by Antonio Cocchi in 1726, with a parallel Greek and Latin text. Bürger borrowed this volume from the Göttingen University Library in December, 1770, and again in January, 1771.[55] When he finally published the work in 1775, he noted on the title page that it had been translated from the Greek. While it is quite probable that he consulted the Greek, it is likely that he found it simpler to read the parallel Latin text, an assumption supported by the fact that in Bürger's translation all the place names have been Latinized and, indeed, even the gods, such as Eros, have been given their Roman equivalents (i.e., Amor). Whether from Latin or Greek, Bürger's concern for the accuracy of the translation was minimal, for as he wrote to Boie, "es kommt nicht ein Pfifferling drauf an, ob die Übersetzung überall getreu ist, wenn sie sich nur rein und fließend lesen läßt" ("it doesn't matter a whit, whether the translation is everywhere faithful, if it only reads easily and smoothly").[56]

Bürger made no secret of his disdain for the work. In addition to the disparaging attitude he assumed toward it in his letters to Boie (where he called it "Quark" ("trash"),[57] or "ein elendes Groschenwerklein" ("a miserable two-penny novel"),[58] he noted in the preface that he could have spent his time better than in translating an "albernes Romanlein" ("silly little novel"). He was probably right, at least from a financial standpoint, since Weygand, who published the work in 1775, paid him a total of six ducats—for which Bürger called him "einen rechten Filz" ("a real skinflint").

The plot of the romance is vastly complicated. It centers on the adventures and trials of Abrocomas, the embodiment of male beauty, and Anthia, a girl of surpassing beauty. Abrocomas, having grown up in Ephesus, has developed many skills and talents, but he is aware of his beauty and is supremely vain, so vain, in fact, that he will hear of no beauty other than his own. In his vanity he mocks Amor, who takes umbrage and decides to punish him. The basis of the plot is thus established, and it only remains for Abrocomas to fall mortally in love with Anthia. They wed and then set out on a grand journey, despite the warning of the oracle not to undertake a voyage. Almost immediately disaster strikes; the lovers are separated and spend many years searching for each other before they are finally reunited. After their separation the plot advances by moving back and forth between Anthia and Abrocomas, and their misfortunes run remarkably parallel. Both are constantly assailed by lovers of both sexes, but they never yield or succumb to temptation. Both are sold into slavery; they are nearly killed on numerous occasions, and their paths are continually crossed by third parties who move inadvertently from one camp to the other.

Anthia und Abrocomas is a moral tale conceived in the manner of a tragedy. There is a basic flaw, disproportionate pride, for which Abrocomas is made to suffer, although, in the end, he and Anthia are brought together again. Despite the fact that it is a tale of love, it is not one of passion. It is a novel of virtue, and although none of the characters may surpass either Anthia or Abrocomas in virtue, almost uniformly they are drawn sympathetically and are represented as honest, straightforward, loyal, and generous.[59]

In its totality, the work lacks proportion and is quite uneven. In the early chapters it moves rather swiftly, but it quickly loses momentum and never regains it. There is no attempt whatever at making transitions, and the reader finds himself abruptly shifted from the misadventures of Anthia to the adventures of Abrocomas. Moreover, Xenophon never ceases to introduce new characters, and even the most insignificant figures are given names. Yet despite these drawbacks, there is much grace in the work, and the scenes involving both Anthia and Abrocomas are drawn with considerable charm and delicacy. It is perhaps not a great work, but even as Bürger conceded in his Introduction, "hin und wieder sind Schilderei und Ausdruck ganz lieblich, süß und artig" ("now and again the descriptions and expressions are quite lovely, sweet and attractive").

In his correspondence with Boie concerning *Anthia and Abrocomas*, Bürger made it clear that he did not wish his name to be associated with the work when it was published. Two years later, when he published his *Dido* fragment, he again wished to remain anonymous, but for different reasons. He had been inspired by Gleim to try his hand at translating a portion of the *Aeneid*, but he was actively motivated by his determination to show the public that he, too, could turn out hexameters like Friedrich Leopold Stolberg, who at the time posed a threat to Bürger with his Homeric translations. Bürger's letter to Boie explains the reason for his undertaking his *Dido* fragment with unabashed candor: "Es geschieht bloß um Fritzen zu zeigen, daß ich sie [Hexameter], wenn ich will, so gut als Einer machen kann" ("It is only done, in order to show Fritz that I can make them [hexameters] as well as any one if I wish to.")[60]

The fragment was published by Boie in the *Deutsches Museum* in March, 1777. Bürger introduced the translation with a letter, ostensibly written by a friend of the young man who had done the translation. The friend has 'read Stolberg's and Bürger's Homeric attempts as well as Bürger's essay rejecting hexameters and agrees strongly with Bürger's point of view.' Bürger had the anonymous contributor indicate that he was writing from Bamberg, in order to throw people off the scent, but the letter and the fragment are so thoroughly Bürger's in character that Klopstock recognized him immediately, as did Voß and a host of others.

Bürger translated from the Fourth Canto and demonstrated a genuine facility with hexameters. The language is properly elevated, and the rhythm is delicately and subtly varied. Inevitably, Bürger expanded Virgil's ca. 400 lines to 448, breaking off as Dido finishes her accusation of Aeneas, and having fainted, is carried off to her bed. In general Bürger remained relatively close to the original.

Two further fragments from Bürger's hand demonstrate, once again, his inclination for taking up a project with vigor and enthusiasm, only to lose interest and move on to something else. In 1791, at the time Bürger was planning an edition of *One Thousand and One Nights*, he was urged by the physician Gramberg to prepare a modernized edition of Georg Rollenhagen's *Froschmäusler* and accompany it with an introductory essay. For some reason, Bürger responded enthusiastically and immediately sent off to

Göttingen to find out what editions were available in the University Library. At the same time, he borrowed two editions from Gramberg. The latter convinced a Bremen publisher, Cramer, of the excellence of the plan, and the work was to get under way immediately. Bürger, for his part, very soon forwarded 98 lines as a sample, and Gramberg predicted that *Rollenhagio redivivo* would be a "Masterpiece."[61] Gramberg was not a gifted prophet. Eight years later, when it finally became apparent that there would be no *Rollenhagio redivivo,* he politely requested the return of his books, but it took him another year and a half to retrieve them, and when they did come back, Bürger confessed that he could not find a manuscript essay by Gramberg on Rollenhagen, but would search for it "soon" [!].

The extract from the *Froschmäusler* that Bürger submitted consisted of about half of the Prologue and a section from the chapter "Von Bröseldiebs, des Mäusekönigs Sohns, Kundschaft bei dem Froschkönig." Bürger had retained the verse in his revision.

Another fragment, "Bellin," is a free adaptation of the twenty-eighth Canto of Ariosto's *Orlando Furioso,* and contains twenty-six ottave rime. Bürger undertook the project during the late fall, 1789, and sent the lines which have survived to Boie. He subsequently published them in the *Akademie der schönen Redekünste* (1791) but never completed the translation. As late as October, 1791, he wrote to Boie that his translation was progressing; but no more was forthcoming. It was at Boie's suggestion that Bürger changed the name from "Jukund" ("Giocondo") to "Bellin." Although Boie heartily disapproved of the name, he greeted the verse with delight, "Deine Stanzen sind bis zum Bewundern leicht gearbeitet, und zeigen, was alle bisherigen Versuche bezweifeln lassen wollten, die Möglichkeit sich auch in so schweren Fesseln noch mit Grazie zu bewegen" ("Your stanzas are worked with admirable lightness and show—what has driven all earlier attempts nearly to despair—the possibility of moving gracefully even in such confining fetters").[62] In a sense, one must agree that Bürger demonstrated skill in his handling of the verse form. The stanzas move with considerable ease but otherwise it is a leaden affair. Bürger tried to salt the fragment with the perennial Hans Quast and Jan Spleen, but without success. It also contains a heavyhanded sneer for the noted pedagogue and author, Johann Heinrich Campe, who, because of his association with the Enlightenment, finds himself rhymed with "Lampe" and then reflected in Heinrich Hampe. Altogether it is a rather tasteless effort, and one can agree with Boie who stated, in one of his rare moments of candor: "Ich mag dein Jukund nicht" ("I don't like your Jukund").[63]

It was a basic characteristic of Bürger's work that he allowed his private sentiments and passions to operate in his poetry, whether in major endeavours such as the "Elegie" or "Das hohe Lied" or in a minor production like "Bellin." It is probable that he himself recognized this aspect of this work, as did Schiller, and a number of friends evidently tried to persuade him to resist this urge. In a letter to F. L. W. Meyer, Caroline Böhmer mentions that Bürger had just finished his "Heloise an Abelard" (July, 1792) and had asked for her opinion. "Er schickte mirs ... und wollte strenge Critik, die ihm geworden ist—Eloise war ein paarmal Bürger geworden" ("He sent it to me ... and wanted frank criticism, which he got—Eloise, a few times, had become Bürger").[64]

Bürger first mentioned his translation of Pope's "Eloïsa to Abelard" in a letter to A. W. Schlegel written in October, 1791. He spoke of it almost in passing, but noted that it is "ein gar feines Werklein" ("a splendid little work").[65] Bürger continued to have a high opinion of the piece, and when he published it in the *Musen-Almanach* for 1793 he wrote to A. W. Schlegel, " ...Und diese Heloise ist nicht das einzige Stück. Mein Köcher ist noch voll goldner Pfeile" (" ...And this Heloise is not the only piece. My quiver is still full of golden arrows").[66] When it appeared in print, it bore the appropriate note after the title, "Frei nach Pope" ("Freely from Pope").

Pope's "Eloïsa to Abelard" (1717) is an heroid or heroic epistle. Eminently characteristic of Pope's style, the work is precise, formal, classic, and immensely literary. Johnson ranked it among "the happiest productions of the human mind," and it was otherwise received with great enthusiasm. Pope worked from a prose translation (based on a French version), which he expanded and refined. He regarded and treated it as a vehicle for demonstrating his prodigious virtuosity, and the result is a bravura performance, as well as a "repertory of literary effects." Pope's "Argument," which Bürger omitted, gives the design and direction of the poem, and it also provides the obvious clue as to why it attracted Bürger:

Abelard and Eloïsa flourished in the twelfth century; they were two of the most distinguished persons of their age in learning and beauty, but for nothing more famous than for their unfortunate passion. After a long course of calamaties, they retired each to a several convent, and consecrated the remainder of their days to religion. It was many years after this separation that a letter of Abelard's to a friend, which contained the history of his misfortune, fell into the hands of Eloïsa. This awakening of her tenderness, occasioned those celebrated letters (out of which the following is partly extracted) which gives so lively a picture of the struggles of grace and nature, virtue and passion.

Pope's poem is approximately 370 lines long, but Bürger's adaptation runs to some 635 lines, nearly double the length of the original. Moreover, Bürger changed Pope's iambic pentameter to trochaic pentameter, and the movement of the piece is thus markedly retarded. With obvious intent, Bürger sought to make the work his own, and the result is that it has more in common with his earlier "gothick" ballads than with Pope's cool and refined elegance. Characteristic of Bürger's adaptation is his treatment of Pope's "moss-grown domes with spiry turrets crowned,/Where awful arches make the noonday night,/And the dim windows shed a solemn light," which suggest something considerably more vivid to Bürger's mind, and in adapting them, he tried to heighten their effect:

> *In den Dom, vom Efeu grün bedacht,*
> *Rund umkränzt mit schlanken Pyramiden*
> *Und in seiner hohen Wölbung Nacht,*
> *Wo hinein durch schmale trübe Fenster*
> *Wie ein stilles hehres Mondenlicht*
> *In der Wanderstunde der Gespenster,*
> *Selbst der sonnenhellste Mittag bricht,*

(/Into the cathedral, covered green with ivy,/ Circled round with slender pyramids,/ And in its high vaulting night,/ Into which, through narrow, dim windows,/ Like a quiet lofty moonlight/ In the hour when ghosts are abroad,/ Even the brightest noon streams in,/)

Pope's classically precise language has given way to melodramatic expression, and the austerity of the original has succumbed to extravagance. Bürger also tended to expand a turn of phrase in Pope, though he gained little in meaning or effect: " . . . from

Abelard/ And Eloïsa yet must kiss the name" becomes "Muß ich den geliebten Namen küssen,/ Welcher mir so unvergeßlich ward" ("Must I kiss the beloved name,/ Which became so unforgettable to me"). As a result of Bürger's changes, the poem has gained in tangible imagery and intensity, but in achieving these effects Bürger forfeited the character of the original.

The most successful part of the poem occurs at the conclusion where Bürger found Pope's lines an inspiration for his own invention:

> *And sure, if fate some future bard shall join*
> *In sad similitude of griefs to mine,*
> *Condemned whole years in absence to deplore*
> *And image charms he must behold no more;*
> *Such if there be, who loves so long, so well;*
> *Let him our sad, our tender story tell!*

As was so often the case, Bürger reacted to the suggestion of his own experience, and the last twenty lines of his adaptation represent his last literary apostrophe to Molly:

> *Wenn das Glück nicht meinen Nachruhm neidet,*
> *So erhebt ein Sänger sich vielleicht,*
> *Der an einer Seelenwunde leidet,*
> *Die der meinigen an Tiefe gleicht;*
> *Der umsonst, umsonst durch lange Jahre*
> *Seiner Hochgeliebten nachgeweint,*
> *Bis ihn noch mit ihr—doch vor der Bahre!—*
> *Das Geschick minutenlang vereint; . . .*

(/If Fortune does not grudge my posthumous fame,/ Perhaps a poet will arise,/ Who suffers from a wound in his soul,/ Which is as deep as mine;/ Who vainly, vainly, through long years/ Has lamented the death of his Most Beloved,/ Until with her—though before the bier!—/ Fate united them for a brief moment./)

In the final two years of his life, Bürger's financial situation took such a turn for the worse that his earlier complaint to Dieterich about having to turn his talents to cash rang with even greater truth. Translation offered a meager but likely reward, and Bürger prepared a translation of Benjamin Franklin's *Autobiography* which was published in 1792 by H. A. Rottmann in Berlin. The title page simply stated that the work had been translated by G. A. Bürger, which was accurate, but it did not note that he had translated it from the French version, published by Buisson (Paris, 1791). Reinhard subsequently revealed that fact in his 1817 edition of Bürger's works, though later editions stated that it had been translated from the English. The answer is easy: Bürger had to translate from the French edition, since there was no English version. The first English edition was itself a translation from the French and did not appear until a year after Bürger's German translation (Paris, 1793).

It is interesting, though perhaps not especially profitable, to speculate on the possibility that Bürger may have been the author of a Swedish translation which was published anonymously in Stockholm in the same year (1792) in which Bürger's German version appeared. There is a remark in Dr. Althof's biography to the effect that Bürger had learned Swedish under the tutelage of one Dr. Canzler, and that he had pursued his study, "mit einem beharrlichen Eifer" ("with a very persistent zeal").[67]

Bürger's German translation is singularly faithful, as he follows the French with precision and accuracy. Understandably, he makes the same mistakes that Buisson had made before him. Following his normal practice, Bürger worked with an eye toward his German audience, and he translated everything, including proper names and place names. Thus Banbury in Oxfordshire became Banburg, John became Johann, and Fisher, Fischer. Franklin's brother-in-law, Holmes, is consistently called Holmer, and the compositor, Whitemarsh, became Wite-Mach (apparently because there had been a break in the line in Buisson and Bürger assumed it was a hyphenated name). *The Busy-Body* is translated as the *Thualles, The Lighthouse Tragedy* is the *Tragödie des Pharus,* and *The Spectator,* as to be expected, is *Der Zuschauer* (the title given it by Frau Gottsched when she translated it). The most original (and amusing) of these Germanizations was Bürger's translation of *The Crooked Billet,* which was the name of an inn located at the wharves above Chestnut Street in Philadelphia. Unaware that billets are accommodations, Bürger must have been rather puzzled, but not easily intimidated, he gave the inn the ingenious, though somewhat eccentric name *Zum zusammengelegten Zettel.*

Bürger's other nonfictional prose work of this period was *Die Republik England,* which was written for publication in the bimonthly journal *Politische Annalen* (1793). In 1793 Bürger had joined with the politically active Göttingen physician and professor, Dr. Christoph Girtanner, and together they decided upon the journal as a cooperative venture. Bürger had many misgivings about the arrangement, and he was particularly anxious that his name should not be associated with it.

In its own way, *Die Republik England* is an extraordinary work, although it can hardly be classified as history. Wolfgang Friedrich views it as a means of determining—in one further way—Bürger's position vis-à-vis the French Revolution, and certainly, at the very outset, Bürger points up the resemblance between the material in his essay and the current happenings in France.[68] This question aside, the essay still remains a most curious document.

Die Republik England begins with a quotation from *Ossian:* "A tale of the times of old! The deeds of the days of other years!" and then moves immediately into the commentary, with the suggestion that history tends to repeat itself, and Bürger asks rhetorically, who could have foreseen the most recent events in France by studying the Civil War in England. Bürger moves quickly backward in time and begins his study with the events leading up to and surrounding the Irish massacre of the English on October 22, 1641. He then carries his reader through the conquest and settlement of Ireland during the following four years, at which point he abruptly turns his attention to the situation in Scotland, as it developed after the Covenant of 1638. The remainder of the work concerns itself with the deterioration of the monarchy, the increased powers assumed by the House of Commons, and the decline of Charles I, paralleled by the ascendency of Oliver Cromwell. The final section begins with the invasion of Scotland in July, 1650, but abruptly breaks off after the defeat of Charles II at Worcester (September 3, 1651).

It is difficult to imagine Bürger as the author of this fragmentary essay, and much internal evidence suggests that it is a translation or adaptation rather than an original piece. The language is so rabid, and the style so radical that the work assumes a bizarre and grotesque quality, in which historical events are subverted to personal prejudices. It purports to be an historical commentary on the English Commonwealth period or the times of the Civil War, but it is only peripherally concerned with these matters. The trial and execution of Charles I are barely accorded a word (even the date is wrongly given as 1648), although the author lingers for eight pages over the atrocities committed at the massacre of the English colonists (October 22, 1641). The reader is borne along for page after page with battles, sieges, invasions, passing before him, but with scarcely a date assigned to them. The author is as frugal with his statistics as he is generous with his prejudices. When he supplies them, however, his dates are generally accurate, although his figures for armies, battle deaths, etc., do not agree with the standard histories, such as Burnet, Clarendon, Whitelock, or Tindal. Bürger's sources still remain to be identified.

The last work of any length that Bürger suceeded in completing was a verse setting of Stanislas de Boufflers's prose tale, *La Reine de Golconde*. There is no mention of it in his correspondence, but it was completed in 1793 and published in the *Musen-Almanach* for 1794.

The tale is contained within a framework, and the poet gives himself over to his pen to let it write to please him. In his reverie, the poet returns to his youth and a fateful meeting with the milk maid, Aline. He was sixteen years old and she fifteen, and in the meadow where they met, they had learned to love for the first time. The poet saw her but this once, and he gave her a gold ring by which to remember him. Many years later he meets her again in Paris, but recognizes her only when she shows him the ring. Through her wit, charm, and grace she has prospered and moved into the great world, where she has married and acquired a title. The poet spends the night with her but the experience is passion without love, and the next day he leaves her for new distractions. Another fifteen years pass, and in India he meets Aline again. She has now become the wise and beloved Queen of Golconda. The poet is led to a hamlet and meadow which correspond exactly to the place where he had first met Aline, and when she appears to him, they renew their love. Upon his return to Paris, his fortunes fluctuate and eventually he falls into poverty and disgrace. As the work concludes he finds himself telling his story to an old lady in a meadow, who turns out to be Aline. They were once lovely and handsome; but now they should become wise.

> *Den ganzen Tag sucht' ich mein Glück vergebens;*
> *Ich fand es erst am Abend meines Lebens.*

(/The whole day I sought my happiness in vain,/ I found it only in the evening of my life./)

The Chevalier de Boufflers (1738–1815) wrote *La Reine de Golconde* in 1761, and the brief tale is quite characteristic of his style and manner. The French original is a succinct vignette with little adornment. Boufflers was known for his light and graceful style, and this example of his work also shows a delicate clarity which is neither lax nor precious. In rendering the work into German Bürger succeeded to an unusual degree in retaining the lightness and grace of his model. Bürger's clear and precise language reflect his close adherence to the French, and although he could not always resist expanding an image, his German version is not appreciably longer than the original.

The work is essentially a moral tale in praise of love, rather than desire, and is told in the evening of the narrator's life. Love is portrayed as the central virtue of existence and the goal of man's eternal quest. In addition, Boufflers extolls freedom as a moral virtue (i.e., as it obtained under a benign monarch). He does not dismiss passion or pleasure, but he makes them subsidiary concerns. Finally, "Die Königin von Golkonde" was the tale of a woman, who, by the grace of her love, became the wise and benevolent monarch, whose reign nurtured freedom, tolerance, and respect. Even as Queen, Aline kept her milk-maid's dress,

> *Es wird sie überall den Stand der Menschheit ehren*
> *Und besser als ein Buch, die Kunst zu herrschen lehren.*

(/It will teach her above all to honor the condition of men,/ And teach her the art of ruling, better than a book./)

Boufflers's moral tale held an understandable attraction for Bürger, who could regard the love of the Chevalier and Aline as a reflection of his own love for Molly. At the same time, he also reacted positively to the liberal political views he found in the original. In 1793 *The Queen of Golconda* offered Bürger an opportunity to reflect not only on the transitory power of monarchs, but on the eternal power of love.

Conclusion

POSTERITY has not been inordinately kind to Bürger, and it is still a difficult task to acquire a balanced view of the man and his achievements. The difficulties are enhanced by sympathetic and hostile critics alike, since both have exaggerated those aspects of his character and poetry they wish to emphasize.

It is a rare event for a critic to undertake the kind of sweeping overall assessment of a living poet, as Schiller did with Bürger. In doing so—and with such force—Schiller set the tone, in one way or another, for all subsequent criticism. He became the yardstick or criterion against which, or in accord with which, all subsequent critics have measured Bürger.

In his opportunistic essay, "Bürger 1800," A. W. Schlegel was even less justified than Schiller and lacked, in addition, Schiller's reasoned argument. He also stands at the beginning of a long tradition of hyperbolic criticism, in which Bürger was regarded either with disdain or rapture: from Wolfgang Menzel's caustic impeachment to Eduard Grisebach, and from Friedrich Gundlof to Wilhelm Dilthey's vision of Bürger suffused in a roseate glow. Like a tragic flaw, the lack of impartiality has haunted Bürger scholarship for over a century, but it is, in some degree, a measure of the man's versatility that he called forth such extremes of critical response. In more recent times, scholars like Emil Staiger, Albrecht Schöne, and Götz Hübner have significantly contributed towards establishing a more objective image of Bürger and the many dimensions of his character.

Between the polarities of Menzel and Dilthey there has never ceased to be a visible and appreciative audience for Bürger's poetry. Moreover, it is evidence of the breadth of his vision that he found sympathetic response in such disparate poetic natures as Heinrich Heine and Hermann Löns. Similarly, after many years of neglect, critics are once again looking closely at some of Bürger's poems other than "Lenore." The most recent attempts of this kind include Walter Naumann's sensitive and perceptive reading of

"Trauerstille" and Martin Stern's critical discussion of "An das Herz."

For some years, there has been a very active interest in Bürger among the scholars of the German Democratic Republic. The only critical assessment ever done on *Die Republik England* (by Wolfgang Friedrich), appeared in the *Weimarer Beiträge,* and the only edition of Bürger's works currently in print (excepting the reprint of Karl Reinhard's edition) is the selection edited by Lore Kaim-Kloock and published as part of the series *Bibliothek Deutscher Klassiker.*

It is perhaps not realistic to envisage a full-scale Bürger renaissance within the foreseeable future, but many of the issues Bürger dealt with, such as freedom, tolerance, the importance of the individual, and human rights are particularly germane at the present. More important, however, are the timeless qualities and aspects of the human condition to which Bürger, the poet, addressed himself; and to the extent that his expressions were honest and genuine, his audience will ultimately transcend national and temporal boundaries.

Notes and References

Chapter One

1. Heinrich Pröhle, *Gottfried August Bürger. Sein Leben und seine Dichtung* (Leipzig, 1856), p. 25.

2. Dr. Ludwig Christoph Althof, Bürger's long-time physician and friend, as well as his first biographer, writes that the birthplace of Bürger's father was "Pomsfelde." See *Gottfried August Bürger's Sämmtliche Werke,* ed. Karl Reinhard. (Vienna, 1844), IX, 193. Hereafter cited as *Werke*-R. or-Althof, as appropriate.

3. Wolfgang Wurzbach, *Gottfried August Bürger. Sein Leben und seine Werke* (Leipzig, 1900), p. 6. Hereafter cited as Wurzbach.

4. *Werke*-Althof, IX, 197.

5. Wurzbach, pp. 15–16.

6. *Werke*-Althof, IX, 199.

7. Bürger's law briefs were generally recognized as excellent, and Dr. Justus Claproth asked the poet's permission to publish one in his *Nachtrag zu der Sammlung verschiedener gerichtlichen vollständigen Acten* (Göttingen, 1782).

8. Karl Goedeke, *Gottfried August Bürger in Göttingen und Gelliehausen* (Hannover, 1873), p. 83 ff.

9. *Briefe von und an Gottfried August Bürger,* ed. Adolf Strodtmann, 4 vols. (Berlin, 1874), I, 123. Hereafter cited as Strodtmann.

10. *Ibid.,* III, 143.

11. Wurzbach, p. 32.

12. *Ibid.,* p. 59.

13. Goedeke, *op. cit.,* recommendations from Von Selchow et al., pp. 82–83.

14. Gottfried August Bürger, *Gedichte,* ed. Arnold E. Berger (Leipzig and Vienna, 1891). Cited by Berger in his Introduction, p. 11. Hereafter cited as *Gedichte*-B.

15. Strodtmann, I, 176.

16. *Ibid.,* I, 185.

17. *Ibid.,* IV, 19–29.

18. *Ibid.,* I, 204.

19. *Ibid.,* I, 233.

20. *Ibid.,* I, 266.

21. Wurzbach, p. 139.

22. Strodtmann, III, 12.

23. Wurzbach, p. 175.

24. *Ibid.,* p. 186.

25. Strodtmann, III, 103.

26. I make this comparison only because both letters were utilitarian in purpose. In his dealings with Goethe, Bürger failed to sense a change of tone from the poet's earlier letters, and continued to think of Goethe as he had been at the time of writing *Götz.*

27. Strodtmann, III, 138.

28. Siegfried Kadner, *Gottfried August Bürgers Einfluß auf August W. Schlegel* (Kiel, 1919), pp. 7–8. Hereafter cited as Kadner.

29. *Ibid.*

30. Cited by Wurzbach, p. 248 (March 2, 1786).

31. Wurzbach, p. 331.

32. Strodtmann, IV, 113.

33. Friedrich Schiller, *Werke,* ed. E. von der Hellen, 16 vols. (Stuttgart, 1904–1905—Säkularausgabe). Hereafter cited as Schiller.

34. Gottfried August Bürger, *Sämtliche Werke,* ed. Wolfgang Wurzbach, 4 vols. in 1 (Leipzig, 1902), III, 178. Hereafter cited as *Werke.*

35. Walter Müller-Seidel, "Schillers Kontroverse mit Bürger und ihr geschichtlicher Sinn," *Formwandel: Festschrift für Paul Böckmann* (Hamburg, 1964), p. 295.

36. Kadner, p. 109.

Chapter Two

1. Eduard Grisebach, *Die deutsche Literatur—1770–1870* (Vienna, 1876), pp. 120 ff.

2. Strodtmann, I, 175–76.

3. August Barth, *Der Stil von G. A. Bürgers Lyrik* (Marburg, 1911), p. 7.

4. Wurzbach, p. 288; see also Strodtmann, IV, 19–29.

5. Strodtmann, II, 278.

6. Schiller, p. 230.

7. *Werke,* III, 153.

8. Wurzbach, p. 152.

9. *Ibid.*

10. *Ibid.,* p. 257.

11. *Werke,* III, 171.

12. *Werke,* III, 88. The original title indicated that the Latin poem was by Catullus, "nach Catullus." There is no evidence, however, that Catullus was the author, and in later editions Bürger omitted the reference.

13. *Werke,* III, 90–91.

14. John E. Sandys, *A Companion to Latin Studies* (Cambridge, ³1921), 953.

15. *Werke,* III, 105.

16. *Ibid.,* III, 93, fn.

17. *Ibid.,* III, 116.

18. *Ibid.,* III, 112–17. Schiller also translated the "Pervigilium veneris" as "Der Triumph der Liebe" (1781).

19. Wurzbach, p. 162.

20. Gottfried August Bürger, *Leben, Briefe und Prosa Schriften,* ed. Eduard Grisebach (Berlin, 1872), p. xvi. Hereafter cited as *Werke*-G.

21. Barth, *op. cit.,* p. 126.

22. The number may vary, depending upon the selection of a particular editor. In the last century, editors frequently and mistakenly included the two sonnets, "Der Entfernten," which were actually written in honor of Frau Dr. Kaulfuss.

23. Wurzbach, p. 122.

24. *Ibid.,* p. 123.

25. *Ibid.,* p. 122.

26. The long and convoluted "Das hohe Lied von der Einzigen" offers similar problems.

27. Strodtmann, II, 231.

28. *Werke*-R, III, 192. "Kritische Anmerkungen zu einigen Gedichten."

29. Grisebach, *op. cit.,* p. 140.

30. *Werke*-G, p. xxxvi.

31. It would not have been the first time; see, "Die Hexe, die ich meine," or "An Themire," a travesty based on Horace.

32. Schiller, p. 241.

33. Wurzbach, p. 263.

34. Barth, *op. cit.,* p. 45.

35. Strodtmann, III, 215.

36. A. W. Schlegel, "Über Bürgers Hohes Lied," *Neues Deutsches Museum,* II, Feb. 1790, p. 345.

37. A. W. Schlegel, "Bürger 1800" in *Werke,* ed. E. Böcking. (Leipzig, 1846–1847), XII, 132. Hereafter cited as Schlegel.

38. Schiller, p. 240.

39. *Ibid.*

40. Barth, *op. cit.,* p. 46.

Chapter Three

1. Lore Kaim-Kloock, *Gottfried August Bürger. Zum Problem der Volkstümlichkeit in der Lyrik* (Berlin, 1963), p. 338. Hereafter cited as Kaim-Kloock.

2. Valentin Beyer, *Die Begründung der ernsten Ballade durch G. A.*

Bürger (Quellen und Forschungen zur Sprach- und Culturgeschichte der Germanischen Völker, XCVII), 1905, p. 26.

3. *Ibid.*

4. Wolfgang Kayser, *Geschichte der deutschen Ballade* (Berlin, 1936), p. 86.

5. Strodtmann, I, 105.

6. *Ibid.,* I, 101.

7. Kayser, *op. cit.,* p. 88.

8. Beyer, *op. cit.,* p. 26.

9. Kayser, *loc. cit.*

10. Hübner, Kaim-Kloock, Staiger, and others.

11. Wurzbach, p. 74.

12. *Ibid.,* p. 75.

13. Kaim-Kloock, p. 166.

14. *Ibid.,* pp. 166–67.

15. Strodtmann, I, 122.

16. *Ibid.,* I, 129–30.

17. *Ibid.,* I, 131.

18. *Ibid.,* I, 137.

19. Wurzbach states that Bürger read his ballad before the group on August 21, but Hübner (*Kirchenliedrezeption und Rezeptionsforschung* [Tübingen, 1969], p. 40) has convincingly shown that Bürger did not, and, in fact, questions whether such a public reading actually took place.

20. Strodtmann, I, 163.

21. *Ibid.,* I, 101.

22. *Ibid.,* footnote.

23. The English journal *The Monthly Magazine,* 1796, cited by Wurzbach, p. 91. See also Hübner, (*Op. cit.* p. 26 and fn. 77.)

24. Boie's letter to Herder (Sept. 22. 1777) with the comment that "Only this summer has Bürger become acquainted with the *Reliques,*" cited in Gottfried August Bürger, *Gedichte,* ed. Ernst Consentius, 2 vols. (Berlin, [2] 1914), II, 310f. Hereafter cited as *Werke* C. Boie's letter also cited by Hübner, p. 25, fn.

25. Hübner, *op. cit.,* pp. 28–29.

26. *Ibid.,* p. 29, fn. 88.

27. Strodtmann, I, 111.

28. *Ibid.,* I, 174.

29. *Ibid.*

30. Wurzbach, p. 97.

31. Hübner, *op. cit.,* p. 18.

32. Wurzbach, p. 98.

33. Strodtmann, I, 175.

34. *Ibid.,* I, 175–76.

35. *Ibid.*, I, 146.

36. Wurzbach, p. 98.

37. Hübner, *op. cit.*, p. 19, fn. 38.

38. Herbert Schöffler, "Bürgers 'Lenore,'" *Die Sammlung,* II (1947), pp. 6–11. Schöffler was one of the last scholars or perhaps the last to address himself to this problem.

39. Albrecht Schöne, *Säkularisation als sprachbildende Kraft* (*Palaestra,* CCXXVI), Göttingen, 1958. Cf., p. 173, fn. 33.

40. *Ibid.*, p. 154.

41. *Ibid.*, p. 181.

42. *Ibid.*, p. 154.

43. Lore Kaim-Kloock, "G. A. Bürgers 'Lenore,'" *Weimarer Beiträge,* II (1956), pp. 42–43, fn. 19.

44. Eduard Stäuble, "Gottfried August Bürgers Ballade 'Lenore,'" *Deutschunterricht* X (1958), p. 107, fn. 18.

45. Kaim-Kloock, pp. 342–43, fn. 51.

46. Emil Staiger, *Stilwandel,* (Zurich, 1963), "Zu Bürger's 'Lenore,'" p. 77.

47. *Ibid.*, pp. 77–78. Also cited by Hübner, *op. cit.*, p. 15.

48. Hübner, *op. cit.*, pp. 13–56.

49. Staiger, *op. cit.*, p. 78.

50. Strodtmann, I, 111.

51. *Ibid.*, I, 120.

52. *Ibid.*

53. *Ibid.*, I, 132 and I, 170.

54. *Ibid.*, I, 164.

55. Stäuble, *op. cit.*, p. 94.

56. Strodtmann, IV, 262.

57. *Ibid.*, I, 132.

58. Gottfried August Bürger, *Gedichte,* ed. August Sauer *(Kürschners Deutsche Nationalliteratur,* vol. 78), Berlin and Stuttgart, 1884. Introduction, p. lvii. Hereafter cited as *Werke*-S. Also cited by Staiger, pp. 75–76.

59. Cited by Hübner, *op. cit.*, p. 14, fn. 7.

60. Strodtmann, I, 105.

61. Wurzbach, p. 104.

62. Strodtmann, I, 287.

63. *Ibid.*, I, 240.

64. Julius Stiefel, *Die deutsche Lyrik des 18. Jahrhunderts* (Leipzig: Wiegand, 1871), p. 109.

65. Strodtmann, I, 329.

66. Helmut Paustian, *Die Lyrik der Aufklärung als Ausdruck der seelischen Entwicklung von 1710–1770* (Berlin, 1933), p. 198.

67. Strodtmann, I, 227.

68. *Ibid.*, I, 231.

69. *Ibid.*, I, 295.

70. *Ibid.*, I, 298.

71. Friedrich Blömker, *Das Verhältnis von Bürgers lyrischer und episch-lyrischer Dichtung zur englischen Literatur* (Münster, 1930), p. 21.

72. Wurzbach, p. 144.

73. Strodtmann, I, 302.

74. Blömker, *op. cit.*, p. 24.

75. *Ibid.*, p. 23.

76. Paustian, *op. cit.*, p. 198.

77. Cf. also the ballad "Der Ritter und sein Liebchen."

78. Strodtmann, II, 82.

79. Penelope Scott, *Gottfried August Bürgers Übersetzungen aus dem Englischen* (Winterthur, 1964), p. 8.

80. *Ibid.*

81. Strodtmann, II, 208.

82. *Ibid.*, II, 202.

83. *Ibid.*, II, 208.

84. *Ibid.*, II, 90.

85. *Ibid.*, II, 93, cf. also Wurzbach, p. 146, fn.

86. Wurzbach, p. 147.

87. Erich Ebstein, "Quellengeschichtliches zu G. A. Bürgers 'Die Kuh,'" *Archiv für neuere Sprachen*, N.F., CLI (1927), p. 77.

88. Strodtmann, II, 91.

89. Wurzbach, p. 147.

90. Strodtmann, II, 244.

91. *Ibid.*, II, 97.

92. *Ibid.*, II, 98.

93. *Ibid.*, II, 186.

94. *Ibid.*, II, 116.

95. *Ibid.*, II, 276.

96. Wurzbach, p. 142.

97. Scott, *op. cit.*, p. 25.

98. *Ibid.*

99. Strodtmann, I, 341.

100. *Ibid.*, III, 65.

101. *Ibid.*, III, 61, 65.

102. Schlegel, *op. cit.*, p. 114.

103. Kaim-Kloock, p. 220.

104. Schlegel, *op. cit.*, p. 96. Schlegel complains, however, about Bürger's reference to Werther.

105. Scott, *op. cit.*, p. 28.

106. *Ibid.,* p. 27.
107. Strodtmann, III, 147.
108. Wurzbach, p. 203.
109. Ebstein, *op. cit.,* pp. 77–79.
110. Kaim-Kloock, *op. cit.,* p. 256.
111. Ebstein, *op. cit.,* p. 79; M. W. Götzinger, *Deutsche Dichter.* (Leipzig, 1857), Pt. 1, 263.
112. Schlegel, *op. cit.,* p. 113.
113. Ebstein, *op. cit.,* p. 79: Moritz Heyne, *Mitteilungen zur Vorgeschichte der Loge Augusta zum Goldenen Zirkel in Göttingen aus dem 18. Jahrhundert.* (Göttingen, 1896).
114. *Ibid.,* p. 77.
115. Strodtmann, II, 328.
116. *Ibid.*
117. Schlegel, *op. cit.,* pp. 96–98.
118. Kaim-Kloock, *op. cit.,* p. 234.
119. Strodtmann, I, 96.
120. Wurzbach, p. 103.
121. *Ibid.*
122. Strodtmann, I, 208.
123. *Ibid.,* I, 274.
124. *Ibid.,* I, 276–77.

Chapter Four

1. Strodtmann, II, 274.
2. *Ibid.,* I, 31–33.
3. *Ibid.,* I, 351.
4. Wurzbach, p. 167.
5. Strodtmann, III, 175.
6. *Ibid.,* III, 2. *Eulalia,* by A. M. Sprickmann, a tragedy in five acts, was written in 1777.
7. *Ibid.,* III, 148.
8. *Ibid.,* I, 81.
9. *Ibid.,* IV, 219.
10. Blömker, *op. cit.,* p. 66.
11. Barth, *op. cit.,* p. 49.
12. The poem was written with Elise in mind.
13. Barth, *op. cit.,* p. 48.
14. Burkard Waldis (1490–1556), author and editor of *Esopus/Gantz New gemacht und in Reimen gefasst. Mitsammt Hundert Newer Fabeln,* 1548.

15. The parrot was Georg Schatz (1763–1795), who had also reviewed the 1789 *Gedichte* unfavorably.

16. Strodtmann, IV, 215.

17. Wurzbach, pp. 337–38.

18. Strodtmann, *loc. cit.*

19. Schiller, p. 233.

20. Cf. also "Mollys Abschied."

21. Strodtmann, III, 291.

22. Goethe, "Wanderers Nachtlied."

23. Stiefel, *op. cit.*, p. 93. Cf. also Martin Stern's sensitive and perceptive commentary on the same poem in *Literatur und Geistesgeschichte: Festschrift für Heinz Otto Burger* (1968), pp. 171–87.

Chapter Five

1. *Werke,* III, 160.

2. Kaim-Kloock, *op. cit.,* 67.

3. *Werke,* III, 5.

4. "Popularität" is a key word in any consideration of Bürger's thoughts about poetry, as he used it in all his writings on the subject. "Popularity" is not an altogether adequate translation of the word, in the sense in which Bürger used it. For Bürger, "Popularität" seems to have had the meaning of 'universal accessibility and/or appreciation.'

5. *Werke,* III, 11.

6. Herder's *Stimmen der Völker* appeared in 1778–1779.

7. Strodtmann, I, 122.

8. Cited by Kaim-Kloock, *op. cit.,* p. 99.

9. *Werke,* III, 150–151.

10. *Ibid.,* III, 20.

11. *Ibid.,* III, 157.

12. *Ibid.,* III, 159.

13. *Ibid.*

14. *Ibid.,* III, 38.

15. *Ibid.,* III, 40.

16. *Ibid.,* III, 41.

17. Strodtmann, III, 189–90.

18. *Ibid.,* III, 191.

19. *Werke* III, 42–55.

20. *Ibid.,* III, 42.

21. *Ibid.,* III, 47.

22. *Ibid.,* III, 48.

23. *Ibid.,* III, 51.

24. Strodtmann, III, 112.

25. It should be noted that Karl Reinhard also gathered and published Bürger's lecture notes on aesthetics. These appeared, also in Berlin, under the title *Lehrbuch der Aesthetik*, 1825. Christian Janentzky, in his detailed study *G. A. Bürgers Aesthetik* (Berlin, 1909), clearly demonstrates that Bürger was mainly quoting extant and available primary and secondary sources without identifying them. Janentzky identified Sulzer, Steinbar, Adelung, and Mendelssohn as the chief sources.

26. Werke, III, 182.

27. *Ibid.*, III, 184.

28. Strodtmann, IV, 163.

29. *Werke*, III, 70.

30. Wurzbach, p. 343.

31. *Werke*, I, 214, and II, 59.

32. Bürger had chosen legal German as a special target in his "Über Anweisung zur deutschen Sprache und Schreibart auf Universitäten."

33. *Werke*, III, 193.

34. Strodtmann, IV, 29.

35. Wurzbach, p. 352.

36. *Werke*, III, 203.

37. Richard Gosche, "Eine Parabel unter Bürgers Namen," *Archiv für Litteraturgeschichte*, I (1870), pp. 116–17. Although no one seems to have questioned the authenticity of this parable, it has not found its way into subsequent editions, and has never, to my knowledge, been reprinted.

Chapter Six

1. Wurzbach, p. 46.

2. *Werke*, IV, 9.

3. *Ibid.*, IV, 16.

4. *Ibid.*, IV, 18.

5. *Ibid.*, IV, 19.

6. *Ibid.*, IV, 21.

7. *Ibid.*, IV, 22.

8. *Ibid.*, IV, 23.

9. *Ibid.*, IV, 50.

10. Strodtmann, III, 127.

11. Wurzbach, p. 51.

12. Kadner, p. 58.

13. Although *Ossian* is frequently mentioned in the correspondence of the early and mid-1770s, it has not been clearly determined when Bürger first read it.

14. Strodtmann, II, 339.

15. *Ibid.,* II, 319.

16. *Ibid.,* II, 322.

17. *Ibid.,* II, 348.

18. *Ibid.,* II, 337.

19. *Ibid.,* II, 357.

20. *Ibid.,* II, 361.

21. *Ibid.,* II, 357.

22. Cf. Scott, *op. cit.,* p. 39.

23. W. Shaw, *An Inquiry into the Authenticity of the Poems of Ossian,* 1781; Malcolm Laing, *Notes and Illustrations to Ossian,* 1805. Both cited by Eyre-Todd in his edition of *Ossian* (London and New York, ca. 1913).

24. A large part of the information on *Ossian* noted here is taken from the Introduction to George Eyre-Todd's edition of *Ossian,* cf. above, fn. 23.

25. *Ossian,* ed. George Eyre-Todd, cf. fn. 23, p. 46.

26. Rudolf Horstmeyer, *Die deutschen Ossian-Übersetzungen des XVIII. Jahrhunderts* (Greifswald, 1926), p. 112. Also cited by Scott.

27. The manuscript bears the code: MS. M15 4°.

28. Strodtmann, II, 4.

29. *Ibid.,* II, 201.

30. Rudolf Genée, *Geschichte der Shakespearschen Dramen in Deutschland* (Leipzig, 1870), p. 266.

31. Strodtmann, III, 71.

32. *Ibid.,* IV, 116.

33. *Ibid.,* II, 212.

34. *William Shakespeare's Schauspiele,* transl. Johann Joachim Eschenburg (Zurich, 1800); vol. 5 *(Macbeth),* p. 241.

35. Erich Ebstein, "Die Hexenscenen aus Bürgers *Macbeth*-Übersetzung im ersten Entwurf," *Zeitschrift für Bücherfreunde, Neue Folge,* III (1912), 401.

36. Edna Purdie, *Studies in German Literature of the Eighteenth Century* (London, 1965), p. 52.

37. Friedrich Gundolf, *Shakespeare und der deutsche Geist* (Berlin, ²1914), p. 274.

38. Cf. Purdie, *op. cit.,* pp. 53–54.

39. Ebstein, *op. cit.,* p. 402.

40. Strodtmann, II, 212.

41. Schlegel, *op. cit.,* p. 135.

42. Cited by Kadner, p. 58.

43. Michael Bernays, "Ein kleiner Nachtrag zu Bürgers Werken," *Archiv für Litteraturgeschichte,* I (1870), 112.

44. Strodtmann, I, 231.

45. *Ibid.,* I, 266.

46. *Ibid.,* II, 265.

47. *Ibid.,* II, 14.

48. There is wide disagreement on this point. Werner Schweizer regards 1786 as the date of the first edition and furnishes a reproduction of the title page in his book *Münchhausen und Münchhausiaden* (Berne and Munich, 1969). According to E. Wackmann in *The Encyclopaedia Britannica,* this was the second edition, an opinion also held by William Rose in his book *The Travels of Baron Munchausen* (London and New York, 1923). An edition was announced in December, 1785, but if it appeared in 1785 there is no copy known to anyone, except to Penelope Scott. Miss Scott confuses matters considerably: she agrees on 1785 as the date of the first edition, but maintains that "Dieses Buch existiert heute nur noch in einer Kopie, es umfasste 48 Seiten ("This book exists today in but a single copy, it consisted of 48 pages"—p. 79). Since her dissertation was published in 1964, it would seem likely to have come to the attention of one of the most distinguished Münchhausen scholars, Werner Schweizer, between that time and the publication of his most recent book in 1969. Schweizer makes no mention of it, however. Miss Scott also gives no indication as to where the one extant copy of the 1785 edition is located, and she further muddies the waters by noting that it "consisted" of 48 pages. If a 1785 edition exists, it could have had 48 pages; the 1786 copy in the British Museum has 49 pages.

49. Meusel, *Lexikon der vom Jahre 1750 bis 1800 verstorbenen teutschen Schriftsteller* (Leipzig, 1811), XI, 52. Incorrectly cited by Schweizer as being in Vol. II.

50. Strodtmann, IV, 116.

51. *Ibid.*

52. Schweizer, *op. cit.,* p. 56.

53. *Ibid.,* p. 78.

54. *Ibid.*

55. Karl Goedeke, *Gottfried August Bürger in Göttingen und Gelliehausen* (Hannover, 1873), p. 80.

56. Strodtmann, I, 240.

57. *Ibid.,* I, 256.

58. *Ibid.,* I, 309.

59. Xenophon d'Éphèse, *Les Éphésiaques ou le roman d'Habrocomès et d'Anthia,* ed. George Dalmeyda (Paris, 1926), xviii ff.

60. Strodtmann, I, 375.

61. *Ibid.,* II, 48.

62. *Ibid.,* IV, 8.

63. *Ibid.*

64. *Ibid.*, IV, 207.
65. *Ibid.*, IV, 136.
66. *Ibid.*, IV, 209.
67. *Werke*-Althof, IX, 259.
68. Wolfgang Friedrich, "Zu Gottfried August Bürgers Aufsatz 'Die Republik England,'" *Weimarer Beiträge* (1956), p. 219.

Selected Bibliography

Primary Works

BÜRGER, GOTTFRIED AUGUST, "An königl. hohe Landes-Regierung, etc. etc. zu Hannover," *Das Graue Ungeheur,* V (May, 1784), 219–73.

———. "Langbeins Gedichte," *Allgemeine Literatur-Zeitung*—"Intelligenzblatt," LVI (April, 1789), pp. 483–84. Bürger's reply to [Anon.], "*Gedichte,* von August Friedrich Langbein," *A.L.Z.,* XCIII (March, 1789), 732–36.

———. "Gedichte von Karl Theodor Beck," *Allgemeine Literatur-Zeitung,* (August, 1789), p. 325.

———. "Gedichte von F.L.Z. Werner," *Allgemeine Literatur-Zeitung,* (August, 1789), p. 324.

———. *Sämmtliche Werke,* ed. August Wilhelm Bohtz, (in one vol.), Göttingen: Dieterich, 1835.

———. *Sämmtliche Werke,* ed. Karl Reinhard, 9 vols., Vienna: Ignaz Klang, 1844. Neue rechtmäßige Ausgabe.

———. *Werke,* ed. Eduard Grisebach, 2 vols., Berlin: Grote, 1872.

———. *Gedichte,* ed. August Sauer (Kürschners Deutsche National-Literatur. vol. 78), Berlin and Stuttgart, 1884.

———. *Gedichte,* ed. Arnold E. Berger ("Meyers Klassiker-Ausgaben"), Leipzig and Vienna, 1891.

———. *Sämmtliche Werke,* ed. Wolfgang von Wurzbach, 4 vols. (in one), Leipzig: Hesse and Becker, 1902.

———. *Gedichte,* ed. Ernst Consentius, 2 vols., Berlin: Bong, [2]1914.

———. *Briefe, von und an,* ed. Adolf Strodtmann, 4 vols., Berlin: Paetel, 1874. Repr. Berne: Lang, 1970.

———. "Ungedruckte Briefe," *Euphorion,* I (1894), 309–37.

Books and Articles about Bürger and His Work

BARTH, AUGUST. *Der Stil von G. A. Bürgers Lyrik,* Marburg: Hieronymus, 1911. Diss.

BERNAYS, MICHAEL. "Ein kleiner Nachtrag zu Bürgers Werken," *Archiv für Litteratur-Geschichte,* I (1870), 110–15.

BEYER, VALENTIN. *Die Begründung der ernsten Ballade durch G. A. Bürger*

(Quellen und Forschungen zur Sprach- und Culturgeschichte der germanischen Völker), XCVII (1905).

BIEHLER, OTTO. "Bürgers Lyrik im Lichte der Schillerschen Kritik," *Germanisch-Romanische Monatsschrift,* XIII (1927), 259–74.

BLÖMKER, FRIEDRICH. *Das Verhältnis von Bürgers lyrischer und episch-lyrischer Dichtung zur englischen Literatur,* Münster, 1930. Diss.

BÖHME, GABRIELE. *Bänkelsängermoritaten,* Munich, 1920. Diss.

CARGILL, OSCAR. "A New Source for 'The Raven,' " *American Literature,* VIII (1936–1937), 291–94.

DAHINTEN, EGON. *Studien zum Sprachstil der Iliasübersetzungen Bürgers, Stolbergs, und Voßens. Unter Berücksichtigung der Übersetzungstheorien des 18. Jhdts.* Göttingen, 1957. Diss. Masch.

DANIEL, HERMANN ADALBERT. "Bürger auf der Schule," Programm des Kgl. Pädagogiums zu Halle. (Reprinted in the author's *Zerstreute Blätter,* [Halle, 1866], pp. 47 ff.)

DILTHEY, WILHELM. *Die grosse Phantasiedichtung,* Göttingen: Vandenhoeck and Ruprecht, 1954. ("Gottfried August Bürger und sein Kreis," pp. 229–36.)

EBELING, FRIEDRICH WILHELM. *Gottfried August Bürger und Elise Hahn,* Leipzig, 1868.

EBSTEIN, ERICH. "Zu Gottfried August Bürger," *Zeitschrift für deutsche Philologie,* XXXV (1903), 540–53.

———. "Quellengeschichtliches zu G. A. Bürgers 'Die Kuh,'" *Archiv für neuere Sprachen,* N.F. CLI (1927), 77–79.

———. "Gottfried August Bürger und Gustav Friedr. Wilh. Großmann," *Zeitschrift für deutsche Philologie,* LIII (1928), 186–89.

———. "Die Hexenszenen aus Bürgers *Macbeth*-Übersetzung im ersten Entwurf," *Zeitschrift für Bücherfreunde,* N. F. III (1912), 398–402.

———. "Zur Druck- und Quellengeschichte von G. A. Bürgers Übersetzung von *Anthia und Abrocomas,* aus dem Griechischen des Xenophon von Ephesus," *Zeitschrift für deutsche Philologie,* LII (1927), 397–402.

FLUCK, H. *Beiträge zu Bürgers Sprache und Stil mit bes. Berücksichtigung der Ilias-Übersetzung,* Münster, 1914. Diss.

FRANKLIN, BENJAMIN. *Memoires de la Vie privée,* Paris: Buisson, 1791.

———. *Lefwerne,* Stockholm, 1792.

———. *The Private Life,* Paris, 1793.

FREDY, GERHARD. *Stammbaum des Dichters Gottfried August Bürger und der mit ihm verwandten Familien im Ostharz von 1647–1937,* Aschersleben, Halle, 1937.

FRELS, WILHELM. *Deutsche Dichterhandschriften von 1400 bis 1900,* Leipzig: Hiersemann, 1934, pp. 41–42.

FRIEDRICH, WOLFGANG. "Zu Gottfried August Bürgers Aufsatz 'Die Republik England,'" *Weimarer Beiträge,* II (1956), 214–32.

GEIGER, LUDWIG. "Eine Ausgestoßene (Elise Bürger)," *Die Insel,* I (1901), 156–69.

GOEDEKE, KARL. *Grundriß zur Geschichte der deutschen Dichtung* ("Nationale Dichtung," IV/I, 988 ff.).

————. *Gottfried August Bürger in Göttingen und Gelliehausen,* Hannover: Rumpler, 1873.

GOSCHE, RICHARD. "Eine Parabel unter Bürgers Namen," *Archiv für Litteraturgeschichte,* I (1870), 116–17.

GRISEBACH, EDUARD. *Die Deutsche Literatur, 1770–1870,* Vienna: Rosner, 1876. ("G. A. Bürger," pp. 108–74.)

GUNDOLF, FRIEDRICH. *Shakespeare und der deutsche Geist,* Berlin: Bondi, ²1914, pp. 271–76.

HAIGHT, ELIZABETH H. *Essays on the Greek Romances,* New York: Longmans, Green, 1943.

HARDINA, EMIL. *Dämonen der Tiefe, ein Gottfried August Bürger Roman,* Reichenberg: Stiepel, 1922.

HOENIG, BERTHOLD. "G. A. Bürgers 'Nachtfeier der Venus' und Schillers '"Triumph der Liebe in ihrem Verhältnis zu dem lateinischen 'Pervigilium Veneris'" *Neues Jahrbuch für Philosophie und Pädagogik* (1894), pp. 177 ff, 223 ff, 321 ff.

————. "Nachträge und Zusätze zu den bisherigen Erklärungen Bürgerscher Gedichte," *Zeitschrift für deutsche Philologie,* XXVI (1894), 493 ff.

HÜBNER, GÖTZ E. *Kirchenliedrezeption und Rezeptionsforschung,* Tübingen: Niemeyer, 1969.

JAHN, MORITZ. *Die Gleichen. Eine Erzählung um Gottfried August Bürger,* Munich: Langen/Müller, 1939, Göttingen: Sachse and Pohl, ²1961.

JANENTZKY, CHRISTIAN. *G. A. Bürgers Aesthetik,* Berlin, 1909.

JOHN, ERHARD. "Einige Bemerkungen zu Gottfried August Bürgers Lehrbuch der Aesthetik," *Weimarer Beiträge,* IX (1963), 42–57.

KADNER, SIEGFRIED. *Gottfried August Bürgers Einfluß auf August W. Schlegel,* Kiel, 1919. Diss.

KAIM-KLOOCK, LORE. *Gottfried August Bürger. Zum Problem der Volkstümlichkeit in der Lyrik,* Berlin: Rütten and Loening, 1963.

KAUENHOWEN, KURT. *Gottfried August Bürgers* Macbeth *Bearbeitung,* Königsberg, 1915. Diss.

KAYSER, WOLFGANG. *Geschichte der deutschen Ballade,* Berlin: Juncker and Dünnhaupt, 1936.

KLEPPER, I. "Berühmte Pastorssöhne in der Literatur," *Zeitwende* (1938), p. 10.

KLINCKOWSTROEM, CARL. "Münchhausiaden vor Münchhausen," *Literarisches Echo*, XXXVIII (1935–1936), 16–18.

KLUCKHOHN, AUGUST. "Bürgers und Höltys Aufnahme in die Deutsche Gesellschaft in Göttingen. Bürgers ursprüngliche Abhandlung über eine deutsche Übersetzung des Homers. Seine Lehrthätigkeit," *Archiv für Litteraturgeschichte*, XII (1884), 61 ff.

KÖHLER, REINHOLD. "Die Quelle von Bürgers Lenardo und Blandine" in *Kleinere Schriften* (Weimar, 1898–1900), III, 173–78.

KÖRNER, JOSEF. *Bibliographisches Handbuch des deutschen Schrifttums*, Bern: Francke, ³1949, pp. 269–71.

KREMBS, B. *Über G. A. Bürgers Stellung zur Literatur seiner Zeit*, Jena, 1875. Diss.

KRIENITZ, ERNST. *G. A. Bürgers Jugendlyrik 1767–1773*, Greifswald, 1929. Diss.

LÜCKE, O. *Bürgers Homerübersetzung*. Programm des kgl. Gymnasiums zu Norden. Berlin, 1890.

MACPHERSON, JAMES. *Poems of Ossian*, ed. George Eyre-Todd. London and New York: Scott, c. 1913.

MAYER, GEORG. "Bürgers 'Lenore'–eine visionäre Ballade," *Neue Jahrbücher für Wissenschaft und Jugendbildung*, III (1927), 153–58.

MEHRING, FRANZ. "Gottfried August Bürger," *Die Wage, Wochenblatt für Politik und Literatur*, XVII (1874), 257 ff.

MEYER, RICHARD M. "Günther und Bürger," *Euphorion*, IV (1897), 485–89.

MINOR, JAKOB. "Zu Bürgers *Macbeth*-Übersetzung," *Jahrbuch der Shakespeare Gesellschaft*, XXXVI (1900), 122 ff.

MOSENTHAL, SALOMON. *Ein deutsches Dichterleben*, Vienna, 1850. Dramatic setting of O. Muller's work.)

MÜLLER, OTTO. *Bürger, ein Dichterleben*, Frankfurt/M. 1845. (Fictional treatment of Bürger.)

MÜLLER-SEIDEL, WALTER. "Schillers Kontroverse mit Bürger und ihr geschichtlicher Sinn," *Formwandel. Festschrift für Paul Böckmann* (Hamburg: Hoffmann and Campe, 1964), pp. 294–318.

NAUMANN, WALTER. *Traum und Tradition in der deutschen Lyrik*, Stuttgart: Kohlhammer, 1966. ("G. A. Bürgers 'Trauerstille,'" pp. 130–36.)

NUTZHORN, KARL. "Aus Bürgers Amtmannstätigkeit," *Hannoversche Geschichtsblätter*, IX (1903), 385.

PARSONS, COLEMAN O. "Scott's Translation of Bürger's 'Das Lied von Treue,'" *Journal of English and Germanic Philology*, XXXIII (1934), 240–49.

PAUSTIAN, HELMUT. *Die Lyrik der Aufklärung als Ausdruck der seelischen Entwicklung von 1710–1770*, Berlin: Juncker and Dünnhaupt, 1933.

PONGS, HERMANN. *Das Bild in der Dichtung,* Marburg: Elwert, 1926, ²1960. ("Bürgers 'Lenore.' " III, 71–83.)

PRÖHLE, HEINRICH. *Gottfried August Bürger. Sein Leben und seine Dichtung,* Leipzig, 1856.

PURDIE, EDNA. *Studies in German Literature of the Eighteenth Century,* London: The Athlone Press, 1965. ("Observations on some Eighteenth-Century German Versions of the Witches' Scenes in *Macbeth,*" pp. 47–61.)

ROHDE, ERWIN. *Der griechische Roman und seine Vorläufer,* Hildesheim: Olms, ⁴1960.

ROSE, WILLIAM, ed. *The Travels of Baron Munchausen. Gulliver revived, or the Vice of Lying properly exposed,* London: Routledge and Sons; New York: Dutton, 1923.

SANDYS, JOHN E. *A Companion to Latin Studies,* Cambridge University Press, ³1921.

SCOTT, PENELOPE E. A. L. *Gottfried August Bürgers Übersetzungen aus dem Englischen,* Winterthur: Schellenberg, 1964. Diss.

SCHILLER, FRIEDRICH. "Über Bürgers Gedichte." *Werke,* ed. E. von der Hellen, Stuttgart: Cotta, 1904–1905. Säkularausgabe, XVI, 226–50.

SCHLEGEL, AUGUST W., *Werke,* ed. E. Böcking, Leipzig: Weidmann, 1846–1847. ("Bürger, 1800," XII, 64–139.)

––––––. "Über Bürgers hohes Lied," *Neues deutsches Museum,* II (Feb., Mar. 1790), 205–14 and 306–48.

SCHMIDT, ERICH. *Charakteristiken,* Berlin: Weidmann, 1886. ("Bürgers 'Lenore,' " pp. 199–248.)

SCHMIDT-KASPAR, HERBERT. "Gottfried August Bürger, 'Lenore.' " *Wege zum Gedicht,* II. Munich and Zurich: Schnell and Steiner, 1963, ²1968.

SCHNORR VON CAROLSFELD, FRANZ. "Bürger und A. W. Schlegel." *Archiv für Litteraturgeschichte,* III (1873), 435–51.

SCHÖFFLER, HERBERT, "Bürgers 'Lenore.'" *Die Sammlung,* II (1947), 6–11.

SCHÖNE, ALBRECHT. *Säkularisation als sprachbildende Kraft.* Palestra, vol. 226, Göttingen: Vandenhoeck and Ruprecht, 1958. ("Weltliche Kontrafaktur: Gottfried August Bürger," pp. 158–189.)

SCHRÖDER, ERNST. *Die Pfarrerstochter von Taubenhain,* Kiel, 1933. Diss.

SCHÜDDEKOPF, CARL. "Nachlese zu Bürger," *Euphorion,* (3. Ergänzungsheft) (1897), 101–49.

SCHWEIZER, WERNER R. *Die Wandlungen Münchhausens,* Leipzig: Dieterich, 1921.

––––––. *Münchhausen und die Münchhausiaden,* Berne and Munich: Francke, 1969.

SHAKESPEARE, WILLIAM. *Schauspiele,* transl. Johann Joachim Eschenburg, Zurich: Orell, Füssli and Co., 1800. (*Macbeth* in V, 222–347.)

SPAMER, A. "Bänkelsang," *Sachwörterbuch für Deutschkunde,* I (1930), 85 ff.

STÄUBLE, EDUARD. "Gottfried August Bürgers Ballade, 'Lenore,'" *Deutschunterricht,* X (1958), 85–114.

STAIGER, EMIL. *Stilwandel,* Zurich: Atlantis, 1963. ("Zu Bürgers 'Lenore,'" pp. 75–119.)

STAMMLER, W. and MERKER, P. *Reallexikon,* 4 vols., Berlin: De Gruyter, 1925–1931. ("Münchhauseniade," pp. 423–25.)

STERN, MARTIN. "Bürger, 'An das Herz,'" *Literatur und Geistesgeschichte. Festschrift für Heinz Otto Burger,* Berlin: Schmidt, 1968, pp. 171–87.

STIEFEL, JULIUS. *Die deutsche Lyrik des 18. Jahrhunderts,* Leipzig: Wiegand, 1871.

STRODTMANN, ADOLF. "Bürgers politische Ansichten," *Blumenthals Neue Monatshefte für Dichtkunst und Kritik,* I, 3 (1875), 216 ff.

WACKERNAGEL, WILHELM. "Zur Erläuterung und Beurteilung von Bürgers 'Lenore,'" Baseler Programm, (1835) (in *Kleinere Schriften,* II, 426 ff.).

WEINHOLD, KARL. *H. Chr. Boie,* Halle, 1868.

WURZBACH, WOLFGANG. *Gottfried August Bürger. Sein Leben und seine Werke.* Leipzig: Dieterich, 1900.

XENOPHON D'ÉPHÈSE. *Les Éphésiaques ou le Roman d'Habrocomès et d'Anthia,* ed. George Dalmeyda. Paris: Société d'Éditions "Les Belles Lettres," 1926.

ZAUNERT, PAUL. *Bürgers Verskunst,* Marburg, 1911. Repr. New York: Johnson, 1969. Diss.

Index

PART II